ARMSTRONG'S HANDBOOK

OF MANAGEMENT
AND LEADERSHIP

ARMSTRONG'S HANDBOOK

OF MANAGEMENT
AND LEADERSHIP

A guide to managing for results

2ND EDITION

Michael Armstrong

KOGAN
PAGE

London and Philadelphia

Publisher's note

Every possible effort has been made to ensure that the information contained in this book is accurate at the time of going to press, and the publishers and author cannot accept responsibility for any errors or omissions, however caused. No responsibility for loss or damage occasioned to any person acting, or refraining from action, as a result of the material in this publication can be accepted by the editor, the publisher or the author.

First published in Great Britain and the United States in 2005 by Kogan Page Limited
Second edition 2009

120 Pentonville Road
London N1 9JN
United Kingdom
www.koganpage.com

525 South 4th Street, #241
Philadelphia PA 19147
USA

© Michael Armstrong and Tina Stephens, 2005
© Michael Armstrong, 2009

ISBN 978 0 7494 5417 3

British Library Cataloguing-in-Publication Data

A CIP record for this book is available from the British Library.

Library of Congress Cataloging-in-Publication Data

Armstrong, Michael, 1928–
  Armstrong's handbook of management and leadership : a guide to managing for results / Michael Armstrong.
      p. cm.
  Rev. ed. of: A handbook of management and leadership : a guide to managing for results / Michael Armstrong, Tina Stephens. 2005.
  Includes index.
  ISBN 978-0-7494-5417-3
  1. Management--Handbooks, manuals, etc. 2. Leadership--Handbooks, manuals, etc. I. Armstrong, Michael, 1928- Handbook of management and leadership. II. Title.
  HD38.15.A76 2009
  658.4'092--dc22
                                    2009008237

Typeset by Saxon Graphics Ltd, Derby
Printed and bound in India by Replika Press Pvt Ltd

Contents

Preface to the Second Edition

This book is primarily about the practice of management – the art and science of getting things done. But it is also about leadership – how things get done through people. Management and leadership are different but complementary activities, as explained in Chapter 1.

The activities of management and leadership take place in order to make things happen – to get results. The book therefore also examines the process of managing for results, a phrase first used by Peter Drucker (1963) in his book of that name. Drucker is quoted extensively in this book – simply because, as stated in the *Harvard Business Review* (Drucker, 2006): 'He is the pre-eminent management thinker of our time'.

The book is divided into the following six parts:

- The practice of management
- Approaches to management
- Organizations
- Delivering change
- Enhancing customer relations
- Enabling continuous improvement

The content of this book has been extensively revised in this edition but, as set out in the Appendix, it is still aligned to the *Managing for results* professional standards of the Chartered Institute of Personnel and Development, which form part of the overall *Leadership and management* professional standards.

Drucker, P (1963) *Managing for Results*, Heinemann, London
Drucker, P (2006) What executives should remember, *Harvard Business Review*, February, pp 145–52

Part I
The Practice of Management

The Processes of Management and Leadership

'Let's stop the dysfunctional separation of leadership from management. We all know that managers who don't lead are boring, dispiriting. Well, leaders who don't manage are distant, disconnected.'

Henry Mintzberg (2004) Enough leadership, *Harvard Business Review*, November, p 22

The key purpose of management and leadership as described by the Management Standards Centre (2004) is to 'provide direction, facilitate change and achieve results through the efficient, creative and responsible use of resources'. Effective management is the process of harmonizing individual endeavour to the common good. This introductory chapter sets the scene for the rest of the book by defining and distinguishing between the processes of management and leadership. It also deals with the influences that affect management in the shape of codes of practice and organizational and legal requirements.

Management

To manage means to bring about, to accomplish, to have charge of or responsibility for, to conduct. Management is the process of deciding what to do and then getting it done through the effective use of resources. It is about what managers do to make things happen. They define goals, determine the resources – people, finance, work systems and technology – required to achieve the goals, allocate those resources to opportunities and planned activities and ensure that those activities take place as planned in order to achieve predetermined objectives. All this adds up to managing for results.

Purpose of management

The primary function of management in profit-making firms is to satisfy a range of stakeholders. This means making a profit and creating value for shareholders, producing and delivering valued products and services at a reasonable cost for customers, and providing rewarding employment and development opportunities for employees. In the public sector, management is there to ensure that the services the community requires are delivered effectively. In the voluntary sector, management is there to ensure that the purposes of the charity are achieved and also to keep the faith of the community and donors.

The processes of management

The overall process of management as defined above is divided into a number of individual processes, which are methods of operation designed to assist in the achievement of objectives. Their purpose is to bring as much system, order, predictability, logic and consistency to the task of management as possible in the ever-changing, varied and turbulent environment in which managers work.

These processes were defined by the classical theorists of management such as Henri Fayol (1916), who stated that: 'All undertakings require planning, organizing, command, coordination and control to function properly'. But this classical view has been challenged by the empiricists such as Henry Mintzberg (1973) and Rosemary Stewart (1967). They believed that management could not be treated as a group of formal activities as defined by Fayol and other classical writers. Based on their research into what managers actually do, the empiricists regarded management as a process involving a mix of rational, logical, problem-solving, decision-making activities, and intuitive, judgemental activities. It was therefore both science and art. However, the classical theorists were defining the main processes of management; they were not attempting to describe how managers actually spend their time.

Leadership

To lead is to inspire, influence and guide. Leadership is the process of getting people to do their best to achieve a desired result. It involves developing and communicating a vision for the future, motivating people and gaining their engagement. Other definitions (there are many) include:

- Ivancevich *et al* (2008): Leadership is 'the process of influencing people to enable the achievement of relevant goals'.

- Goleman (2000): 'A leader's singular job is to get results'.

- House *et al* (2004): 'Leadership is the ability to motivate, influence and enable individuals to contribute to the objectives of organizations of which they are members'.

- Stogdill (1974): 'Leadership is an influencing process aimed at goal achievement'.

- Dixon (1994) 'Leadership is no more than exercising such an influence on others that they tend to act in concert towards the achievement of a goal that they might not have achieved so readily had they been left to their own devices'.

The significance of leadership

The consulting firm Hay McBer, as reported by Goleman (2000), in a study of 3,871 executives selected from a database of more than 20,000 executives worldwide, found that leadership had a direct impact on organizational climate, and that climate in turn accounted for nearly one-third of the financial results of organizations. The conclusion from research conducted by Professor Malcolm Higgs (2006) was that leadership behaviour accounts for almost 50 per cent of the difference between change success and failure. Research by Northouse (2006) into 167 US firms in 13 industries established that over a 20 year period, leadership accounted for more variations in performance than any other variable.

Leadership theories

There are many theoretical explanations and descriptions of the process of leadership. Three of the more important ones are summarized below.

Contingent leadership

The theory of contingent leadership developed by Fiedler (1967) states that the type of leadership exercised depends to a large extent on the situation and the ability of the leader to understand it and act accordingly. This is sometimes called situational leadership. Fiedler wrote: 'Leadership performance... depends as much on the organization as on the leader's own attributes. Except perhaps for the unusual case, it is simply not meaningful to speak of an effective leader or an ineffective leader. We can only speak of a leader who tends to be effective in one situation and ineffective in another.'

The performance of a group, as Fiedler pointed out, is related both to the leadership style and to the degree to which the situation provides the leader with the opportunity to exert influence. He referred to the concepts originated by Halpin and Winer (1957) on the basis of their research into how aircraft captains acted as leaders. Two dimensions of leadership were identified: (1) initiating structure, a task-orientated approach that focuses on defining the task and how it should be carried out, and (2) consideration, a people-orientated approach where the emphasis is on maintaining good relations through behaviour indicative of trust, respect and warmth.

Fiedler's research revealed that an initiating structure approach worked best for leaders in conditions where the leader has power, formal backing and a relatively well-structured task.

Considerate leaders do better in unstructured or ambiguous situations or where their power as a leader is restricted.

The path-goal model

The path-goal model first developed by Robert House (1971) states that leaders are there to define the path that should be followed by their team in order to achieve its goals. It is the leader's job to guide and help team members to select the best paths towards achieving their own goals and those of the group. A leader's behaviour is acceptable to subordinates when viewed as a source of satisfaction, and it is motivational when need satisfaction is contingent on performance, and the leader facilitates, coaches and rewards effective performance. Leaders have to engage in different types of leadership behaviour depending on the nature and the demands of a particular situation. It is the leader's job to assist followers in attaining goals and to provide the direction and support needed to ensure that their goals are compatible with the organization's goals. Path-goal theory identifies four leadership styles: achievement-oriented, directive, participative and supportive. These are described in Chapter 3.

Leader-member exchange theory (LMX)

The leader-member exchange theory of leadership as formulated by Graen (1976) focuses on the two-way relationship between supervisors and subordinates. It is linked to social exchange theory, which explains social change and stability as a process of negotiated exchanges between parties.

Leaders usually have special relationships with an inner circle of assistants and advisors, who often get high levels of responsibility and access to resources. This is called the 'in-group', and their position can come with a price. These employees work harder, are more committed to task objectives, and share more administrative duties. They are also expected to be totally committed and loyal to their leader. Conversely, subordinates in the 'out-group' are given low levels of choice or influence and put constraints on the leader. These relationships start very soon after a person joins a team and follow these three stages:

1. Role-taking: The member joins the team and the leader evaluates their abilities and talents. Based on this, the leader may offer opportunities to demonstrate capabilities.

2. Role-making: In the second phase, the leader and member take part in an unstructured and informal negotiation whereby a role is created for the member and the unspoken promise of benefit and power in return for dedication and loyalty takes place. Trust-building is very important in this stage, and any feelings of betrayal, especially by the leader, can result in the member being demoted to the out-group. This negotiation includes relationship factors as well as purely work-related ones, and a member who is similar to the leader in various ways is more likely to succeed.

3. Routinization: In this phase, a pattern of ongoing social exchange between the leader and the member becomes established. Being a successful or in-group member usually requires

being similar in many ways to the leader. These members work hard at building and sustaining trust and respect. They are often empathetic, patient, reasonable, sensitive, and good at seeing the viewpoint of other people, especially their leader. Aggression, sarcasm and a self-centred view are qualities seen in the out-group.

The quality of the LMX relationship varies. It is better when the challenge of the job is extremely high or extremely low. The size of the group, financial resource availability and the overall workload are also important. The theory can work upwards as well. Leaders can gain power by being members of their manager's inner circle, which they can then share with their subordinates.

The problem with the leadership concept

In spite of all the research and theorizing, the concept of leadership is problematic. As Meindl *et al* (1985) commented: 'It has become apparent that, after years of trying, we have been unable to generate an understanding of leadership that is both intellectually compelling and emotionally satisfying. The concept of leadership remains elusive and enigmatic'.

In *The Arts of Leadership*, Keith Grint (2000) made the case that leadership is not accessible to scientific approaches because it is essentially a constitutive process (ie leaders shape and are shaped by the situation they are in). Instead, he suggests we should think of leadership as an art because: 'It appears to have more to do with invention than analysis, despite claims to the contrary; it operates on the basis of indeterminacy, whilst claiming to be deterministic; it is rooted in irony, rather than the truth; and it usually rests on a constructed identity but claims a reflective identity'.

These problems may arise because, as a concept, leadership is difficult to pin down. There are many different types of situations in which leaders operate, many different types of leaders and many different leadership styles. Producing one theory that covers all these variables is difficult if not impossible. All that can be done is to draw on the various theories that exist to explain different facets of leadership, without necessarily relying on any one of them for a comprehensive explanation of what is involved. Perhaps leadership is best defined as being what leaders do. This will be considered in Chapter 3.

Management and leadership compared

Some commentators link leadership closely with the idea of management, some regard the two as synonymous, others consider management a subset of leadership and yet others praise leadership and demonize management.

Hersey and Blanchard (1998) claimed that management merely consists of leadership applied to business situations; or in other words, management forms a subset of the broader process of leadership. They put it this way: 'Leadership occurs any time one attempts to influence the behaviour of an individual or group, regardless of the reason. Management is a kind of leadership in which the achievement of organizational goals is paramount'.

Abraham Zaleznik (2004) saw leaders as inspiring visionaries, concerned about substance; while managers are planners who are concerned with process.

Bennis and Nanus (1985) wrote that: 'there is a profound difference between management and leadership and both are important'. They went on famously to explain that 'Managers do things right, leaders do the right things'. This aphorism owes a lot to Peter Drucker's distinction (1967) between efficiency and effectiveness, which was taken up by Bill Reddin (1970), who wrote that concentrating on efficiency rather than effectiveness meant that managers 'do things right rather than do right things'. But Drucker and Reddin (not acknowledged by Bennis and Nanus) were focusing on managers, not making invidious comparisons between managers and leaders. And it seems to be perfectly possible that managers often do the right things, while leaders often get things right.

In his role as a demonizer of managers, Bennis (1989) identified 12 invidious distinctions between managers and leaders:

1. Managers administer, leaders innovate.
2. Managers ask how and when, leaders ask what and why.
3. Managers focus on systems, leaders focus on people.
4. Managers do things right, leaders do the right things.
5. Managers maintain, leaders develop.
6. Managers rely on control, leaders inspire trust.
7. Managers have a short-term perspective, leaders have a longer-term perspective.
8. Managers accept the status quo, leaders challenge the status quo.
9. Managers have an eye on the bottom line, leaders have an eye on the horizon.
10. Managers imitate, leaders originate.
11. Managers emulate the classic good soldier, leaders are their own person.
12. Managers copy, leaders show originality.

Paul Birch (1999) also saw a distinction between leadership and management and, without denigrating management, gave pre-eminence to leadership. He observed that, as a broad generalization, managers concerned themselves with tasks, while leaders concerned themselves with people. However, one of the main things that characterize great leaders is the fact that they achieve. The difference is that leaders realize that tasks are achieved through the goodwill and support of others (influence), while managers may not. This goodwill and support originates in the leader seeing people as people, not as another resource for use in getting results. The manager has the role of organizing resources to get something done. People form one of these resources, and poor managers treat people as just another interchangeable factor of production.

More positive distinctions between management and leadership were made by Kotter (1991), as set out in Table 1.1.

Table 1.1   Distinctions between management and leadership (Kotter, 1991)

Management involves	Leadership involves
Focusing on managing complexity by planning and budgeting with the aim of producing orderly results, not change.	Focusing on producing change by developing a vision for the future along with strategies for bringing about the changes needed to achieve that vision.
Developing the capacity to achieve plans by creating an organization structure and staffing it – developing human systems that can implement plans as precisely and efficiently as possible.	Aligning people by communicating the new direction and creating coalitions that understand the vision and are committed to its achievement.
Ensuring plan accomplishment by controlling and problem-solving – formally and informally comparing results to the plan, identifying deviations and then planning and organizing to solve the problems.	Using motivation to energize people, not by pushing them in the right direction as control mechanisms do, but by satisfying basic human needs for achievement, a sense of belonging, recognition, self-esteem, a feeling of control over one's life and the ability to live up to one's ideals.

Conclusions

The answer to the issues raised by these various comparisons is that management and leadership are indeed different. Management is concerned with the effective use of all resources, including people, while leadership concentrates on getting the best out of people. However, both are needed. As Mintzberg (2004) commented, 'instead of isolating leadership we need to diffuse it throughout the organization... It's time to bring management and leadership down to earth'.

Perhaps the most familiar definition of management was made by Mary Parker Follett (1924), a pioneering writer on management. She defined it as 'the art of getting results through people', thus combining the concepts of management and leadership.

Rather than pursuing the Manichean view ('leaders good, managers bad') it is better to accept that managers have to be leaders and leaders are often, but not always, managers. It is necessary to allow for a reciprocal relationship between leadership and management, implying that an effective manager should possess leadership skills, and an effective leader, at least in business, should demonstrate management skills.

Influences on management

The process of management is influenced by codes of practice (professional, industrial and official). These codes provide guidance on behaviour and the procedures to be followed and, in the case of professional codes and some industry codes, are supported by disciplinary sanctions. They usefully define expectations, but the extent to which they can be enforced may be limited, except that contravention of some official codes is taken into account in Employment Tribunal cases. Management processes are also influenced by procedures and legal and corporate governance (organizational) requirements.

Professional codes of practice

Professional codes of practice lay down the behaviours expected of the members of a profession. They are supported by disciplinary procedures, which hold members to account for serious contraventions of the code.

For example, the Chartered Management Institute has a code of professional management practice that sets out the professional standards required of members of the Institute as a condition of membership. It states in the introduction that: 'As a member, you must demonstrate high standards of professional conduct, competence, judgement and honesty in your actions as a practising manager'. The code has sections dealing with standards for individual managers, relationships with others, supporting policies and practices of the organization, and dealing with external relationships and the wider community. The section dealing with individual managers states that: 'As a professional manager you will:

- Pursue managerial activities with integrity, accountability and competence.

- Disclose any personal interest which might be seen to influence managerial decisions.

- Practise an open style of management so far as it is consistent with business needs.

- Keep up-to-date with developments in best management practice and continue to develop personal competence.

- Adopt an approach to the identification and resolution of conflicts of values, including ethical values, which is reasonable and justifiable.

- Safeguard personal information and not seek personal advantage from it.

- Exhaust all available internal remedies for dealing with matters perceived as improper before resorting to public disclosure.

- Encourage the development of quality and continuous improvement in all management activities.'

The code of the Chartered Institute of Personnel and Development (CIPD) includes the statement that in all circumstances CIPD members 'must endeavour to enhance the standing of the profession; adherence to this professional code of conduct is an essential aspect of this'.

Industrial codes of practice

Industrial codes of practice lay down rules for how an industry should conduct its work. For example, The Recruitment and Employment Confederation (REC) has a code of practice that aims to ensure that employment and recruitment agencies meet ethical and legal requirements. Amongst its general provisions are:

- Members will comply with any REC guidance on ethical, commercial or statutory issues in the operation of their businesses.

- Members and their staff will deal with and represent themselves to work-seekers, hirers and others fairly, openly, honestly and courteously at all times.

- Any selection tests used, including psychometric and personality questionnaires, should be relevant, properly validated and, where appropriate, conducted by trained or licensed personnel.

The British Computer Society has a Code of Good Practice, the purpose of which is defined as being to describe 'standards of practice relating to the contemporary multifaceted demands found in Information Technology (IT)'. Its provisions include the requirement to maintain technical competence, adhere to regulations, act professionally as a specialist, use appropriate methods and tools, and respect the interests of customers. Specific guidance is given on the whole range of work carried out by IT specialists; for example, the guidelines on designing software include the requirement to 'achieve well-engineered products that demonstrate fitness for purpose, reliability, efficiency, security, maintainability and cost effectiveness'.

Industrial codes of practice in the United Kingdom are also developed by official bodies such as OFTEL (the Office of Telecommunications). This has overseen the development of codes of practice for a considerable number of communication service providers. OFTEL has stated that these codes are 'primarily aimed at providing consumers with a clear statement of the range of policies, services and support activities offered by individual communication suppliers – they should provide sufficient information for any consumer to understand the range of services available, how to contact the supplier in order to, for example, obtain a new service, clarify the provider's terms and conditions, obtain support, or make a complaint'.

Official codes

A large number of codes of practice have been issued by the government, government agencies or bodies sponsored by the government. Examples include the code on job evaluation schemes free of sex bias issued by the Equal Opportunities Commission (now the Equality and Human Rights Commission), the code on disciplinary and grievance procedures issued by ACAS (Advisory, Conciliation and Arbitration Service) and various practice codes issued by the Health and Safety Executive.

Procedures

Procedures are formal statements of how particular issues should be dealt with. They affect the way in which people handle certain matters in organizations. Typical procedures are concerned with people management on such matters as discipline, grievances, redundancy and equal opportunities, although procedures can be produced for any aspect of administration, such as handling customer complaints.

Legal requirements

Management takes place within a framework of employment, health and safety, company, commercial and other legislation. Necessarily, this places obligations and constraints on managements in general and on individual managers.

Organizational requirements and corporate governance

Organizational requirements are expressed in the concept of 'corporate governance', which refers to the system by which businesses are directed and controlled. The Organisation for Economic Co-operation and Development (OECD), in the Preamble to its Principles, has defined corporate governance as follows:

> *Corporate governance is one key element in improving economic efficiency and growth as well as enhancing investor confidence. Corporate governance involves a set of relationships between a company's management, its board, its shareholders and other stakeholders. Corporate governance also provides the structure through which the objectives of the company are set and the means of attaining these objectives and monitoring performance are determined. Good corporate governance should provide proper incentives for the board and management to pursue objectives that are in the interests of the company and its shareholders and should facilitate effective monitoring.*

Corporate governance is regulated by The Companies Acts, 1985 and 1989. A Combined Code on Corporate Governance was produced by the Hampel Committee.

The issues covered by the Hampel and other reports include:

- board structure and membership;
- board management;
- directors' remuneration;
- financial controls;
- accountability and audit;
- relations with shareholders.

References

Bennis, W (1989) *On Becoming a Leader*, Addison Wesley, New York

Bennis, W and Nanus, B (1985) *Leaders: The strategies for taking charge*, Harper & Row, New York

Birch, P (1999) *Instant Leadership: Reach your potential now*, Kogan Page, London

Dixon, N F (1994) *On the Psychology of Military Incompetence*, Pimlico, London

Drucker, P (1967) *The Effective Executive*, Heinemann, London

Fayol, H (1916) *Administration Industrielle et General*, translated by C Storrs (1949) as *General and Industrial Management*, Pitman, London

Fiedler, F E (1967) *A Theory of Leadership Effectiveness*, McGraw-Hill, New York

Follett, M P (1924) *Creative Experience*, Longmans Green, New York

Goleman, D (2000) Leadership that gets results, *Harvard Business Review*, March–April, pp 78–90

Graen, G (1976) Role-making processes within complex organizations, in *Handbook of Industrial and Organizational Psychology*, ed M D Dunnette, pp 1201–45, Rand McNally, Chicago, IL

Grint, K (2000) *The Arts of Leadership*, Oxford University Press, Oxford

Halpin, A W and Winer, B J (1957) *A Factorial Study of the Leader Behaviour Descriptions*, Ohio State University Press, Ohio

Hersey, P and Blanchard, K H (1998) *Management of Organizational Behaviour*, Prentice Hall, Englewood Cliffs, NJ

Higgs, M (2006) *Change and its Leadership*, Rowland, Fisher, Lennox Consulting [Online] www.rflc.co.uk

House, R J (1971) A path-goal theory of leader effectiveness, *Administrative Science Quarterly*, **16**, pp 321–38

House, R et al (2004) *Culture, Leadership and Organization: The GLOBE study of 62 societies*, Sage, Thousand Oaks, CA

Ivancevich, J M, Konopaske, R and Matteson, M T (2008) *Organizational Behavior and Management*, 8th edn, McGraw-Hill/Irwin, New York

Kotter, J P (1991) Power, dependence and effective management, in *Managing People and Organizations*, ed J Gabarro, pp 33–49, Harvard Business School Publications, Boston, MA

Management Standards Centre (2004) *Management Standards* [Online] www.management-standards.org

Meindl, J R, Ehrlich, S B and Dukerich, J M (1985) The romance of leadership, *Administrative Science Quarterly*, **30**, 78–102

Mintzberg, H (1973) *The Nature of Managerial Work*, Harper & Row, New York

Mintzberg, H (2004) Enough leadership, *Harvard Business Review*, November, p 22

Northouse, P G (2006) *Leadership: Theory and practice*, 4th edn, Sage, Thousand Oaks, CA

Reddin, W J (1970) *Managerial Effectiveness*, McGraw-Hill, London

Stewart, R (1967) *Managers and Their Jobs*, Macmillan, London

Stogdill, R (1974) *Handbook of Leadership: A survey of theory and research*, Free Press, New York

Zaleznik, A (2004) Manager and leaders: are they different? *Harvard Business Review*, January, pp 74–81

The Role of the Manager

'The manager is the dynamic, life-giving element in every business.'
Drucker, P (1955) *The Practice of Management*, Heinemann, London

This chapter answers five questions about managers:

1. What is a manager?

2. What do managers do?

3. How do they do it?

4. What is an effective manager?

5. What do line/middle managers contribute?

What is a manager?

Managers are there to get results by ensuring that their function, unit or department operates effectively. They manage people and their other resources – finance, facilities, knowledge, information, time and themselves. They are accountable for attaining goals, having been given authority over those working in their unit or department. Accountability means that they are responsible (held to account) for what they do and what they achieve. Authority means having the right or power to get people to do things. Authority is exercised through leadership and personal influence arising from position, personality and knowledge.

The manager's role

Managers are like everyone else in an organization in that they carry out roles. A role is the part people play in fulfilling their responsibilities. A role is not the same as a job, as set out in a job description, which is a list of duties and, perhaps, a statement of the overall purpose of the job. The role someone plays describes how they carry out their job.

The concept of a role distinguishes between the role demands and situational pressures that confront individuals in organizational positions, and their conception and performance of a role. The demands of a role can be classified in terms of explicitness, clarity and coherence. They can refer to expectations – what must be done, what should be done and what can be done. Role expectations consist of what individuals perceive to be their positions and the demands attached to them. People interpret what they are expected to do in the light of their perceptions of the context in which they work. When confronted with new demands or pressures from outside the organization or from people within the organization they may have to reinterpret their roles and be prepared to respond flexibly.

Roles, especially managerial roles, can therefore be fluid, and managers have to adapt rapidly – they cannot remain within the rigid confines of a prescribed set of duties. Role performance refers to managers' actual behaviour – either in response to perceived expectations or in pursuing individual aims and projects. Managers may have to work in conditions of role ambiguity, when they are not sure of what they are expected to do, or role conflict, when what they feel that they should do is not in accord with what others believe they should do.

Activities and tasks

In carrying out their roles managers are engaged in activities and tasks. Activities comprise what managers do – their behaviour. Tasks are what managers are expected or seek to achieve. In defining managerial work a distinction has been made by Hales (1986) between their behaviours and actions and the desired outcomes of those behaviours. This can be described as an input-process-output model in which inputs are the knowledge and skills managers bring to their role, process is their behaviour in using their knowledge and skills to make decisions and take action, and output is the result or outcome of the behaviour.

Silverman and Jones (1976) have suggested that managers actively define their own work and create its constituent activities. Communication is the medium through which managerial work is constituted. As Hales (1986) points out: 'The work of managers is the management of their work'.

The role of the manager in a variety of different contexts

The roles of managers vary according to the context in which they work. They will be dependent on their function, level, organization (type, structure, culture, size, system of work and technology) and their working environment generally (the extent to which it is turbulent, predictable, settled, pressurized, steady). Individual managers will adapt to these circumstances in different ways and will operate more or less successfully in accordance with their perceptions of the behaviour expected of them, their experience of what has or has not worked in the past, and their own personal characteristics.

The added value contribution of managers

Managers exist to add value. The term 'added value' was originally used in accountancy where it is defined as the value added to the cost of raw materials and bought-out parts by the processes of production and distribution. The term is often used colloquially to indicate the development and use of any resource in such a way as to ensure that it yields a substantial and sustainable higher return on whatever has been invested in it. Even more colloquially, to add value means making any contribution that delivers additional benefits to the organization in the shape of increased effectiveness, competitive advantage, better customer service and higher levels of quality. Managers make an added value contribution when they ensure that they and the resources they control generate levels of income, productivity and operational effectiveness that provide a satisfactory return on the money, time and effort invested in those resources. A value-added approach to management means the creation of more out of less.

Added value is produced by managers and the people they manage. It is managers at various levels who create visions, define values and missions, set goals, develop strategic plans, and implement those plans in accordance with the underpinning values. Added value will be enhanced by anything that is done to obtain and develop the right sort of people, to motivate and manage them effectively, to gain their commitment to the organization's values, and to build and maintain stable relationships with them based on mutual trust.

What do managers do?

The traditional model of what managers do is that it is a logical and systematic process of planning, organizing, motivating and controlling. However, this is misleading. Managers often carry out their work on a day-to-day basis in conditions of variety, turbulence and unpredictability. Managers may have to be specialists in ambiguity, with the ability to cope with conflicting and unclear requirements.

Classical concepts of what managers do

The classical writers on management set out to define the nature of managerial work in terms of universal basic elements. These were believed to provide a framework for the analysis and conduct of the managerial task. The classical framework was developed in 1916 by a pioneer writer on management, Henri Fayol (1916), who based it on an analysis of his experience as a practising manager and defined the five elements of managerial work as planning, organizing, commanding, coordinating and controlling. Apart from the substitution of 'commanding' with 'motivating', Fayol's analysis is still the common parlance of management, but its usefulness and universality have been challenged.

Challenges to the classical school

Sune Carlsson (1951), a researcher into management, wrote that: 'If we ask a managing director when he is coordinating, or how much coordination he has been doing during the day, he would not know, and even the most highly skilled observer would not know either. The same holds true of the concepts of planning, command, organization and control.'

Rosemary Stewart (1967) pointed out that: 'They [the management theorists] could talk about the manager's job because their description of his functions was so general as to be universally valid; but such a level of generalisation has a very limited usefulness in practice.' Common sense as well as the evidence collected by the empirical researchers as described later tells us that managers do not sit down and divide their day into neat segments labelled planning, organizing, motivating and controlling.

However, the classical concept of management should not be dismissed out of hand. Planning, organizing, motivating and controlling are what managers do at least some of the time, even if they take place haphazardly, almost unconsciously, during a complex working day. And it is clear that when the originator of this school, Henri Fayol, wrote about management, he was writing about management in general, not the behaviour of individual managers. In fact, the classical theorists tried to describe what management is. They did not attempt to describe how individual managers behave.

The role of managers as strategic and visionary thinkers

Managers are doers. They make things happen. They deal with events as they occur. But they must also be concerned with where they are going. This requires strategic and visionary thinking, especially at higher levels.

Strategic thinking

As strategic thinkers, managers develop a sense of purpose and frameworks for defining intentions and future directions. This aspect of the manager's role is dealt with more comprehensively in Chapter 5.

Visionary thinking

As visionary thinkers, managers set out an imaginative, inspirational and insightful picture of what can and should be attained – a state of future being that is significantly superior to the present state. They define and describe goals. If this is carried out and presented convincingly, it can enhance, indeed drive, commitment to the achievement of what the organization or an individual manager believes to be important.

Management standards

What managers do can be defined in terms of the standards they are expected to achieve. The following management standards have been produced by the Management Standards Centre (2004).

Providing direction

- Develop a vision for the future.
- Gain commitment and provide leadership.
- Provide governance – comply with values, ethical and legal frameworks and manage risks in line with shared goals.

Facilitating change

- Lead innovations.
- Manage change.

Achieving results

- Lead the business to achieve goals and objectives.
- Lead operations to achieve specific results.
- Lead projects to achieve specified results.

Meeting customer needs

- Promote products and/or services to customers.
- Obtain contracts to supply products and/or services.
- Deliver products and/or services to customers.
- Solve problems for customers.
- Assure the quality of products and/or services.

Working with people

- Build relationships.
- Develop networks and partnerships.
- Manage people.

Using resources

- Manage financial resources.
- Procure products and/or services.
- Manage physical resources and technology.
- Manage information and knowledge.

Managing self and personal skills

- Manage own contribution.
- Develop own knowledge, skills and competence.

How do managers do it?

A number of researchers have studied how managers carry out their work and four of the leading studies are summarized below. These and other projects have led to conclusions about the fragmented nature of the work of managers and its characteristics.

Sune Carlsson

Sune Carlsson (1951) studied the work of nine Swedish managing directors, and his findings can be summarized under three headings:

1. Working time

    Executives were alone for not more than one hour a day but the typical 'alone' intervals were only of 10–15 minutes' duration. They spent their days being constantly interrupted and they had remarkably little control over how they spent their time.

2. Communication patterns

    Chief executives initiate far fewer letters a day than they receive. The average time spent with visitors was three and a half hours a day.

3.   Work content

One of the main activities of the chief executives was to keep themselves informed.

Rosemary Stewart

Rosemary Stewart (1967) studied 160 senior and middle managers for four weeks each. Her main findings on how they spent their time were:

- The managers worked an average of 42 hours per week.

- Discussions took 60 per cent of their time – 43 per cent informal, 7 per cent in committee, 6 per cent telephoning and 4 per cent social activity (if this research were repeated today, e-mailing would no doubt take up a lot of time).

- They spent 34 per cent of their time alone, 25 per cent with their immediate subordinates, 8 per cent with their superiors, 25 per cent with colleagues and 5 per cent with external contacts.

- Fragmentation in work was considerable. In the four-week period, managers averaged only nine periods of 30 minutes or more without interruption and averaged 20 contacts a day, 12 of them fleeting ones (less than five minutes' duration).

Henry Mintzberg

Henry Mintzberg (1973) observed five chief executives over a period of five weeks. He found that the proportion of time they spent on different activities was as shown in Table 2.1.

Table 2.1   Time spent on different activities by chief executives (Mintzberg, 1973)

Activities	Average (%)	Range (%)
Desk work	22	16–38
Telephone calls	6	4–9
Scheduled meetings	59	38–75
Unscheduled meetings	10	3–8
Tours	3	0–10
Proportion of activities lasting less than 9 minutes	49	40–56
Proportion of activities lasting longer than 60 minutes	10	5–13

The managers' days were characterized by a large number of brief, informal two-person contacts (telephone calls and unscheduled meetings) and relatively few scheduled meetings, which nevertheless took most of their time. Subordinates consumed about half the managers' contact time and were involved in two-thirds of the contacts. The managers initiated less than one-third of their contacts and only 5 per cent were scheduled regularly.

The broad conclusions emerging from this study confirmed that management is:

- highly interactive;
- very much concerned with communication;
- about getting things done with or through other people;
- not much about office work.

Mintzberg also contrasted findings such as these on the work of managers with the classical school, stating that the former 'paint an interesting picture, one as different from Fayol's view as a cubist abstract is from a Renaissance painting'.

Leonard Sayles

Leonard Sayles (1964) interviewed 75 lower and middle-level managers in a large US corporation. He identified three aspects of managerial work in his analysis.

1. Managers as participants in external work flows, which leads to the following basic relationships with people outside their immediate managerial responsibility:

    - trading relationships: making arrangements with other members of the organization to get work done;
    - work-flow relationships: making contacts concerning the work preceding or following that supervised by the manager;
    - service relationships: contacts concerning the giving or receiving of services or support by specialist groups, for example market research or maintenance;
    - advisory relationships: provision of counsel and advice to line managers by experts, for example industrial relations;
    - auditing relationships: contacts with those who evaluate or appraise organizational work, for example management accounts or quality control;
    - stabilization relationships: contacts with those who are empowered to limit or control the manager's decisions in accordance with organizational policy, for example production planning and control;
    - innovative relationships: contacts with groups specially isolated to perform a research function.

2. Managers as leaders, which results in three basic types of leadership behaviour:

    ● leadership as direction: getting subordinates to respond to the requests of the manager;

    ● leadership as response: responding to initiatives from subordinates who are seeking aid or support;

    ● leadership as representation: representing subordinates in contact with other parts of the organization.

3. Managers as monitors, in which managers follow the progress of work through the system, detect variations and initiate action as required.

Characteristics of how managers work

The typical characteristics of how managers work as identified by the researchers in this field are described below.

The nature of the work

As Hales (1986) points out, the nature of work varies by duration, time span, recurrence, unexpectedness and source. Little time is spent on any one activity and in particular on the conscious, systematic formulation of plans. Planning and decision-making tend to take place in the course of other activities. Managerial activities are riven by contradictions, cross-pressures, and the need to cope with and reconcile conflict. A lot of time is spent by managers accounting for and explaining what they do, in informal relationships and in networking.

Reaction and non-reflection

Hales also suggests that much of what managers do is, of necessity, an unreflecting response to circumstances. Managers are usually not so much slow and methodical decision-makers as doers who have to react rapidly to problems as they arise and think on their feet. Much time is spent on day-to-day troubleshooting.

Choice

Stewart *et al* (1980) established that managers exercise choice about their work. They informally negotiate widely different interpretations of the boundaries and dimensions of ostensibly identical jobs, with particular emphasis upon the development of 'personal domain' (ie establishing their own territory and the rules that apply within it). Stewart (1967) also identified the choices that operate within the demands and constraints of managerial work. She suggested that the choices common to all managerial jobs are concerned with content (aspects of a job a manager chooses to emphasize, selections between aspects, and choices about risk-taking) and methods (how work is done). This is why the concept of discretionary behaviour is so important when describing how managers operate. This refers to the fact that most managers have quite a lot of discretion about how they carry out their roles, especially when dealing with people.

Communication

Much managerial activity consists of asking or persuading others to do things, which involves managers in face-to-face verbal communication of limited duration. Managers spend a great deal of time communicating – orally, by e-mail or (to a lesser extent) in writing.

Identification of tasks

Silverman and Jones (1976) suggested that the typical work of a junior manager is the 'organizational work' of drawing upon an evolving stock of knowledge about 'normal' procedures and routines in order to identify and negotiate the accomplishment of problems and tasks.

The fragmentary nature of managerial work

The research described earlier into the behaviour of managers and how they spend their time confirmed that because of the open-ended nature of their work, managers feel compelled to perform a great variety of tasks at an unrelenting pace. Mintzberg (1973) commented that managers actually appear to prefer brevity and interruption to their work. They become conditioned by their workload; they develop an appreciation of the opportunity cost of their own time; and they live continuously with an awareness of what else might or must be done at any time. Superficiality is an occupational hazard. Managers gravitate to the more active elements of their work – the current, the specific, the well-defined, the non-routine activities.

Mintzberg also noted that even senior managers spend little time on planning, are subject to constant interruption, hold short face-to-face meetings that flit from topic to topic, and respond to the initiatives of others far more than they initiate themselves.

Fragmentation, variety and brevity in managerial work arise for the following six reasons:

1. Managers are largely concerned with dealing with people – their staff and their internal and external customers. But people's behaviour is often unpredictable; their demands and responses are conditioned by the constantly changing circumstances in which they exist, the pressures to which they have to respond and their individual wants and needs. Conflicts arise and have to be dealt with on the spot.

2. Managers are not always in a position to control the events that affect their work. Sudden demands are imposed upon them from other people within the organization and/or from outside. Crises can occur that they are unable to predict.

3. Managers are expected to be decisive and deal with situations as they arise. Their best laid plans are therefore often disrupted; their established priorities have to be abandoned.

4. Managers are subject to the beck and call of their superiors, who also have to respond instantly to new demands and crises.

5. Managers often work in conditions of turbulence and ambiguity. They are not clear about what is expected of them when new situations arise. They therefore tend to be reactive rather than proactive, dealing with immediate problems rather than trying to anticipate them.

6. For all the reasons given above, managers are subject to constant interruptions. They have little chance to settle down and think about their plans and priorities, or to spend enough time in studying control information to assist in maintaining a 'steady state' as far as their own activities go.

What is an effective manager?

Managerial effectiveness 'denotes the extent to which what managers actually do matches what they are supposed to do' (Hales, 1986). It is about performance, which refers both to what people do (their achievements) and how people do it (their behaviour). To measure effectiveness it is necessary to understand and define both sides of the equation; that is, inputs (skills and behaviour) and outputs (results). The measurement of effectiveness and performance therefore compares expectations about achievements and behaviour with actual results and behaviour. Effective managers:

- get the things done that they are expected to get done;
- exercise visionary leadership;
- understand the business and its key drivers and act accordingly;
- plan the effective use of the resources allocated to them;
- set the direction and ensure that everyone knows what is expected of them;
- initiate and manage change designed to improve performance;
- adapt and respond rapidly to changing demands and circumstances;
- anticipate problems but deal promptly with those that arise unexpectedly; and
- monitor performance so that swift corrective action can be taken when necessary.

Managerial skills

To meet these onerous demands managers require a wide range of skills. These include coaching, communicating, delegating, facilitating, leadership, measuring and managing performance, motivating, networking, problem-solving and decision-making, and providing feedback.

Tamkin *et al* (2003) suggest that managers need the ability to:

- empower and develop people – understand and practise the process of delivering through the capability of others;

- manage people and performance – maintain morale while also maximizing performance;

- work across boundaries, engaging with others, working as a member of a team, thinking differently about problems and their solutions;

- develop relationships and a focus on the customer, building partnerships with both internal and external customers;

- balance technical and generic skills – the technical aspects of management and the management of human relationships.

Managerial competencies

Managerial competencies are the behaviours that will produce effective performance. They refer to characteristics of managers in such areas as leadership, team working and communication. They are defined in the competency frameworks and profiles that many organizations use to inform decisions on selection, learning and development and, sometimes, increases in pay. They can be used as criteria for assessing performance. A competency framework or profile also provides guidance to managers on the sort of behaviour expected of them.

The following is an example of a competency framework.

- Achievement orientation: The desire to get things done well and the ability to set and meet challenging goals, create own measures of excellence and constantly seek ways of improving performance.

- Business awareness: The capacity to continually identify and explore business opportunities, to understand the business priorities of the organization and constantly seek methods of ensuring that the organization becomes more businesslike.

- Communication: The ability to communicate clearly and persuasively, orally or in writing.

- Customer focus: The exercise of unceasing care in looking after the interests of external and internal customers to ensure that their wants, needs and expectations are met or exceeded.

- Developing others: The desire and capacity to foster the development of members of their team, providing feedback, support, encouragement and coaching.

- Flexibility: The ability to adapt to and work effectively in different situations and to carry out a variety of tasks.

- Leadership: The capacity to inspire individuals to give of their best to achieve a desired result and to maintain effective relationships with individuals and the team as a whole.

- Planning: The ability to decide on courses of action, ensuring that the resources required to implement the action will be available, and schedule the programme of work required to achieve a defined end result.

- Problem-solving: The capacity to analyse situations, diagnose problems, identify the key issues, establish and evaluate alternative courses of action, and produce a logical, practical and acceptable solution.

- Teamwork: The ability to work cooperatively and flexibly with other members of the team, with a full understanding of the role to be played as a team member.

Some organizations illustrate their competency frameworks with examples of positive or negative indicators of behaviour under each heading. These provide a useful checklist for managers willing to measure their own performance in order to develop their career. Here is an extract (Table 2.2) from a framework used by a large housing association.

What do line/middle managers contribute?

Line or middle managers form the essential link between top managers, who are concerned with broad strategic issues and the overall direction of the organization, and the employees who carry out the detailed work. Line managers are intermediaries and this can make their lives difficult. They have to interpret and apply corporate strategies, plans and policies and ensure that these are implemented by their teams, on whom they depend to get results.

The research conducted by Professor John Purcell and colleagues (2003) showed that the role of line managers is crucial: 'The way line managers implement and enact policies, show leadership in dealing with employees and in exercising control come through as a major issue'. It is line managers who bring organizational policies to life. Further work by Sue Hutchinson and John Purcell (2003) found that the responsibilities of line managers covered a wide range of duties, ranging from traditional supervisory duties – such as work allocation and monitoring

Table 2.2 Positive and negative indicators of performance

Manage performance	
Do things well and achieve the objectives and standards agreed for the role	
positive indicators	carries out work as required completes work on time meets quality/service standards works accurately sees things through asks for ground rules committed to achieving high-quality results shows commitment to make it happen seeks to raise quality standards puts measures in place actions match words takes ownership of things to be done evaluates and revises deadlines as necessary takes responsibility for outcomes always has a follow-up course of action makes contingency plans does everything within their means to ensure that things get done to the best of their ability confronts issues
negative indicators	frequently forgets things has to be chased to meet deadlines not concerned with quality does not learn from mistakes does not follow instructions often late in delivering expected results work not up to standard makes too many mistakes does minimum they can get away with relies on others to complete actions no pride in the job blames others for personal failure conceals situations when things go wrong focuses on less important activities builds achievements to be greater than they are agrees unrealistic deadlines prioritizes badly

quality – to newer management activities, such as people management. In some cases it included cost control/budgeting. The role typically included a combination of the following activities:

- people management;
- managing operational costs;
- providing technical expertise;
- organizing, such as planning work allocation and rotas, monitoring work processes;
- checking quality;
- dealing with customers/clients;
- measuring operational performance.

In addition, mangers promote appropriate behaviours by serving as role models and exemplars, influencing the activities of their team members by what they do and how they do it. They are there to provide guidance and support to their staff through leadership and performance management processes (agreeing roles and expectations, providing feedback and reviewing performance in order to formulate improvement and personal development plans). They promote development by acting as coaches and mentors – advising, helping people to learn by doing, and complementing learning on the job by functioning as mentors (experienced and trusted advisors).

The variety of these activities demonstrates the complexity of the role and why the work of line managers is often fragmented.

References

Carlsson, S (1951) *Executive Behaviour: A study of the workload and the working methods of managing directors*, Strombergs, Stockholm

Fayol, H (1916) *Administration Industrielle et General*, translated by C Storrs (1949) as *General and Industrial Management*, Pitman, London

Hales, C P (1986) What managers do: a critical review of the evidence, *Journal of Management Studies*, **23** (1), pp 88–115

Hutchinson, S and Purcell, J (2003) *Bringing Policies to Life: The vital role of front line managers in people management*, CIPD, London

Management Standards Centre (2004) *Management Standards* [Online] www.management-standards.org

Mintzberg, H (1973) *The Nature of Managerial Work*, Harper & Row, New York

Purcell, J et al (2003) *Understanding the People and Performance Link: Unlocking the black box*, CIPD, London

Sayles, L (1964) *Managerial Behaviour*, McGraw-Hill, New York

Silverman, D and Jones, J (1976) *Organisational Work*, Macmillan, London
Stewart, R (1967) *Managers and their Jobs*, Macmillan, London
Stewart, R *et al* (1980) *The District Administrator in the National Health Service*, Pitman, London
Tamkin, P, Hirsh, W and Tyers, C (2003) *Chore to Champion: The making of better people managers, Report 389*, Institute of Employment Studies, Brighton

3

The Role of the Leader

A leader is best when people barely know that he exists.
Not so good when people obey and acclaim him.
Worst when they despise him.
Fail to honour people, they fail to honour you.
But a good leader who talks little,
When his work is done, his aim fulfilled,
They will all say, 'We did this ourselves'.

Lao-Tzu, 6th century BC

This chapter answers the following questions about leaders:

- What is a leader?
- What are the main types of leaders?
- What do leaders do?
- How do they do it (leadership styles)?
- What makes a good leader?
- What is the significance of followers?

What is a leader?

Leaders get things done through people. They set the direction and get other people to follow them. As Ted Johns (2008) says: 'A leader takes people where they want to go. A great leader takes people where they don't necessarily want to be, but ought to be.'

There are a number of types of leaders who adopt different styles. Approaches to leadership will vary according to the situation, the personality of the leader and the characteristics of the leader's followers.

Types of leaders

Leaders have been classified into a number of different types as described below.

Transactional leaders

Transactional leaders, as originally described by Burns (1978), identify the expectations of their followers and respond to them by establishing a close link between effort and reward. Power is given to the leader to evaluate, correct and train subordinates when performance needs to be improved and to reward effectiveness when the required outcomes are achieved.

Transformational leaders

Transformational leaders, as defined by Bass (1985), empower their followers and encourage them to 'do more than they originally expected to do'. Transformational leaders motivate followers to perform at higher levels, to exert greater effort, and to show more commitment. Bass identified three principal leadership processes for achieving such outcomes: (1) heightening followers' awareness about the importance and value of designated goals and the means to achieve them; (2) inducing followers to transcend their self-interests for the good of the group and its goals; and (3) meeting followers' higher-order needs. Transformational leaders provide encouragement and support to followers, assist their development by promoting growth opportunities, and show trust and respect for them as individuals. They build self-confidence and heighten personal development.

Charismatic leaders

Charismatic leaders have compelling personalities and the ability to rouse people to follow them through the sheer force of the impression they make. As originally described by Weber (1947), charismatic leaders are achievement orientated, calculated risk-takers and good communicators. They achieve motivational outcomes through four mechanisms: (1) changing follower perceptions of the nature of work itself; (2) offering an appealing future vision; (3) developing a deep collective identity among followers; and (4) heightening both individual and collective self-efficacy (people's belief in themselves and what they can do). There is a strong affinity between the charismatic and the transformational leader.

Situational leaders

As originally described by Hersey and Blanchard (1969), a situational leader is one who can adopt different leadership styles depending on the situation. The behaviour of leaders towards their followers can take the following forms:

- Directing leaders define the roles and tasks of their followers, and supervise them closely. Decisions are made and announced by the leader, so communication is largely one-way.

- Delegating leaders are still involved in decisions and problem-solving, but control is with the follower. The follower decides when and how the leader will be involved.

- Coaching leaders still define roles and tasks, but seek ideas and suggestions from the followers. Decisions remain the leader's prerogative, but communication is much more two-way.

- Supporting leaders pass day-to-day decisions, such as task allocation and processes, to followers. Leaders facilitate and take part in decisions, but control is with the follower.

Effective leaders are versatile in being able to move between the styles according to the situation, so there is no one right style. However, people tend to have a preferred style and should understand what that is.

What do leaders do?

Leaders have three essential roles. They have to:

1. Define the task – they must make it clear what the group is expected to do.

2. Achieve the task – that is why the group exists. Leaders ensure that the group's purpose is fulfilled. If it is not, the result is frustration, disharmony, criticism and perhaps eventually disintegration of the group.

3. Maintain effective relationships – between themselves and the members of the group, and between the people within the group. These relationships are effective if they contribute to achieving the task. They can be divided into those concerned with the team and its morale and sense of common purpose, and those concerned with individuals and how they are motivated.

John Adair (1973), the leading British expert on leadership, explained that these demands are best expressed as three areas of need that leaders are there to satisfy. These are: (1) task needs – to get the job done; (2) individual needs – to harmonize the needs of the individual with the needs of the task and the group; and (3) group maintenance needs – to build and maintain team spirit. As shown in Figure 3.1, he models these demands as three interlocking circles.

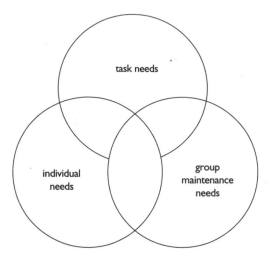

Figure 3.1 The John Adair three circle leadership model

This model suggests that the task, individual and group needs are interdependent. Satisfying task needs will also satisfy group and individual needs. Task needs, however, cannot be satisfied unless attention is paid to individual and group needs, and looking after individual needs will also contribute to satisfying group needs and vice versa. There is a danger in becoming so task orientated that individual and group or team needs are ignored, and it is just as dangerous to be too people orientated, focusing on meeting individual or group needs at the expense of the task. The best leaders are those who keep these three needs satisfied and in balance according to the demands of the situation.

How do leaders do it?

Leaders adopt different leadership styles, sometimes called management styles. To varying degrees leaders can be achievement orientated, task orientated or people orientated. They can be:

- Charismatic/non-charismatic: Charismatic leaders rely on their personality, their inspirational qualities and their 'aura'. Non-charismatic leaders rely mainly on their know-how (authority goes to the person who knows), their quiet confidence and their cool, analytical approach to dealing with problems.

- Autocratic/democratic: Autocratic leaders impose their decisions, using their position to force people to do as they are told. Democratic leaders encourage people to participate and involve them in decision-taking.

- Enabler/controller: Enablers inspire people with their vision of the future and empower them to accomplish team goals. Controllers command people to obtain their compliance.

- Transactional/transformational: Transactional leaders trade money, jobs and security for compliance. Transformational leaders motivate people to strive for higher-level goals.

Other classifications of leadership styles have been produced by House (1971) – the path-goal model – and by Hay McBer, as reported by Goleman (2000).

Path-goal leadership styles

Path-goal leadership theory identifies the following styles:

- Achievement-oriented – the leader sets challenging goals for followers, expects them to perform at their highest level, and shows confidence in their ability to meet this expectation. This style is appropriate when the follower suffers from a lack of job challenge.

- Directive – the leader lets followers know what is expected of them and tells them how to perform their tasks. This style is appropriate when the follower has an ambiguous job.

- Participative – the leader consults with followers and asks for their suggestions before making a decision. This style is appropriate when the follower is using improper procedures or is making poor decisions.

- Supportive – the leader is friendly and approachable and shows concern for the psychological well-being of followers. This style is appropriate when the followers lack confidence.

Hay McBer

Research conducted by the consulting firm Hay McBer (as reported by Goleman, 2000) identified six leadership styles:

1. Coercive: Demands immediate compliance – 'do what I tell you'.

2. Authoritative: Mobilizes people towards a vision – 'come with me'.

3. Affiliative: Creates harmony and builds emotional bonds – 'people come first'.

4. Democratic: Forges consensus through participation – 'what do you think?'

5. Pacesetting: Sets high standards for performance – 'do as I do'.

6. Coaching: Develops people for the future – 'try this'.

Choice of style

There is no such thing as an ideal leadership style. The situation in which leaders and their teams function will influence the approaches that leaders adopt. It all depends. The factors affecting the degree to which a style is appropriate will be the type of organization, the nature of the task, the characteristics of the group and, importantly, the personality of the leader.

An achievement-orientated approach may be appropriate when expectations of the results the team has to produce are high and team members can be encouraged to rise to the occasion. A task-orientated approach (autocratic, controlling and directive) may be best in emergency or crisis situations or when the leader has power, formal backing and a relatively well-structured task. In these circumstances the group is more ready to be directed and told what to do. In less well-structured or ambiguous situations, where results depend on the group working well together with a common sense of purpose, leaders who are concerned with maintaining good relationships (democratic, participative or supportive) are more likely to obtain good results.

Good leaders are capable of flexing their style to meet the demands of the situation. Normally democratic or participative leaders may have to shift into more of a directive mode when faced with a crisis, but they make clear what they are doing and why. Poor leaders change their style arbitrarily so that their team members are confused and do not know what to expect next.

Effective leaders may also flex their style when dealing with individual team members according to their characteristics. Some people need more positive direction than others. Other people respond best if they are involved in decision-making with their boss. But there is a limit to the degree of flexibility that should be used. It is unwise to differentiate too much between the ways in which individuals are treated.

The kind of leadership exercised will indeed be related to the nature of the task and the people being led. But it also depends on the context and, of course, on leaders themselves. People who have a natural leadership style that works have to be careful about changing it arbitrarily or substantially.

However, Charles Handy (1994) believes that intelligent organizations have to be run by persuasion and consent. He suggests that the heroic leader of the past 'knew all, could do all and could solve every problem'. Now, the post-heroic leader has come to the fore, who 'asks how every problem can be solved in a way that develops other people's capacity to handle it'.

What makes a good leader?

There is no universal answer to this question but recent thinking about leadership has indicated that good leaders are confident and know where they want to go and what they want to do. They have the ability to take charge, convey their vision to their team, get their team members into action and ensure that they achieve their agreed goals. They are trustworthy, effective at influencing people and earn the respect of their team. They are aware of their own strengths and weaknesses and are skilled at understanding the needs, attitudes and perspective of team members. They appreciate the advantages of consulting and involving people in decision-making. They can switch flexibly from one leadership style to another to meet the demands of different situations and people.

Many lists and explanations of the qualities required by leaders have been produced, which complement or enhance the definition of a good leader given above. Here are a few of the better known ones.

John Adair

John Adair (1973) listed the following qualities that good leaders possess:

- enthusiasm – to get things done, which they can communicate to other people;
- confidence – belief in themselves, which again people can sense (but this must not be over-confidence, which leads to arrogance);
- toughness – resilient, tenacious and demanding high standards, seeking respect but not necessarily popularity;
- integrity – being true to oneself – personal wholeness, soundness and honesty, which inspires trust;
- warmth – in personal relationships, caring for people and being considerate;
- humility – willingness to listen and take the blame, not being arrogant and overbearing.

Leadership competencies

It was argued by Bennis and Thomas (2002) that the competencies of leaders (ie their skills, attributes and behaviours) are outcomes of their formative experiences. The key competencies are adaptive capacity, an ability to engage others in shared meanings, a compelling voice and integrity. They claimed that one of the most reliable indicators and predictors of 'true leadership' is an individual's ability to find meaning in negative situations and to learn from trying circumstances.

The Industrial Society

An extensive survey conducted by the Industrial Society, now the Work Foundation (1997), revealed that what good leaders do is to make the right space for people to perform well without having to be watched over. The top 10 requirements for leader behaviour as ranked by respondents were:

1. Shows enthusiasm.

2. Supports other people.

3. Recognizes individual effort.

4. Listens to individuals' ideas and problems.

5. Provides direction.

6. Demonstrates personal integrity.

7. Practises what they preach.

8. Encourages teamwork.

9. Actively encourages feedback.

10. Develops other people.

Leadership and emotional intelligence

Emotional intelligence is a combination of skills and abilities such as self-awareness, self-control, empathy and sensitivity to the feelings of others. The notion of emotional intelligence was first defined by Salovey and Mayer (1990), who proposed that it involves the capacity to perceive emotion, integrate emotion in thought, understand emotion and manage emotions effectively.

Goleman (1995) popularized the concept. He defined emotional intelligence as: 'The capacity for recognizing our own feelings and those of others, for motivating ourselves, for managing emotions well in ourselves as well as others.' The four components of emotional intelligence are:

1. Self-management – the ability to control or redirect disruptive impulses and moods and regulate your own behaviour, coupled with a propensity to pursue goals with energy and persistence. The six competencies associated with this component are self-control, trustworthiness and integrity, initiative, adaptability (comfort with ambiguity), openness to change, and a strong desire to achieve.

2. Self-awareness – the ability to recognize and understand your moods, emotions and drives as well as their effect on others. This is linked to three competencies: self-confidence, realistic self-assessment and emotional self-awareness.

3. Social awareness – the ability to understand the emotional makeup of other people and skill in treating people according to their emotional reactions. This is linked to six competencies: empathy, expertise in building and retaining talent, organizational awareness, cross-cultural sensitivity, valuing diversity, and service to clients and customers.

4. Social skills – proficiency in managing relationships and building networks to get the desired result from others and reach personal goals, coupled with the ability to find

common ground and build rapport. The five competencies associated with this component are leadership, effectiveness in leading change, conflict management, influence/communication, and expertise in building and leading teams.

What is the significance of followers?

A report on Robert Graves by his CO in the First World War said that 'The men will follow this young officer if only to know where he is going'. This is a good start but it is not enough. Successful leaders depend on followers who want to feel that they are being led in the right direction. They need to know where they stand, where they are going and what is in it for them. They want to feel that it is all worthwhile. They have three requirements of their leaders:

1. Leaders must fit their followers' expectations – they are more likely to gain the respect and cooperation of their followers if they behave in ways that people expect from their leaders. These expectations will vary according to the group and the context but will often include being straight, fair and firm – as a nineteenth century schoolboy once said of his headmaster: 'He's a beast but a just beast'. People also appreciate leaders who are considerate, friendly and approachable but don't want them to get too close – leaders who spend too much time courting popularity are not liked.

2. Leaders must be perceived as the 'best of us' – they have to demonstrate that they are experts in the overall task facing the group. They need not necessarily have more expertise than any members of their group in particular aspects of the task, but they must demonstrate that they can get the group working purposefully together and direct and harness the expertise shared by group members to obtain results.

3. Leaders must be perceived as 'the most of us' – they must incorporate the norms and values that are central to the group. They can influence these values by visionary powers but they will fail if they move too far away from them.

Kelley (1991) suggested that the role of the follower should be studied as carefully as that of the leader. Leaders need effective followers and one of the tasks of leaders is to develop what Kelley calls 'followership' qualities. These include the ability to manage themselves well, to be committed to the organization, to build their competence and to focus their efforts for maximum impact. Keith Grint (2005) points out that 'the trick of the leader is to develop followers who privately resolve the problems leaders have caused or cannot resolve, but publicly deny their intervention'.

References

Adair, J (1973) *The Action-Centred Leader*, McGraw-Hill, London
Bass, B M (1985) *Leadership and Performance Beyond Expectations*, Free Press, New York

Bennis, W G and Thomas, R J (2002) *Geeks and Geezers: How era, values and defining moments shape leaders*, Harvard University Press, Boston, MA

Burns, J M (1978) *Leadership*, Harper & Row, New York

Goleman, D (1995) *Emotional Intelligence*, Bantam, New York

Goleman, D (2000) Leadership that gets results, *Harvard Business Review*, March–April, pp 78–90

Grint, K (2005) *Leadership: Limits and possibilities*, Palgrave Macmillan, Basingstoke

Handy, C (1994) *The Empty Raincoat*, Hutchinson, London

Hersey, P and Blanchard, K H (1969) Life cycle theory of leadership, *Training and Development Journal*, **23** (2), pp 26–34

House, R J (1971) A path-goal theory of leader effectiveness, *Administrative Science Quarterly*, **16**, pp 321–38

Industrial Society (1997) *Leadership – Steering a new course*, Industrial Society, London

Johns, E (2008) *Out to Lunch: back in six hours*, Institute of Customer Service, London

Kelley, R E (1991) In praise of followers, in *Managing People and Organizations*, ed J J Gabarro, pp 143–53, Harvard Business School Publications, Boston, MA

Salovey, P and Mayer, J D (1990) Emotional intelligence, *Imagination, Cognition and Personality*, **9**, pp 185–211

Weber, M (1947) *The Theory of Social and Economic Organizations*, translated by A M Henderson and T Parsons, ed T Parsons, Free Press, New York

Part II

Approaches to Management

4

Managing for Results

'Work, to achieve results, has to be thought through and done with direction, method and purpose.'

Peter Drucker (1963) *Managing for Results*, Heinemann, London

Management was defined in Chapter 1 as the process of deciding what to do and then getting it done through the effective use of resources. It is about what managers do to make things happen. They define goals, determine the resources – people, finance, work systems and technology – required to achieve the goals, allocate those resources to opportunities and planned activities and ensure that those activities take place as planned in order to achieve predetermined objectives. All this adds up to managing for results.

Peter Drucker (1963) wrote that managers must be committed to 'the systematic, purposeful and organized discharge' of the tasks in their jobs. He emphasized the need for a unified, organization-wide programme for performance and for a unified, organization-wide plan for the work to be done. The foundations for these activities are decisions on the idea of the business and its objectives, on the areas of excellence and on priorities and strategies. This leads to an assessment of the efforts required and to the selection of the resources to be committed. Performance becomes a job for which someone is responsible: 'If it is to be real assignment, there has to be a deadline; work without deadlines is not work assigned but work toyed with'.

Managing for results involves planning, setting objectives, organizing, and generally making things happen. These are covered in turn in this chapter.

Planning

Planning is a key aspect of managing for results. Planning involves deciding on a course of action, ensuring that the resources required to implement the action will be available, and scheduling and prioritizing the work required to achieve a defined end result.

The aim of planning is to enable managers to complete tasks on time by making the best use of the resources available to them. They need to avoid crises and the high costs that they cause; to have fewer 'drop everything and rush this' problems. Contingency or fall-back plans are prepared if there is any reason to believe that the initial plan may fail for reasons beyond the manager's control.

When managers plan, they may choose certain courses of action and rule out others; that is to say, they lose flexibility. This will be a disadvantage if the future turns out differently from what was expected – which is only too likely. Managers should try to make plans that can be changed without undue difficulty. It is a bad plan that admits no change.

Planning ingredients

Most of the planning managers carry out is simply a matter of thinking systematically and using common sense. Every plan contains four key ingredients:

1. The objective – what is to be achieved.
2. The action programme – the specific steps required to achieve the objective.
3. Resource requirements – what resources, in the shape of money, people, facilities and time, will be required.
4. Impact assessment – determining the impact made on the organization by achieving the plan (assessed in terms of costs and benefits).

Planning activities

There are 10 planning activities:

1. Defining goals – what has to be achieved through the plan.
2. Organizing – deciding how the work and the people who carry it out should be organized.
3. Forecasting what sort of work has to be done, how much and by when, and how the workload might change.
4. Prioritizing – deciding the sequence and timescale of operations.
5. Programming the activities and events required to produce results on time.

6. Workforce planning – deciding how many and what type of people are needed and considering the feasibility of absorbing peak loads by means of overtime, temporary staff, subcontracting or outsourcing.

7. Establishing detailed performance requirements – for output, sales, times, quality, costs or for any other aspect of the work where performance should be planned, measured and controlled.

8. Procedure planning – deciding how the work should be done and planning the actual operations by defining the systems and processes required.

9. Materials planning – deciding what materials, bought-in parts or subcontracted work are required and ensuring that they are made available in the right quantity at the right time.

10. Facilities planning – deciding on the plant, equipment, tools and space required.

Setting objectives and targets

One of the most important tasks carried out by managers as leaders is to manage expectations. Each individual and the team as a whole must know what they have to do and achieve. The task is to ensure that performance requirements developed in the planning stage are expressed as objectives or goals.

What are objectives?

An objective describes something that has to be accomplished – a point to be aimed at. Objectives or goals (the terms are interchangeable) define what organizations, functions, departments, teams and individuals are expected to achieve. There are two main types of objectives: work and personal.

Work objectives

Work or operational objectives refer to the results to be achieved or the contribution to be made to the accomplishment of team, departmental and corporate objectives. At corporate level they are related to the organization's mission, core values and strategic plans. At departmental or functional level they are related to corporate objectives, spelling out the specific mission, targets and purposes to be achieved by a function or department. At team level they will again be related specifically to the purpose of the team and the contribution it is expected to make to achieving departmental and corporate goals. At individual level they are role-related, referring to the principal accountabilities, main activity areas or key tasks that constitute the individual's role. They focus on the results individuals are expected to achieve and how they contribute to the attainment of team, departmental and corporate goals and to upholding the organization's core values.

Personal objectives

Personal or learning objectives are concerned with what individuals should do and learn to improve their performance (performance improvement plans) and/or their knowledge, skills and overall level of competency (learning and personal development plans).

How are individual work objectives expressed?

Individual objectives define the results to be achieved and the basis upon which performance in attaining these results can be measured by the use of key performance indicators (KPIs) or measures. They can take the form of targets, standing objectives or project objectives.

Targets

Individual objectives can be expressed as quantified output or improvement targets (open 24 new accounts by 30 November, reduce cost per unit of output by 2.5 per cent by 30 June), or in terms of projects to be completed (open distribution depot in Northampton by 31 October). Targets may be reset regularly, say once a year or every six months, or be subject to frequent amendments to meet new requirements or changed circumstances.

Standing objectives

Objectives for some aspects of a role (or for all aspects of some roles) can be what might be described as 'standing objectives'. These are concerned with the permanent or continuing features of a role and may be incorporated in a role profile, which specifies what has to be achieved in terms of key result areas. They can lead to defined standards of performance.

Qualitative standing objectives may also be defined for behaviour that will contribute to upholding the core values of the organization. For example, if one of the core values relates to the development of the skills and competencies of employees, a performance standard for employee development could be one of the objectives agreed for all managers and team leaders.

Project objectives

Project objectives define what has to be achieved by an individual who is managing or contributing to a project. They will define the purpose of the project and the success criteria – how the conduct and impact of the project will be measured.

What is a good work objective?

Good work or operational objectives are:

- Consistent with the values of the organization and departmental and organizational objectives.

- Precise: clear and well defined, using positive words.

- Challenging: to stimulate high standards of performance and to encourage progress.

- Measurable: they can be related to quantified or qualitative performance measures.

- Achievable within the capabilities of the individual. Account should be taken of any constraints that might affect the individual's capacity to achieve the objectives; these could include lack of resources (money, time, equipment, support from other people), lack of experience or training, external factors beyond the individual's control, etc.

- Agreed by the manager and the individual concerned. The aim is to provide for the ownership, not the imposition, of objectives, although there may be situations where individuals have to be persuaded to accept a higher standard than they believe themselves capable of attaining.

- Time-related – achievable within a defined timescale (this would not be applicable to a standing objective).

- Teamwork orientated – emphasize teamwork as well as individual achievement.

- The acronym SMART is often used to define a good objective: S = stretching; M = measurable; A = agreed; R = realistic; T = time-related.

Defining work objectives

The process of agreeing objectives need not be unduly complicated. It starts with the agreement of the key result areas, which define broadly what role holders are expected to achieve in each of the main elements of their role (these are sometimes called principal accountabilities or main tasks). For example, a key result area for the head of a distribution centre may be to ensure that agreed levels of service delivery are achieved. It is then a matter of jointly examining each area and agreeing targets and standards of performance as appropriate. In the case of a head of distribution, a service-level agreement might be set out that specifies standards in such areas as turning round dispatch orders, delivery within a time limit and number of customer complaints. Agreement can also be reached on any projects to be undertaken that might be linked to a specific accountability, or maybe more general projects that fall broadly within the remit of the role holder. Defining objectives involves agreeing targets and standards of performance.

Defining targets

Targets are quantified and time based – they always define specific and measurable outputs and when they have to be reached. The target may be to achieve a specified level of output or to improve performance in some way. Targets may be expressed in financial terms such as profits to be made, income to be generated, costs to be reduced or budgets to be worked within. Or they may be expressed in numerical terms as a specified number of units to be processed, sales volume to be achieved, responses to be obtained or clients or customers to be contacted over a period of time.

Output targets are expressed in financial or unitary terms, for example:

- Achieve sales of £1.6 million by 30 June.

- Maintain inventory levels at no more than £12 million.

- Maintain throughput at the rate of 800 units a day.

Performance improvement targets may be expressed in terms such as:

- Increase sales turnover for the year by 8 per cent in real terms.

- Reduce the overhead to sales ratio from 22.6 to 20 per cent over the next 12 months.

- Increase the ratio of successful conversions (enquiry to sales) from 40 to 50 per cent within six months.

- Reduce the number of customer complaints to 0.5 per cent of deliveries made.

Defining performance standards

A performance standard definition should take the form of a statement that performance will be up to standard if a desirable specified and observable result happens. Performance standards are broadly defined in outcome terms in the key result area definitions contained in a role profile. But the broad definition should be expanded and as far as possible quantified, by reference to levels of service or speed of response, for example. Where the standard cannot be quantified, a more qualitative approach may have to be adopted, in which case the standard of performance definition would in effect state: 'This job or task will have been well done if... [these things happen]'. Junior or more routine jobs are likely to have a higher proportion of standing objectives to which performance standards are attached than senior and more flexible or output-orientated jobs. A qualitative standard could be expressed as: 'Performance will be up to standard if requests for information are dealt with promptly and helpfully on a can do/will do basis and are delivered in the form required by the user'.

It is often assumed that qualitative performance standards are difficult to define. But all managers make judgements about the standards of performance they expect and obtain from their staff, and most people have some idea of whether or not they are doing a good job. The problem is that these views are often subjective and are seldom articulated. Even if, as often happens, the final definition of a performance standard is somewhat unspecific, the discipline of working through the requirements in itself will lead to greater mutual understanding of performance expectations.

Organizing

To achieve their goals, managers have to ensure that they have the resources required and that the human element of those resources is properly organized in the sense of deciding what needs to be done, grouping activities together, establishing lines of communication and control and defining responsibilities and accountabilities.

Managers or team leaders may have been promoted, transferred or recruited into a post and presented with an established organization structure. Very occasionally, they may have to set up their own organization. More frequently, they may feel that there are improvements that can usefully be made to the structure or to the ways in which responsibilities and tasks are allocated to members of their team.

The aim of organizing can be defined as being to optimize the arrangements for conducting the affairs of the business or business unit. To do this it is necessary, as far as circumstances allow, to:

- clarify the overall purposes of the organization or organizational unit;

- define the key activities required to achieve that purpose;

- group these activities logically together to avoid unnecessary overlap or duplication;

- provide for the integration of activities and the achievement of cooperative effort and teamwork in pursuit of the common purpose;

- build flexibility into the system so that organizational arrangements can adapt quickly to new situations and challenges;

- clarify individual roles, accountabilities and authorities;

- design jobs to make the best use of the skills and capacities of the job holders and to provide them with high levels of intrinsic motivation.

The process of organization and of designing and developing organizations is dealt with in more detail in Part 3 of this book.

Making things happen

Managing for results is ultimately about making things happen; getting things done. Managers have to be achievers, taking personal responsibility for delivering what they are there to do. John Harvey-Jones, in *Making it Happen* (1984), said of the approaches used by successful business managers:

- Nothing will happen unless everyone down the line knows what they are trying to achieve and gives of their best to achieve it.

- The whole of business is taking an acceptable risk.

- The process of deciding where you take the business is an opportunity to involve others, which actually forms the motive power that will make it happen.

This section of the chapter first poses and answers three basic questions on how to make it happen. An analysis is then conducted of what makes achievers tick and what achievers do. The section continues by considering a key quality required to make things happen, namely decisiveness, and concludes with a discussion of how managers can analyse and improve their capacity to get things done.

How to make it happen: basic questions

It is said that there are three sorts of managers: those who make things happen, those who watch things happening, and those who don't know what is happening. Before finding out how to get into the first category, there are three questions to answer:

1. Is making things happen simply a matter of personality – characteristics like drive, decisiveness, leadership, ambition, a high level of achievement motivation – which some people have and others haven't?

2. And if people haven't got the drive, decisiveness and so forth that it takes, is there anything they can do about it?

3. To what extent is an ability to get things done a matter of using techniques that can be learnt and developed?

The significance of personality

Personality is important. Without the drive to achieve nothing will happen. But remember that personality is a function of both nature and nurture. People are born with genes that influence certain characteristics of their behaviour, but upbringing, education, training and, above all, experience develop them into the person they are.

Doing something about it

People may not be able to change their personality, which, according to Freud, is formed in the first few years of their life. But they can develop and adapt it by consciously learning from their experience and analysing other people's behaviour.

Using techniques

Techniques for achieving results such as setting objectives, planning, organizing, delegating, motivating and monitoring performance can be learnt. But these techniques are only as effective as the person who uses them. They must be applied in the right way and in the right circumstances. And you still have to use your experience to select the right technique and your personality to make it work.

What makes achievers tick?

People who make things happen have high levels of achievement motivation – a drive to get something done for the sheer satisfaction of achieving it. David McClelland (1961) of Harvard University identified three needs through his research, which he believed were key factors in motivating managers. These were:

1. The need for achievement.

2. The need for power (having control and influence over people).

3. The need for affiliation (being accepted by others).

All effective managers need to have each of these needs to a certain degree but by far the most important is achievement. This is what counts and achievers, according to McClelland, have these characteristics:

- They set themselves realistic but achievable goals with some 'stretch' built in.

- They prefer situations that they can influence rather than those that are governed by chance.

- They are more concerned with knowing that they have done well than with the rewards that success brings.

- They get their rewards from their accomplishment rather than from money or praise. This does not mean that high achievers reject money, which can in fact motivate them as long as it is seen as a realistic measure of their performance.

- High achievers are most effective in situations where they can get ahead by their own efforts.

What do achievers who make things happen do?

High achievers do many, if not all, of these things:

- They define to themselves precisely what they want to do.

- They set demanding but not unattainable timescales and deadlines in which to do it, which they meet.

- They convey clearly what they want done and by when.

- They are single-minded about getting where they want to go, showing perseverance and determination in the face of adversity.

- They demand high performance from themselves and equally expect high performance from everyone else.

- They work hard and well under pressure; in fact, it brings out the best in them.

- They tend to be dissatisfied with the status quo.

- They are never completely satisfied with their own performance and continually question themselves.

- They take calculated risks.

- They snap out of setbacks and quickly regroup their forces and ideas.

- They are enthusiastic about the task and convey their enthusiasm to others.

- They are decisive in that they are able to quickly sum up situations, define alternative courses of action, determine the preferred course, and convey to the members of their team what needs to be done.

- They continually monitor their own performance and that of their team so that any deviation can be corrected in good time.

On being decisive

To make things happen people have to be decisive. This means being prepared to make decisions and live with the consequences. A consultant in a New York hospital promoted a registrar because he was a good decision-maker. When asked why she had promoted someone whose decisions were not always right, the consultant replied 'I said he was a good decision-maker, not that he made good decisions'. Being decisive means that people sometimes have to take risks. They may be calculated but they do not always work. But indecisiveness is even worse. As long as people learn from their mistakes and avoid repeating them, the occasional and inevitable poor decision need not matter unduly. There is more about being decisive in Chapter 8.

Analysing and improving how you make things happen

Improving your ability to make things happen means analysing how you get things done, identifying areas for improvement and taking action. It is no good trying to assess your performance as a doer unless you have criteria against which you can measure that performance. You have to set standards for yourself and if you don't meet them, ask yourself why. The answer should tell you what to do next time.

The questions you should ask yourself are:

- What did I set out to do?

- Did I get it done?

- If I did, why and how did I succeed?

- If not, why not?

The aim is to make the best use of your experience in getting things done.

Use the list of what high achievers do to check your own behaviour and actions. If your performance has not been up to scratch under any of these headings, ask yourself what went wrong and decide how you are going to overcome this difficulty next time. This is not always easy. It is hard to admit to yourself, for example, that you have not been sufficiently enthusiastic. It may be even harder to decide what to do about it. You don't want to enthuse all over the place, indiscriminately. But you can consider whether there are better ways of displaying and conveying your enthusiasm to others in order to carry them with you.

References

Drucker, P (1963) *Managing for Results*, Heinemann, London
Harvey-Jones, J (1984) *Making it Happen*, Collins, Glasgow
McClelland, D C (1961) *The Achieving Society*, Van Norstrand, New York

5

Managing Strategically

The purpose of strategic management is to 'elicit the present actions for the future ... – integrating and institutionalising mechanisms for change'.
Rosabeth Moss Kanter (1984) *The Change Masters,* **Allen & Unwin, London**

Managing strategically involves adopting a broader and longer-term view of what needs to be done and ensuring that the activities you carry out contribute to achieving the organization's strategic goals. In this chapter: (1) the underpinning concept of strategy is defined; (2) the concept of strategic management is examined; (3) consideration is given to the development of a shared vision; (4) the process of developing strategy is explained; and (5) the meaning and importance of strategic capability as a necessary requirement of managing strategically is explored.

Strategy

Strategy consists of a statement or an understanding of what the organization or a part of it wants to become, where it wants to go and, broadly, how it means to get there. Business strategy in a commercial enterprise answers the questions: 'What business are we in?' and 'How are we going to make money out of it?'

Strategy determines the direction in which the enterprise is going in relation to its environment in order to achieve sustainable competitive advantage. The emphasis is on focused actions that differentiate the firm from its competitors. It is a declaration of intent that defines means to achieve ends, and is concerned with the long-term allocation of significant resources and with matching those resources and capabilities to the external environment. Strategy is a perspective on the way in which critical issues or success factors can be addressed, and strategic decisions aim to make a major and long-term impact on the behaviour and success of the organization.

Individual managers develop strategies for the accomplishment of their longer-term objectives. Again, these are directions of intent and definitions of how it is proposed those intentions should be put into effect.

Strategies are developed to provide for the realization of visions – views on what the future should be.

Strategic management

Strategic management is what managers do when they look ahead at what they need to achieve in the middle or relatively distant future. Although, as Fombrun *et al* (1984) put it, the managers are aware of the fact that businesses, like managers, must perform well in the present to succeed in the future, they are concerned with the broader issues they are facing and the general directions in which they must go to deal with these issues and achieve longer-term objectives. They do not take a narrow or restricted view.

Strategic management has been described by Rosabeth Moss Kanter (1984) as follows: 'Strong leaders articulate direction and save the organization from change by drift... They see a vision of the future that allows them to see more clearly what steps to take, building on present capacities and strengths'.

Strategic management deals with both ends and means. As an end it describes a vision of what something will look like in a few years' time. As a means, it shows how it is expected that the vision will be realized. Strategic management is therefore visionary management, concerned with creating and conceptualizing ideas of where the organization should be going. But it is also empirical management, which decides how in practice it is going to get there.

The focus is on identifying the organization's mission and strategies, but attention is also given to the resource base required to make it succeed. It is always necessary to remember that strategy is the means to create value. Managers who think strategically will have a broad and long-term view of where they are going. But they will also be aware that they are responsible first for planning how to allocate resources to opportunities that contribute to the implementation of strategy, and secondly for managing those opportunities in ways that will significantly add value to the results achieved by the firm.

The process of strategic management is modelled in Figure 5.1. It involves defining the organization's mission, analysing the internal and external environment, exercising strategic choice (there is always choice), formulating corporate and functional strategies and goals, implementing strategies, and monitoring and evaluating progress in achieving goals. But in practice, it is not as simple and linear as that. Boxall and Purcell (2003) believe that strategic management 'is a mixed, impure, interactive process, fraught with difficulties, both intellectually and politically'.

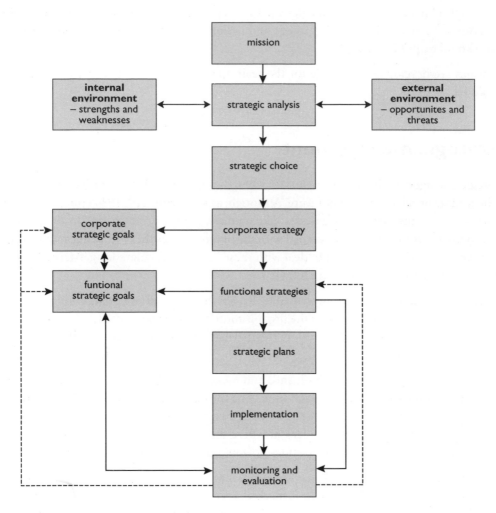

Figure 5.1   A strategic management model

Developing a shared vision

A vision provides a broad picture of what the future might look like. It provides the basis for formulating and implementing strategic plans. Visionary management is the process of developing, sharing and implementing a view of what needs to be done. It is much more than a process in which managers sit in their offices and indulge in pipe dreams about the future. A vision can only be realized if it is shared with those who have to act upon it order to obtain their commitment and engagement. To gain support for the vision it is necessary to present it in language that people can understand and to discuss with those concerned its implications in terms of the part they will play and the benefits that will ensue for themselves as well as the organization. They need to be given a voice in deciding what needs to be done so that they become parties to the vision rather than simply being at the receiving end. They should be regarded as stakeholders who have a legitimate interest in what the vision means and their role in making it real.

Developing strategic plans

The formulation of strategic plans can be defined as a process for developing a sense of direction. It has often been described as a logical, step-by-step affair, the outcome of which is a formal written statement that provides a definitive guide to the organization's or the manager's long-term intentions. Many people still believe and act as if this were the case, but it is a misrepresentation of reality. This is not to dismiss completely the ideal of adopting a systematic approach – it has its uses as a means of providing an analytical framework for strategic decision-making and a reference point for monitoring the implementation of strategy. But in practice the formulation of strategy can never be as rational and linear a process as some managers attempt to make it.

Strategy formulation can best be described as 'problem-solving in unstructured situations' (Digman, 1990) and strategies will always be formed under conditions of partial ignorance. The difficulty is that strategies are often based on the questionable assumption that the future will resemble the past. Robert Heller (1972) criticized the cult of long-range planning: 'What goes wrong,' he wrote, 'is that sensible anticipation gets converted into foolish numbers, and their validity always hinges on large loose assumptions'. Faulkner and Johnson (1992) have said of long-term planning that it:

> was inclined to take a definitive view of the future, and to extrapolate trend lines for the key business variables in order to arrive at this view. Economic turbulence was insufficiently considered, and the reality that much strategy is formulated and implemented in the act of managing the enterprise was ignored. Precise forecasts ending with derived financials were constructed, the only weakness of which was that the future almost invariably turned out differently.

Strategy formulation is not necessarily a rational and continuous process, as was pointed out by Mintzberg (1987). He believes that, rather than being consciously and systematically developed, strategy reorientation happens in what he calls brief 'quantum loops'. A strategy, according to Mintzberg, can be deliberate – it can realize the intentions of management, for example to attack and conquer a new market. But this is not always the case. In theory, he says, strategy is a systematic process: first we think, then we act; we formulate, then we implement. But we also 'act in order to think'. In practice, 'a realized strategy can emerge in response to an evolving situation' and the strategic planner is often 'a pattern organizer, a learner if you like, who manages a process in which strategies and visions can emerge as well as be deliberately conceived... Strategy is a pattern in a stream of activities.' Mintzberg (1994) also contended that 'the failure of systematic planning is the failure of systems to do better than, or nearly as well as, human beings'. He went on to say that 'real strategists get their hands dirty digging for ideas, and real strategies are built from the nuggets they discover', and 'sometimes strategies must be left as broad visions, not precisely articulated, to adapt to a changing environment'.

Again, it is important to involve people in the process of strategic planning so they understand what is to be accomplished, why it needs to be accomplished and the part they will play in accomplishing it. A stakeholder approach is required. Everyone involved should be treated as stakeholders because they have a personal interest in the outcome, as it affects not only the organization but also themselves. As stakeholders they have the right to comment on proposals and put forward their own ideas. In this way the original concept can be refined so that it becomes more achievable with the participation of the stakeholders.

Strategic capability

To manage strategically requires strategic capability – the capacity to create an achievable vision for the future, to foresee longer-term developments, to envisage options (and their probable consequences), to select sound courses of action, to rise above the day-to-day detail, to see the big picture, and to challenge the status quo.

Managers with high levels of strategic capability will:

- understand the strategic goals of the organization or unit and appreciate the business imperatives and performance drivers relative to these goals;

- comprehend how sustainable competitive advantage can be obtained through their efforts;

- contribute to the development of a clear vision and a set of integrated values for the business;

- ensure that senior management understands the business implications of the function or activity they control;

- be aware of the broader context (the competitive environment and the business, economic, social and legal factors that affect it) in which the organization operates;

- think in terms of the bigger and longer-term picture of where their unit, function or department should go and how it should get there;

- be capable of making a powerful business case for any proposals on the development of business strategies in their area;

- be able to introduce and manage change within their area.

References

Boxall, P F and Purcell, J (2003) *Strategy and Human Resource Management*, Palgrave Macmillan, Basingstoke

Digman, L A (1990) *Strategic Management: Concepts, decisions, cases*, Irwin, Georgetown, Ontario

Faulkner, D and Johnson, G (1992) *The Challenge of Strategic Management*, Kogan Page, London

Fombrun, C J, Tichy, N M, and Devanna, M A (1984) *Strategic Human Resource Management*, New York, Wiley

Heller, R (1972) *The Naked Manager*, Barrie & Jenkins, London

Kanter, R M (1984) *The Change Masters*, Allen & Unwin, London

Mintzberg, H (1987) Crafting strategy, *Harvard Business Review*, July–August, pp 66–74

Mintzberg, H (1994) The rise and fall of strategic planning, *Harvard Business Review*, January–February, pp 107–14

6

Managing for Performance

'All proposals for new ventures, capital investment, or new products and services should be directed towards the company's programme for performance.'
Peter Drucker (1963) *Managing for Results*, Heinemann, London

Managing for results means managing for performance. This involves developing a high-performance culture and high-performance work systems for the organization as a whole, and managing the performance of individuals and teams.

High-performance culture

A high-performance culture is one in which striving for improved performance is a recognized way of life. The characteristics of an organization in which such a culture exists can be as follows:

- people know what's expected of them – they are clear about their goals and accountabilities;

- people have the skills and competencies to achieve their goals;

- high-performance is recognized and rewarded accordingly;

- people feel that their job is worth doing, and that there's a strong fit between the job and their capabilities;

- managers act as supportive leaders and coaches, providing regular feedback, performance reviews and development;

- a pool of talent ensures a continuous supply of high performers in key roles;

- there's a climate of trust and teamwork, aimed at delivering a distinctive service to the customer.

Examples of high-performance working in a number of companies are given in Table 6.1.

Table 6.1   Examples of high-performance working ingredients

Organization	High-performance working ingredients
Halo Foods	A strategy that maintains competitiveness by increasing added value through the efforts and enhanced capability of all staff. The integration of technical advance with people development. Continuing reliance on team working and effective leadership, with innovation and self- and team management skills.
Land Registry	Organizational changes to streamline processes, raise skill levels and release talents. Managers who could see that the problems were as much cultural as organizational. Recruitment of people whose attitudes and aptitudes match the needs of high-performance work practices.
Meritor Heavy Vehicle Braking Systems	Skill enhancement, particularly of management and self-management skills, using competence frameworks. Team working skills and experience used in improvement projects. Linking learning, involvement and performance management.
Orangebox	A strategy that relies on constant reinvention of operational capability. Engagement and development of existing talent and initiative in productivity improvement. Increasing use of cross-departmental projects to tackle wider opportunities.
PerkinElmer	A vision and values worked through by managers and supervisors. Engagement of everyone in the organization and establishment of a continuous improvement culture. Learning as a basis for change.
United Welsh Housing Association	Linking of better employment relations with better performance. Using staff experience to improve customer service. Focusing management development on the cascading of a partnership culture.

Source: Stevens (2005)

Developing a high-performance culture

A high-performance strategy focuses on what needs to be done to reach the organization's goals. The approach to development is therefore based on: (1) an understanding of what those goals are and how people can contribute to their achievement; and (2) assessing what type of performance culture is required. This provides the basis for creating a high-performance work system.

High-performance work systems

High-performance work systems provide the means for creating a performance culture. They embody ways of thinking about performance in organizations and how it can be improved. They are concerned with developing and implementing bundles of complementary practices that as an integrated whole will make a much more powerful impact on performance than if they were dealt with as separate entities.

As defined by Appelbaum *et al* (2000), a high-performance work system (HPWS) consists of practices that can facilitate employee involvement, skill enhancement and motivation. Research conducted by Armitage and Keble-Allen (2007) indicated that people management basics formed the foundation of high-performance working. They identified three themes underpinning the HPWS concept:

1. An open and creative culture that is people-centred and inclusive, where decision-taking is communicated and shared through the organization.

2. Investment in people through education and training, loyalty, inclusiveness, and flexible working.

3. Measurable performance outcomes such as benchmarking and setting targets, as well as innovation through processes and best practice.

Sung and Ashton (2005) defined what they call high-performance work practices as a set of 35 complementary work practices covering three broad areas: high employee involvement work practices; human resource practices; and reward and commitment practices. They refer to them as 'bundles' of practices.

As described by Appelbaum *et al* (2000), a HPWS is 'generally associated with workshop practices that raise the levels of trust within workplaces and increase workers' intrinsic reward from work, and thereby enhance organizational commitment'.

Components of a HPWS

Descriptions of high-performance systems usually include lists of desirable practices and therefore embody the notion of 'best practice'. However, such lists vary considerably and doubt can be expressed over any concept of best practice that implies that there are ways of doing things that are universally applicable. The practices adopted by an organization must fit their circumstances. Best fit is more important than best practice.

However, there are a number of typical features of a HPWS, such as those listed by Thompson and Heron (2005):

- information sharing;
- sophisticated recruitment;
- formal induction programme;
- five or more days of off-the-job training in the last year;
- semi- or totally autonomous work teams, continuous improvement teams, problem-solving groups;
- interpersonal skill development;
- performance feedback;
- involvement – works council, suggestion scheme, opinion survey;
- team-based rewards, employee share ownership scheme, profit-sharing scheme.

Impact of high-performance working

US studies conducted by Appelbaum *et al* (2000), King (1995), Varma *et al* (1999) and others have demonstrated that high-performance work systems are associated with high-performance.

In the United Kingdom, Sung and Ashton (2005) conducted a survey of 294 UK companies. Their research included 10 case studies. Its aim was to study the relationship between the adoption of high-performance working practices and a range of organizational outcomes. A list of 35 high-performance practices was drawn up under the three headings of high-involvement practices, human resource practices, and reward and commitment practices. The survey provided evidence that the level of high-performance practice as measured by the number of practices in use is linked to organizational performance. Those adopting more of the practices as 'bundles' had greater employee involvement and were more effective in delivering adequate training provision, managing staff and providing career opportunities.

Developing a high-performance work system

The development programme requires strong leadership from the top. Stakeholders – line managers, team leaders, employees and their representatives – should be involved as much as possible through surveys, focus groups and workshops. The steps required are described below.

1. Analyse the business strategy:

    –   where is the business going?

    –   what are the strengths and weaknesses of the business?

    –   what threats and opportunities face the business?

    –   what are the implications of the above on the type of people required by the business, now and in the future?

    –   to what extent do we – can we – obtain competitive advantage through people?

2. Define the desired performance culture of the business and the objectives of developing a HPWS – use the list of characteristics above as a starting point and produce a list that is aligned to the culture and context of the business and a statement of the objectives of developing a HPWS.

3. Analyse the existing arrangements – start from the headings defined at stage 2 and analyse against each heading:

    –   what is happening now in the form of practices, attitudes and behaviours (what should people do differently)?

    –   what should be happening?

    –   what do people feel about it (the more involvement in this analysis from all stakeholders the better)?

4. Identify the gaps between what is and what should be – clarify specific practices where there is considerable room for improvement.

5. Draw up a list of practices that need to be introduced or improved – at this stage only a broad definition should be produced of what ideally needs to be done.

6. Establish links – identify the practices that can be related together in 'bundles' in order to complement and support one another.

7. Assess practicality – the ideal list of practices, or preferably bundles of practices, should be subjected to a reality check:

    –   is it worth doing? What's the business case in terms of added value? What contribution will it make to supporting the achievement of the organization's strategic goals?

    –   can it be done?

    –   who will do it?

    –   have we the resources to do it?

    –   how do we manage the change?

8. Prioritize – in the light of the assessment of practicalities, decide on the priorities that should be given to introducing new or improved practices. A realistic approach is essential. There will be a limit on how much can be done at once or at any future time. Priorities should be established by assessing:

   – the added value the practice will create;

   – the availability of the resources required;

   – anticipated problems in introducing the practice, including resistance to change by stakeholders (too much should not be made of this as change can be managed, but there is much to be said for achieving some quick wins);

   – the extent to which they can form bundles of mutually supporting practices.

9. Define project objectives – develop the broad statement of objectives produced at stage 2 and define what is to be achieved, why and how.

10. Get buy-in – this should start at the top with the chief executive and members of the senior management team, but as far as possible it should also extend to all the other stakeholders (easier if they have been involved at earlier stages and if the intentions have been fully communicated).

11. Plan the implementation – this is where things become difficult. Deciding what needs to be done is fairly easy; getting it done is the hard part. The implementation plan needs to cover:

    – who takes the lead – this must come from the top of the organization; nothing will work without it;

    – who manages the project and who else is involved;

    – the timetable for development and introduction;

    – the resources (people and money required);

    – how the change programme will be managed, including communication and further consultation;

    – the success criteria for the project.

12. Implement – too often, 80 per cent of the time spent on introducing a HPWS is spent on planning and only 20 per cent on implementation. It should be the other way round. Whoever is responsible for implementation must have considerable project and change management skills.

Managing individual performance

The management of individual performance involves five elements: agreement, measurement, feedback, positive reinforcement and dialogue. The process of performance management is illustrated in Figure 6.1.

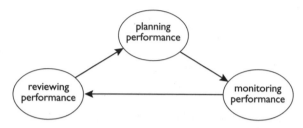

Figure 6.1   The performance management cycle

This model illustrates that performance management is a continuous process – it proceeds from planning (defining expectations) to monitoring (managing performance throughout the year) to reviewing performance against expectations and reformulating the plan on the basis of that review.

Planning performance

Performance planning involves managers and individuals reporting to them reaching an agreement (often called a performance and development agreement) on what needs to be done by both parties to improve performance. The starting point for the plan is a role profile, which defines the results, knowledge, skills and behaviours required. This should be agreed as the basis for deciding on objectives and performance measures or key performance indicators. Performance development plans are derived from an analysis of role requirements and an assessment of the performance displayed in meeting them.

Monitoring performance

Performance management is what managers do. It is an integral part of the continuing process of management. Managers should therefore be ready, willing and able to deal with performance issues as they arise. It should not be left to the annual performance review. The process of continuing assessment should be carried out by reference to agreed objectives and to work, development and improvement plans. Progress reviews can take place informally or through an existing system of team meetings. But there should be more formal interim reviews at predetermined points in the year, eg quarterly. For some teams or individual jobs these points could be related to 'milestones' contained in project and work plans. Deciding when such meetings should take place would be up to individual managers in consultation with their staff and would not be a laid-down part of a 'system'. Managers should be encouraged to consider how to accommodate the need for regular dialogue within the established pattern of briefings, team or group meetings, or project review meetings.

In addition to the collective meetings, managers may have regular one-to-one meetings with their staff. If performance management is to be effective, there needs to be a continuing agenda through these regular meetings to ensure that good progress is being made towards achieving the objectives agreed for each key result area.

Reviewing performance

Although performance management is a continuous process, it is still necessary to have a formal review once or twice yearly. This acts as a focal point for the consideration of key performance and development issues, provides an opportunity to take stock, and forms the basis for performance and development planning. Many managers are extraordinarily reluctant to conduct such meetings at all, or at best their reviews are perfunctory. All sorts of reasons are given for this: 'I haven't got enough time', 'It's not necessary – I am already reviewing performance on a day-to-day basis', 'I don't like sitting down and making formal criticisms of someone'. The answers to these objections are simple:

- 'Surely you can spare an hour or so to spend quality time with your staff, if only to show that you are interested in their progress and prepared to give them your support.'

- 'That may well be so, but isn't it a good idea to carry out a systematic review of progress so that both parties are in a better position to plan for the future?'

- 'Performance reviews are not just about criticizing people. They are opportunities to recognize achievements as well as agreeing any areas where improvement is required and planning how this should take place.'

The performance review meeting is the means through which the five primary performance management elements of agreement, measurement, feedback, positive reinforcement and dialogue can be put to good use.

The review should be rooted in the reality of the employee's performance. It is concrete, not abstract, and it allows managers and individuals to take a positive look together at how performance can become better in the future and how any problems in meeting performance standards and achieving objectives can be resolved. Individuals should be encouraged to assess their own performance and become active agents for change in improving their results. Managers are there to carry out their proper enabling role: coaching and providing support and guidance.

There should be no surprises in a formal review if performance issues have been dealt with as they should have been – as they arise during the year. Traditional appraisals are often no more than an analysis of where those involved are now, and where they have come from. This static and historical approach is not what performance management is about. The true role of performance management is to look forward to what needs to be done by people to achieve the purpose of the job, to meet new challenges, to make even better use of their knowledge, skills and abilities, to develop their capabilities by establishing a self-managed learning agenda, and to reach agreement on any areas where performance needs to be improved and how that improvement should take place. This process also helps managers to improve their ability to lead, guide and develop the individuals and teams for whom they are responsible.

Managing team performance

Teams can provide the 'elusive bridge between the aims of the individual employee and the objectives of the organization, [they] provide the medium for linking employee performance targets to the factors critical to the success of the business' (Purcell *et al*, 2003). This is an important aspect of managing performance. How it is applied will be related to the following factors that affect team performance:

- the clarity of the team's goals in terms of expectations and priorities;
- how work is allocated to the team;
- how the team is working (its processes) in terms of cohesion, ability to handle internal conflict and pressure, and relationships with other teams;
- the extent to which the team is capable of managing itself – setting goals and priorities and monitoring performance;
- the quality of leadership – even self-managed teams need a sense of direction, which they cannot necessarily generate by themselves;
- the level of skill possessed by individual team members (including multi-skilling);
- the systems and resources support available to the team.

Team performance management processes

Team performance management involves the team in agreeing work and process activities and conducting team performance reviews. The aim should be to give teams and their team leaders the maximum amount of responsibility to carry out all activities. The focus should be on self-management and self-direction.

Setting work objectives

Work objectives for teams are set in much the same way as individual objectives (see Chapter 4). They will be based on an analysis of the purpose of the team and its accountabilities for achieving results. Targets and standards of performance should be discussed and agreed by the team as a whole. These may specify what individual members are expected to contribute. Project teams will agree project plans that define what has to be done, who does it, the standards expected and the timescale.

Setting process objectives

Process objectives are also best defined by the team getting together and agreeing how they should conduct themselves as a team, under headings such as:

- interpersonal relationships;
- the quality of participation and collaborative effort and decision-making;
- the team's relationships with internal and external customers;
- the capacity of the team to plan and control its activities;
- the ability of the team and its members to adapt to new demands and situations;
- the flexibility with which the team operates;
- the effectiveness with which individual skills are used;
- the quality of communication within the team and between the team and other teams or individuals.

Team performance reviews

Team performance review meetings analyse and assess feedback and control information on their joint achievements against objectives and project plans. The agenda for such meetings could be as follows:

1. General feedback review:
    - progress of the team as a whole;
    - problems encountered by the team that have caused difficulties or hampered progress;
    - helps and hindrances to the operation of the team.
2. Work reviews:
    - how well the team has functioned;
    - review of the individual contribution made by each team member – ie peer review;

- discussion of any new problems encountered by individual team members.

3. Group problem-solving:

- analysis of reasons for any shortfalls or other problems;

- agreement of what needs to be done to solve them and prevent their reoccurrence.

4. Update objectives:

- review of new requirements, opportunities or threats;

- amendment and updating of objectives and project plans.

References

Appelbaum, E *et al* (2000) *Manufacturing Advantage: Why high-performance work systems pay off*, ILR Press, Ithaca, New York

Armitage, A and Keble-Allen, D (2007) Why people management basics form the foundation of high-performance working, *People Management*, 18 October, p 48

King, J (1995) High performance work systems and firm performance, *Monthly Labour Review*, May, pp 29–36

Purcell, J *et al* (2003) *People and Performance: How people management impacts on organisational performance*, CIPD, London

Stevens, J (2005) *High Performance Wales: Real experiences, real success*, Wales Management Council, Cardiff

Sung, J and Ashton, D (2005) *High Performance Work Practices: Linking strategy and skills to performance outcomes*, DTI in association with CIPD [Online] http://www.cipd.co.uk/subjects/corpstrtgy/

Thompson, M and Heron, P (2005) Management capability and high-performance work organization, *The International Journal of Human Resource Management*, **16** (6), pp 1029–48

Varma, A *et al* (1999) High performance work systems: exciting discovery or passing fad? *Human Resource Planning*, **22** (1), pp 26–37

7
Managing the Business

'The entrepreneur shifts economic resources out of an area of lower and into an area of higher productivity and greater yield.'
Jean-Baptiste Say (1803) *A Treatise on Political Economy, or the production, distribution and consumption of wealth*

The chief executive of a large charity once said to the author of this book: 'We are not a business but we have to be businesslike'. So does every manager, whether they are line managers directly controlling operational functions or managers in associated functions such as HR (human resources), finance or IT (information technology).

In HR circles much has been made recently of the Dave Ulrich (1998) concept of the HR professional as a business partner, and there are now lots of HR business partners. But there is a lack of clarity about what they do except work alongside their line manager colleagues, and there is nothing new in that. It is preferable to consider them as part of management and not merely partners. The suggestion of Professor Shaun Tyson (1985) that they should act as business managers is nearer the mark. He stated that personnel specialists carrying out this role integrate their activities closely with management and ensure that they serve a long-term strategic purpose. They have the capacity to identify business opportunities, to see the broad picture and to understand how their role can help to achieve the company's business objectives. They anticipate needs, act flexibly and are proactive. In other words, they are businesslike.

This chapter starts by examining what 'being businesslike' means and then deals with four of the key business management activities: preparing the business plan; making a business case; financial budgeting and control; and cost–benefit analysis.

On being businesslike

A businesslike approach to management is one that focuses on allocating resources to business opportunities and making the best use of them to achieve the required results. Managers who are businesslike understand and act upon:

- the business imperatives of the organization: its mission and its strategic goals;

- its business model – the basis upon which its business is done (how its mission and strategic goals will be achieved);

- its business drivers – the characteristics of the business that move it forward;

- its core competences – what the business is good at doing;

- the factors that will ensure the effectiveness of its activities, including specific issues concerning profitability, productivity, financial budgeting and control, costs and benefits and operational performance;

- the key performance indicators (KPIs) of the business, which can be used to measure progress towards attaining goals;

- the factors that will ensure that the firm's resources, especially its human resources, create sustained competitive advantage because they are valuable, imperfectly imitable and non-substitutable (the resource-based view);

- the fact that they are there to create added value through the effective use of resources (cf the quotation from J-B Say at the head of this chapter);

- the need to provide excellent customer service;

- how continuous improvement can be obtained;

- the need to maintain high levels of quality.

Efficiency and effectiveness

It might be thought that being businesslike is simply a matter of being efficient – doing the right things, getting things done on time, ensuring that everything goes smoothly, making more out of less, keeping costs under control and not making mistakes. P G Wodehouse (1929) summed it up in this description of 'the efficient Baxter':

> We have called Rupert Baxter efficient and efficient he was. The word, as we interpret it, implies not only a capacity for performing the ordinary tasks of life with a smooth firmness of touch, but in addition a certain alertness of mind, a genius for seeing clearly, thinking swiftly and Doing it Now.

This sort of efficiency is important in a business but it is even more important to be effective. Peter Drucker (1963), a pioneer thinker in this aspect of management, as in many others, summed it up when he wrote:

> *Management, we are usually told, should concern itself with efficiency, that is with doing better what is already being done. It should therefore focus on costs. But the entrepreneurial approach focuses on effectiveness, that is, on the decision what to do. It focuses on opportunities to produce revenue, to create markets and to change the economic characteristics of existing products and markets. It asks not: how do we do this or that? It asks: which of the products really produce economic results or are capable of producing them? which of the markets and/or uses are capable of producing extraordinary results? It then asks: to what results should therefore the resources and efforts of the business be allocated so as to produce extraordinary results rather than the 'ordinary' results which is all efficiency can possibly produce.*

Drucker was concentrating on profit-making firms but the same principle applies in the public and not-for-profit sectors. They have to focus on the delivery of public services or the provision of effective services that meet crucial needs in the community. They have to do this efficiently but it is the results of their activities that matter.

The difference between efficiency and effectiveness was summed up by Reddin (1970) as follows: 'Efficiency is doing things right; effectiveness is doing the right things'. The danger of placing too much emphasis on efficiency is that the object of the exercise becomes obscured by the bureaucratic machinery set up to achieve it. To be businesslike, the approach should be – in Drucker's phrase again – to manage for results. It's the end that counts, not the means, although it is necessary to adopt the most efficient way of getting from here to there. Costs must be controlled, and if they are excessive, cost-cutting exercises may be necessary, even drastic ones like a 10 per cent cut 'across the board'. But money is not made and results are not attained by cutting costs. Organizations must go for growth and/or continuous improvement. They must invest in success and in profit-making firms they often have to spend money to make money.

How to be businesslike

Managers who are businesslike are concerned generally with understanding the business they are in and with being effective rather than merely efficient. In particular, they need to understand how to prepare a business plan, how to make a business case, how to control their financial budgets and how to conduct a cost–benefit analysis.

Preparing a business plan

A business plan sets out what a business or an individual intends to achieve and how it will be achieved, in order to attract any investment required. The plan includes financial projections of revenue and profit based on business forecasts covering the planned levels of sales or activity, the income they will generate and the investment required to get the expected results. Additionally, it will provide information in sufficient but not excessive detail on how those results will be achieved.

A business plan may be required to convince some person or organization – a senior executive in the company, a bank, a finance company – to invest in an idea (ie spend money on it) or a business. Importantly, the discipline of producing a business plan and then using it as a point of reference provides the basis for driving and managing a business.

Structuring a business plan

The structure of a business plan will vary according to its purpose and the type of business it is dealing with. The following are typical headings:

- summary;
- the background;
- the proposal;
- financial projections;
- supporting information on the market, operations, finance, control systems, management and personnel;
- a risk assessment;
- conclusion.

Presenting the plan

The plan needs to make a good impression and then hold the attention of the reader. To do this it must be clearly laid out with headings and subheadings to provide signposts to take people through the text. Short, sharp sentences should be used with action words saying what will be done and when. Avoid jargon.

The plan should be evidence-based. Proposals should be supported by reliable and verifiable facts and figures wherever possible.

Making a business case

A business case sets out the reasons why a proposed course of action will benefit the business, how it will provide that benefit and how much it will cost. The case should be made either in added value terms (ie the income generated by the proposal will significantly exceed the cost of implementing it), or on the basis of the return on investment (ie the cost of the investment, say in training, is justified by the financial returns in such areas as increased productivity).

The basis for a business case

A business case is more convincing when it is accompanied by realistic projections of the return on investment. The case for capital expenditure can be made by an analysis of the cash flows associated with the investment and appraisals of the benefits that are likely to arise from them. The object is to demonstrate that in return for paying out a given amount of cash today, a larger amount will be received over a period of time. There are a number of investment appraisal techniques available, such as payback, the accounting rate of return, discounted cash flow and net present value. The case for a new product idea can be based on answers to the following questions:

1. Does it meet a well-defined consumer need?

2. In what segment of the market can this product be sold?

3. In what way does this product provide more value to customers than existing products with which it would compete?

4. Can it be differentiated adequately from alternative products?

5. How well does it fit in with the existing product range?

6. Does it exploit the company's existing skills and resources?

7. What investment is required in developing and marketing the new product?

8. What is the likely return on that investment?

Making the business case can be more difficult in areas where it is hard to generate convincing estimates of future income, for example when justifying investment in training. But an attempt should be made. In the following example training investment was justified because it would:

●   improve individual, team and corporate performance in terms of output, quality, speed and overall productivity;

●   attract high-quality employees by offering them learning and development opportunities, increasing their levels of competence and enhancing their skills, thus enabling them to obtain more job satisfaction, to gain higher rewards and to progress within the organization;

- improve operational flexibility by extending the range of skills possessed by employees (multi-skilling);

- increase the commitment of employees by encouraging them to identify with the mission and objectives of the organization;

- help to manage change by increasing understanding of the reasons for change and providing people with the knowledge and skills they need to adjust to new situations;

- provide line managers with the skills required to manage and develop their people;

- help to develop a positive culture in the organization, for example one that is orientated towards performance improvement;

- help to provide higher levels of service to customers;

- minimize learning costs (reduce the length of learning curves).

Enhancing the business case

A business case will be enhanced if:

- it can be shown convincingly that the return on investment meets or exceeds the amount required by company policy and that the immediate costs are not going to have detrimental effects on cash flow;

- data is made available on the impact the proposal is likely to make on key areas of the organization's operations, eg customer service levels, quality, shareholder value, productivity, income generation, innovation, skills development, talent management;

- it can be shown that the proposal will increase the competitive edge of the business, for example by ensuring that it can achieve competitive advantage through innovation and/or reducing time-to-market;

- there is proof that the innovation has already worked well within the organization (perhaps as a pilot scheme) or represents 'good practice' that is likely to be transferable to the organization;

- it can be implemented without too much trouble, for example it will not take up a lot of managers' time;

- it will add to the reputation of the company by showing that it is a 'world class' organization, ie what it does is as good as, if not better than, the world leaders in the sector in which the business operates (a promise that publicity will be achieved through articles in professional journals, press releases and conference presentations will help);

- the proposal is brief, to the point and well argued – it should take no more than five minutes to present orally and should be summarized in writing on the proverbial one side of one sheet of paper (supplementary details can be included in appendices).

Financial budgeting and control

A businesslike approach means understanding the principles of financial budgeting and budgetary control and putting them into practice.

Financial budgeting

Budgets translate policy into financial terms. They are statements of the planned allocation and use of the company's resources. They are needed to: (1) show the financial implications of plans; (2) define the resources required to achieve the plans; and (3) provide the means of measuring, monitoring and controlling results against the plans.

The procedure for preparing financial budgets consists of the following steps:

1. Budget guidelines are prepared that have been derived from the corporate plan and forecasts. They will include the activity levels for which budgets have to be created and the ratios to be achieved. In a commercial firm these would include return on capital employed, overheads to sales revenue, stock to sales, stock to current assets, and current liabilities to current assets. In a non-commercial organization such as a charity the key ratio may be expenses to revenue. The assumptions to be used in budgeting are also given. These could include rates of inflation and increases in costs and prices.

2. Initial budgets for a budget or cost centre are prepared by departmental managers with the help of budget accountants. They record projected expenditures and activity levels. Increases to budgets that are not in line with changes in activity levels or price/cost assumptions have to be justified. A business case may be required for this purpose. Departmental budgets are checked by the finance department (a management accountant) and then by higher management to ensure that they meet the guidelines and increases are properly justified.

3. Departmental budgets are collated and analysed to produce the master budget. This is reviewed by top management, who may require changes at departmental level to bring it into line with corporate financial objectives and plans.

4. The master budget is finally approved by top management and issued to each departmental (budget centre) manager for planning and control purposes.

Budgetary control

Budgetary control ensures that financial budgets are met and that any variances are identified and dealt with. Control starts with the budget for the cost centre, which sets out the budgeted expenditure under cost headings against which activity levels have been built into the budget. A system of measurement or recording is used to allocate expenditures to cost headings and record activity levels achieved. The actual expenditures and activity levels are compared and positive and negative variances noted. Cost centre managers then act to deal with the variances and report their results to higher management.

Cost–benefit analysis

Cost–benefit analysis is the financial assessment of the total costs and revenues or benefits of a project, paying attention to the social costs and benefits that do not normally feature in conventional costing exercises. The aims are to justify a project, programme or activity and inform the development of a strategy that achieves the maximum benefit for the minimum cost. A cost–benefit analysis is carried out in the following stages:

1. The project and its overall objectives (described as benefits) are defined.

2. A more detailed list is prepared of the anticipated benefits and likely costs. Social benefits and costs will be included in this list.

3. The list of benefits and costs, direct and indirect, is reduced to monetary values to arrive at an estimate of the projected net benefit of the project, if any. This can be a judgemental process.

4. The stream of net benefits is predicted for each year of the project.

5. The stream of annual net benefits is concerned with the capital cost of the project, which can be expressed as a percentage return on investment (RoI). The most common method is discounted cash flow, which converts the time stream of net benefits into present value terms.

References

Drucker, P (1963) *Managing for Results*, Heinemann, London

Reddin, W J (1970) *Managerial Effectiveness*, McGraw-Hill, London

Tyson, S (1985) Is this the very model of a modern personnel manager? *Personnel Management*, **26**, pp 35–39

Ulrich, D (1998) A new mandate for human resources, *Harvard Business Review*, January–February, pp 124–34

Wodehouse, P G (1929) *Summer Lightning*, Penguin Classics, Harmondsworth

8

Management Skills

'The manager of tomorrow... will have to master system and method, will have to conceive patterns and synthesize elements into wholes, will have to formulate general concepts and to apply general principles.'

Peter Drucker (1955) *The Practice of Management*, Heinemann, London

This chapter deals with the following basic skills needed by managers:

- communicating;
- report writing;
- making presentations;
- motivating;
- coaching;
- decision-making;
- delegating;
- facilitating;
- giving feedback;
- networking;
- problem-solving.

Communicating

The manager's role can be said to be 20 per cent doing and 80 per cent putting it across, that is, communicating. People recognize the need to communicate but find it difficult. Like Schopenhauer's hedgehogs, they want to get together, it's only their prickles that keep them apart.

There are two forms of communication:

1. Intra-personal communication, which takes place when we converse with ourselves. We ask ourselves questions, reflect on events and our involvement in them, consider the actions we have taken or not taken, and interpret the factors affecting the decisions we have made in different circumstances.

2. Inter-personal communication, which takes the form of conveying or exchanging information, instructions, observations or comments to and between people.

In inter-personal communications words are used that may sound or look precise, but they are not. All sorts of barriers exist between the communicator and the receiver. Unless these barriers are overcome, the message will be distorted or will not get through. It will fail to persuade or convince. The main barriers and methods of overcoming them are set out in Table 8.1. Methods of communicating through reports and presentations are dealt with in the next two sections of this chapter.

Table 8.1   Barriers to communication

Barriers to communication	Overcoming the barriers
Hearing what we want to hear: What we hear or understand when someone speaks to us is largely based on our own experience and background. Instead of hearing what people have told us, we hear what our minds tell us they have said.	Adjust to the world of the receiver: Try to predict the impact of what you are going to write or say on the receiver's feelings and attitudes. Tailor the message to fit the receiver's vocabulary, interests and values.
Ignoring conflicting information: We tend to ignore or reject communications that conflict with our own beliefs. If they are not rejected, some way is found of twisting and shaping their meaning to fit our preconceptions.	Use feedback: Ensure that you get a message back from the receiver that tells you how much has been understood.

Table 8.1 *continued*

Barriers to communication	Overcoming the barriers
Perceptions about the communicator: It is difficult to separate what we hear from our feelings about the person who says it. Non-existent motives may be ascribed to the communicator. If we like people we are more likely to accept what they say – whether it is right or wrong – than if we dislike them.	Use face-to-face communication: Whenever possible talk to people rather than write to them. That is how you get feedback. You can adjust or change your message according to reactions. You can also deliver it in a more human and understanding way – this can help to overcome prejudices. Verbal criticism can often be given in a more constructive manner than a written reproof, which always seems to be harsher.
Influence of the group: The group with which we identify influences our attitudes and feelings. What a group hears depends on its interests. People are more likely to listen to their colleagues, who share their experiences (their reference group), than to outsiders such as managers.	Involve the group: Get the group involved in the discussion so that feelings can be brought out into the open.
Words mean different things to different people: Essentially language is a method of using symbols to represent facts and feelings. Strictly speaking, we can't convey meaning, all we can do is to convey words. Do not assume that because something has a certain meaning to you, it will convey the same meaning to someone else.	Use direct, simple language: This seems obvious. But many people clutter up what they say with jargon, long words and elaborate sentences.
Emotions: Our emotions colour our ability to convey or to receive the true message.	Control emotion: Try to make your communication as unemotional as possible. Appeal to reason.
Non-verbal communication: When we try to understand the meaning of what people say we listen to the words, but we also use other clues that convey meaning. We attend not only to what people say but to how they say it. We form impressions from what is called body language.	Understand the role of non-verbal communication: Remember that your body language may affect listeners.

Table 8.1 *continued*

Barriers to communication	Overcoming the barriers
Misinterpretation: People can easily misinterpret information for any of the reasons given above.	Get it across: Reinforce written communications with the spoken word. Conversely, an oral briefing should be reinforced in writing.
Size: The larger and more complex the organization, the greater the problem of communication.	Reduce problems of size: Go direst to those who need to get the message.

Report writing

A good report has the following characteristics:

- a logical structure;

- the use of plain words to convey meaning;

- messages presented lucidly, persuasively and, above all, succinctly.

Structure

A report should be structured in a way that ensures the reader is taken through a sequence of sections that are clearly linked to one another and proceed logically from the introduction to the recommendations and conclusions. An executive summary may be included. A typical structure could incorporate the following sections:

Executive summary

If the report is long and/or complex, an 'executive summary' of the findings, recommendations and conclusions is helpful. It concentrates the reader's mind and can serve as an agenda for discussion. The summary should be brief, no more than one side of a sheet of paper, and it should be set out in bullet points.

The introduction

This explains what the report is about, why the report has been written, its aims, its terms of reference, and why it should be read. If the report is divided into sections the readers should be given an indication of the logic of the structure as a signpost to direct them through the report.

The analysis

This is a factual review of the situation or problem. It could describe the present arrangements, breaking them down into their elements – the main areas for attention. It would refer to the data collected as part of the study – the key facts that have been assembled, although too much detail should not be included (this could be attached in an appendix). The analysis would identify the symptoms of any problems and should lead directly to the diagnosis.

The diagnosis

This is prepared by reference to the factual analysis. It indicates the causes of any problems and therefore sets out the issues to be addressed. The diagnosis provides the basis for any recommendations.

Recommendations

The recommendations specify the proposed action(s). They should flow logically and clearly from the analysis and diagnosis. Where there is no obvious solution, alternatives may be presented and evaluated but a clear recommendation should emerge from this evaluation. An indication should be given of what the recommendation involves and why and how it addresses the issue(s).

Action plan

The action plan sets out what needs to be done to implement the recommendations. It should identify:

- what precisely will have to be done;
- who will be responsible;
- the estimated costs;
- the other resources required (internal staff, external advice, materials and equipment);
- the timescale for implementation;
- the programme of work.

Conclusions

The conclusions summarize the main findings (the analysis and diagnosis) and recommendations. An indication of the benefits arising from these proposals should be made (this could be linked to costs in the form of a cost–benefit analysis).

Plain words

Gowers (1987) suggested that in order to convey meaning without ambiguity, and avoid giving the reader unnecessary trouble, it is advisable to:

1. Use no more words than are required to express the meaning, for if too many are used the meaning may be obscured and the reader will be tired. Do not use superfluous adjectives and adverbs, and do not use roundabout phrases where single words would serve.

2. Use familiar words rather than the far-fetched if they express the meaning equally well, for the familiar are more likely to be understood.

3. Use short words with a precise meaning rather than those that are vague, for they will obviously serve better to make the meaning clear; and in particular, prefer concrete words to abstract for they are more likely to have a precise meaning. Too many long words are off-putting.

4. Avoid jargon. If its use is unavoidable, explain what it means in plain language.

Presentation

The way in which the report is presented and written affects its impact and value. The reader should be able to follow the argument easily and not get bogged down in too much detail. If a large amount of supporting data are needed, place these in appendices.

Paragraphs should be short and each one should be restricted to a single topic. It is helpful to use bullet points in order to list and highlight a series of observations or comments.

In long reports it may be a good idea to number paragraphs for ease of reference. Some people prefer the system that numbers main sections 1, 2, etc, subsections 1.1, 1.2, etc, and sub-sub-sections 1.1.1, 1.1.2, etc. However, this can be clumsy and distracting. A simpler system, which eases cross-referencing, is to number each paragraph 1, 2, 3, etc rather than the headings; sub-paragraphs or tabulations can be indicated as 'bullet points'.

Use headings to guide people on what they are about to read and to help them find their way about the report. Main headings should be in capitals or bold lower case, and subheadings should be in bold where capitals have been used for main headings, or italicized lower case where the main headings have been in bold.

The report will make most impact if it is brief and to the point. Read and reread the draft to cut out any superfluous material or flabby writing.

Making presentations

The three keys to effective speaking are:

● thorough preparation;

● good delivery;

● overcoming nervousness.

Thorough preparation

Allow yourself ample time for preparation. You will probably need at least 10 times as much as the duration of your talk. The main stages are:

1. Get informed. Collect and assemble all the facts and arguments you can get hold of.

2. Decide what to say. Define the main messages you want to get across.

3. Limit the number to three or four – few people can absorb more than this number of new ideas at any one time. Select the facts, arguments and examples that support your message.

4. Structure your talk into the classic beginning, middle and end:

   – Start thinking about the middle first, with your main messages and the supporting facts, arguments and illustrations.

   – Arrange your points so that a cumulative impact and a logical flow of ideas is achieved.

   – Then turn to the opening of your talk. Your objectives should be to create attention, arouse interest and inspire confidence. Give your audience a trailer to what you are going to say. Underline the objective of your presentation – what they will get out of it.

   – Finally, think about how you are going to close your talk. First and last impressions are very important. End on a high note.

5. Think carefully about length. Never talk for more than 40 minutes at a time – 20 or 30 minutes is better. Very few speakers can keep people's attention for long. An audience is usually very interested to begin with (unless you make a mess of your opening), but interest declines steadily until people realize that you are approaching the end. Then they perk up. Hence the importance of your conclusion.

6. Keep the audience's attention throughout. Give interim summaries that reinforce what you are saying and, above all, hammer home your key points at intervals throughout your talk.

7. Ensure continuity. You should build your argument progressively until you come to a positive and convincing conclusion. Provide signposts, interim summaries and bridging sections that lead your audience naturally from one point to the next.

8. Prepare your notes. In the first place write out your introductory and concluding remarks in full and set out in some detail the main text of your talk. It is not usually necessary to write everything down. You should then boil down your text to the key headings to which you will refer in your talk. Your aim should be to avoid reading your speech if you possibly can, as this can completely remove any life from what you have to say. So as not to be pinned down behind a lectern, it is better to write your summarized points on lined index cards to which you can refer easily as you go along.

9. Prepare and use visual aids. As your audience will only absorb one-third of what you say, if that, reinforce your message with visual aids. Appeal to more than one sense at a time. PowerPoint slides provide good backup, but don't overdo them and keep them simple. Too many visuals can be distracting (use no more than 15 or so in a half-hour presentation) and too many words, or an over-elaborate presentation, will divert, bore and confuse your audience. As a rule of thumb, try not to put more than five or six bullet points on a slide. Each point should contain not more than six or seven words. Audiences dislike having to read a lot of small print on an over-busy slide. Use diagrams and charts wherever possible to break up the flow of words and illustrate points. If you want the members of your audience to read something fairly elaborate, distribute the material as a handout and take them through it.

10. Rehearse. Rehearsal is vital. It instils confidence, helps you to get your timing right, and enables you to polish your opening and closing remarks and coordinate your talk and visual aids. Rehearse the talk to yourself several times and note how long each section takes. Get used to expanding on your notes without waffling. Practise giving your talk out loud – standing up, if that is the way you are going to present it. Get someone to hear you and provide constructive criticism. It may be hard to take but it could do you a world of good.

11. Check arrangements in the room. Ensure that your projector works and you know how to operate it. Check also on focus and visibility. Before you begin your talk, check that your notes and visual aids are in the right order and to hand.

Good delivery

To deliver a presentation effectively the following approaches should be used:

- Talk audibly and check that you can be heard at the back of the room. Your task is to project your voice. It's easier when there is a microphone, but even then, you have to think about getting your words across.

- Vary the pace (not too fast, not too slow), pitch and emphasis of your delivery. Use pauses to make a point.

- Try to be conversational and as informal as the occasion requires (but not too casual).

- Convey that you truly believe in what you are saying; audiences respond well to enthusiasm.

- Avoid a stilted delivery. That is why you must not read your talk. If you are your natural self people are more likely to be on your side. They will forgive the occasional pause to find the right word.

- Light relief is a good thing but don't drag in irrelevant jokes or, indeed, make jokes at all if you are no good at telling them. You do not have to tell jokes.

- Use short words and sentences.

- Keep your eyes on the audience, moving from person to person to demonstrate that you are addressing them all, and also to gauge their reactions to what you are saying.

- If you can manage without elaborate notes (your slides or a few cards may be sufficient), come out from behind the desk or lectern and get close to your audience. It is best to stand up so that you can project what you say more effectively, unless it is a smallish meeting round a table.

- Use your hands for gesture and emphasis in moderation (don't put them in your pockets – if you have them).

- Don't fidget.

- Stand naturally and upright.

- You can move around the platform a little to add variety – you don't want to look as if you are clutching the lectern for much needed support. But avoid pacing up and down like a caged tiger.

Overcoming nervousness

Some nervousness is a good thing. It makes you prepare, makes you think and makes the adrenalin flow, thus raising performance. But excessive nervousness ruins your effectiveness and must be controlled.

The common reasons for excessive nervousness are: fear of failure; fear of looking foolish; fear of breakdown; a sense of inferiority; and dread of the isolation of the speaker. To overcome nervousness you should:

- Practise. Take every opportunity you can get to speak in public. The more you do it, the more confident you will become. Solicit constructive criticism and act on it.

- Know your subject. Get the facts, examples and illustrations that you need to put across.

- Know your audience. Who is going to be there? What are they expecting to hear? What will they want to get out of listening to you?

- Know your objective. Make sure that you know what you want to achieve. Visualize, if you can, each member of your audience going away having learnt something new that they are going to put into practical use.

- Prepare. If you know that you have prepared carefully, as suggested earlier, you will be much more confident on the day.

- Rehearse. This is an essential method of overcoming nervousness.

Motivating

Leadership, as described in Chapter 1, is about getting people into action and ensuring that they continue taking that action in order to complete the task. It is therefore very much about motivation. This can be defined as the process of getting people to move in the direction the leader wants them to go. The organization as a whole provides the context within which high levels of motivation can be achieved, through reward systems and the provision of opportunities for growth and development. But managers still have a major part to play in deploying their motivating skills to ensure that people give of their best. The aim is to get people to exert the maximum amount of positive discretionary effort – they often have a choice about how they carry out their work and the amount of care, innovation and productive behaviour they display. Discretionary effort makes the difference between people just doing a job and people doing a great job.

What is motivation?

A motive is a reason for doing something. Motivation is concerned with the factors that influence people to behave in certain ways. Motivating other people is about getting them to move in the direction you want them to go in order to achieve a result. Motivation can be described as goal-directed behaviour.

Motivation is initiated by the conscious or unconscious recognition of an unsatisfied need. A goal is then established that it is believed will satisfy this need, and a decision is made on the action that it is expected will achieve the goal. If the goal is achieved the need will be satisfied and the behaviour is likely to be repeated the next time a similar need emerges. If the goal is not achieved the same action is less likely to be repeated. This process is modelled in Figure 8.1.

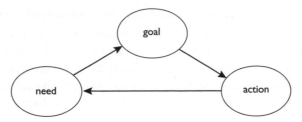

Figure 8.1   The process of motivation

Ten ways of motivating people

1. Agree demanding but achievable goals.

2. Create expectations that certain behaviours and outputs will produce worthwhile rewards when people succeed.

3. Provide feedback on performance.

4. Design jobs that enable people to feel a sense of accomplishment, to express and use their abilities, and to exercise their own decision-making powers.

5. Make good use of the organization's reward system to provide appropriate financial incentives.

6. Provide recognition and praise for work well done.

7. Communicate to your team and its members the link between performance and reward, thus enhancing expectations.

8. Provide effective leadership.

9. Give people the guidance and training that will develop the knowledge and skills they need to improve their performance and be rewarded accordingly.

10. Offer opportunities for learning and development that will enable them to advance their careers.

Coaching

Coaching is a personal (usually one-to-one), on-the-job approach used by managers and trainers to help people develop their skills and levels of competence. As a manager you are there to get results through people; this means that you have a personal responsibility for ensuring that they acquire and develop the skills they need. Other people in the shape of learning and development specialists may help, but because by far the best way of learning is on the job, the onus is mainly on you.

The need for coaching may arise from formal or informal performance reviews, but opportunities for coaching will emerge during normal day-to-day activities. Every time you delegate a new task to someone, a coaching opportunity is created to help the individual learn any new skills or techniques that are needed to do the job. Every time you provide feedback to an individual after a task has been completed, there is an opportunity to help that person do better next time. Methods of giving feedback are described later in this chapter.

Aims of coaching

The aims of coaching are to:

- help people to become aware of how well they are doing, where they need to improve and what they need to learn;

- put controlled delegation into practice; in other words, managers can delegate new tasks or enlarged areas of work, provide guidance as necessary on how the tasks or work should be carried out, and monitor performance in doing the work;

- get managers and individuals to use whatever situations arise as learning opportunities;

- enable guidance to be provided on how to carry out specific tasks as necessary, but always on the basis of helping people to learn rather than spoon-feeding them with instructions on what to do and how to do it.

The coaching sequence

Coaching can be carried out in the following stages:

1. Identify the areas of knowledge, skills or capabilities where learning needs to take place to qualify people to carry out a task, provide for continuous development, enhance transferable skills or improve performance.

2. Ensure that the person understands and accepts the need to learn.

3. Discuss with the person what needs to be learnt and the best way to undertake the learning.

4. Get the person to work out how they can manage their own learning while identifying where they will need help from you or someone else.

5. Provide encouragement and advice to the person in pursuing the self-learning programme.

6. Provide specific guidance as required where the person needs your help.

7. Agree how progress should be monitored and reviewed.

Effective coaching

Coaching will be most effective when the coach understands that their role is to help people to learn, when individuals are motivated to learn, and when they are given guidance on what they should be learning and feedback on how they are doing. The coach should listen to individuals to understand what they want and need, and adopt a constructive approach, building on strengths and experience. It should be remembered that learning is an active, not a passive, process – individuals need to be actively involved with their coach.

Planned coaching

Coaching may be informal but it has to be planned. It is not simply checking from time to time on what people are doing and then advising them on how to do it better. Nor is it occasionally telling people where they have gone wrong and throwing in a lecture for good measure. As far as possible, coaching should take place within the framework of a general plan of the areas and direction in which individuals will benefit from further development. Coaching plans can and should be incorporated into the general development plans set out in performance management discussions.

The manager as coach

Coaching enables you to provide motivation, structure and effective feedback as long as you have the required skills and commitment. As coaches, good managers believe that people can succeed and that they can contribute to their success. They can identify what people need to be able to do to improve their performance. They have to see this as an important part of the role – an enabling, empowering process that focuses on learning requirements.

Decision-making

Good managers are decisive. They can quickly size up a situation and reach the right conclusion about what should be done about it. To say of someone 'He or she is decisive' is praise indeed, as long as the decisions are effective. To be decisive it is first necessary to know something about the decision-making process as summarized in the following section. You should also be familiar with the techniques of problem-solving explained later in this chapter.

Characteristics of the decision-making process

Decision-making is about analysing the situation or problem, identifying possible courses of action, weighing them up and defining a course of action. Peter Drucker (1967) says: 'A decision is a judgement. It is a choice between alternatives. It is rarely a choice between right and wrong.

It is at best a choice between almost right and probably wrong – but much more often a choice between two courses of action neither of which is probably more nearly right than the other.'

You should not expect or even welcome a bland consensus view. The best decisions emerge from conflicting viewpoints. This is Drucker's first law of decision-making: 'One does not make a decision without disagreements'. You can benefit from a clash of opinion as it prevents people falling into the trap of starting with the conclusion and then looking for the facts that support it.

Alfred P Sloan of General Motors knew this. At a meeting of one of his top committees he said: 'Gentlemen, I take it we are all in agreement on the decision here.' Everyone around the table nodded assent. 'Then,' continued Mr Sloan, 'I propose we postpone further discussion of the matter until our next meeting to give ourselves time to develop disagreement and perhaps gain some understanding of what the decision is all about.'

Ten approaches to being decisive

1. Make decisions faster – Jack Welch, when heading General Electric, used to say: 'In today's lightning-paced environment, you don't have time to think about things. Don't sit on decisions. Empty that in-basket so that you are free to search out new opportunities... Don't sit still. Anybody sitting still, you are going to guarantee they're going to get their legs knocked from under them.'

2. Avoid procrastination – it is easy to put an e-mail demanding a decision into the 'too difficult' section of your actual or mental in-tray. Avoid the temptation to fill your time with trivial tasks so that the evil moment when you have to address the issue is postponed. Make a start. Once you have got going you can deal with the unpleasant task of making a decision in stages. A challenge often becomes easier once we have started dealing with it. Having spent five minutes on it, we don't want to feel it was wasted, so we carry on and complete the job.

3. Expect the unexpected – you are then in the frame of mind needed to respond decisively to a new situation.

4. Think before you act – this could be a recipe for delay, but decisive people use their analytical ability to come to swift conclusions about the nature of the situation and what should be done about it.

5. Be careful about assumptions – we have a tendency to leap to conclusions and seize on assumptions that support our case, ignoring the facts that might contradict it.

6. Learn from the past – build on your experience in decision-making; what approaches work best. But don't rely too much on precedents. Situations change. The right decision last time could well be the wrong one now.

7. Be systematic – adopt a rigorous problem-solving approach, as described later in this chapter. This means specifying objectives (what you want to achieve), defining the criteria

for judging whether they have been achieved, getting and analysing the facts, looking for causes rather than focusing on symptoms, developing and testing hypotheses and alternative solutions, and evaluating possible causes of action against the objectives and criteria.

8. Talk it through – before you make a significant decision talk it through with someone who is likely to disagree so that any challenge they make can be taken into account (but you have to canvass opinion swiftly).

9. Leave time to think it over – swift decision-making is highly desirable but you must avoid knee-jerk reactions. Pause, if only for a few minutes, to allow yourself time to think through the decision you propose to make. Confirm that it is logical and fully justified.

10. Consider the potential consequences – McKinsey, the management consultants, call this 'consequence management'. Every decision has a consequence and you should consider very carefully what that might be and how you would manage it. When making a decision it is a good idea to start from where you mean to end – define the end result and then work out the steps needed to achieve it.

Delegating

You can't do everything yourself, so you have to delegate. It is one of the most important things managers do. At first sight delegation looks simple. Just tell people what you want them to do and then let them get on with it. But there is more to it than that. It is not easy. It requires courage, patience and skill. And it is an aspect of your work in which you have more freedom of choice than in any other of your activities. What you choose to delegate, to whom and how, is almost entirely at your discretion.

This section provides answers to the following questions about delegation:

- what is it?
- what are its advantages?
- what are the difficulties?
- when do you delegate?
- how do you delegate?

What is delegation?

Delegation is not the same as handing out work. There are some things that your team members do that go with the territory. They are part of their normal duties and all you have to do is to define what those duties are and allocate work accordingly.

Delegation is different. It takes place when you deliberately give someone the authority to carry out a piece of work that you could have decided to keep and carry out yourself. Bear in mind that what you are doing is delegating authority to carry out a task and make the decisions this involves. You are still accountable for the results achieved. It is sometimes said that you cannot delegate responsibility, but this is misleading if responsibility is defined, as it usually is, as what people are expected to do – their work, their tasks and their duties. What you cannot do is delegate accountability. In the last analysis you as the manager or team leader always carry the can. What managers have to do is to ensure that people have the authority to carry out their responsibilities. A traffic warden without the power to issue tickets would have to be exceedingly persuasive to have any chance of dealing with parking offences.

What are the advantages of delegation?

The advantages of delegation are that:

- It enables you to focus on the things that really matter in your job – those aspects that require your personal experience, skill and knowledge.
- It relieves you of routine and less critical tasks.
- It frees you from being immersed in detail.
- It extends your capacity to manage.
- It reduces delay in decision-making – as long as authority is delegated close to the scene of the action.
- It allows decisions to be taken at the level where the details are known.
- It empowers and motivates your staff by extending their responsibilities and authority and providing them with greater autonomy.
- It develops the knowledge and skills of your staff and increases their capacity to exercise judgement and make decisions.

What are the difficulties of delegation?

The advantages of delegation are compelling but there are difficulties. The main problem is that delegation often involves risk. You cannot be absolutely sure that the person to whom you have delegated something will carry out the work as you would wish. The temptation therefore is to over-supervise, breathe down people's necks and interfere. This inhibits their authority, makes them nervous and resentful and destroys their confidence, thus dissipating any advantages the original act of delegation might have had. Another difficulty is that many managers are reluctant to delegate because they want to keep on top of everything. They really think they know best and cannot trust anyone else to do it as well, never mind better. Finally, some managers are reluctant to delegate simply because they enjoy what they are doing and cannot bear the possibility of giving it away to anyone else.

Approaches to delegation

To a degree, overcoming these difficulties is a matter of simply being aware of them and appreciating that if there any disadvantages, these are outweighed by the advantages. But adopting approaches to delegation such as those discussed in this section is the best way to deal with such difficulties. You need to understand the process of delegation, when to delegate, what to delegate, how to choose people to whom you want to delegate, how to give out the work, and how to monitor performance.

The process of delegation

Delegation is a process that starts from the point when total control is exercised (no freedom of action for the individual to whom work has been allocated) and ends with full devolution (the individual is completely empowered to carry out the work). This sequence is illustrated in Figure 8.2.

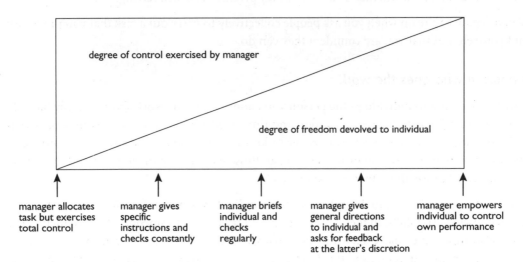

Figure 8.2 The sequence of delegation

When to delegate

You should delegate when you:

- have more work than you can carry out yourself;
- cannot allow sufficient time to your priority tasks;
- want to develop a member of your team;

- believe that it will increase someone's engagement with their job;
- think that the job can be done adequately by the individual or the team to whom you are delegating.

What to delegate

The tasks you delegate are ones that you don't need to do yourself. You are not just ridding yourself of the difficult, tedious or unrewarding tasks. Neither are you trying simply to win for yourself an easier life. In some ways delegation will make your life more difficult, but also more rewarding.

You should delegate routine and repetitive tasks that you cannot reasonably be expected to do yourself – as long as you use the time you have won productively. You can delegate specialist tasks to those who have the skills and know-how to do them. You cannot be expected to do it all yourself. Neither can you be expected to know it all yourself. You have to know how to select and use expertise. There will be no problem as long as you make it clear what you want from the experts and get them to present it to you in a useable way. As their manager, you should know what your specialists can do for you and you should be knowledgeable enough about the subject to understand whether or not what they produce is worth having.

You delegate to a team when you ask people collectively to carry out a task that you previously did yourself and that you are confident they can do.

Choosing who does the work

When delegating to individuals the person you choose to do the work should ideally have the knowledge, skills, experience, motivation and time needed to get it done to your satisfaction. It is your job as a manager or team leader to know your people – their strengths and weaknesses, what they are good at or not so good at, those who are willing to learn and those who, without good cause, think that they know it all.

Frequently you will want to delegate work to an individual who has less than the ideal experience, knowledge or skills. In these cases you should try to select someone who has intelligence, natural aptitude and, above all, willingness to learn how to do the job with help and guidance. This is how people develop, and the development of your team members should be your conscious aim whenever you delegate.

You are looking for someone you can trust. You don't want to over-supervise, so you have to believe that the person you select will get on with it and have the sense to come to you when stuck or before making a bad mistake. Of course you have to make it clear that you are there to give support and guidance when necessary, especially when a person is starting on an unfamiliar task. Initially, you may have to spend time coaching the individual to develop new or improved skills.

How do you know whom you can trust? The best way to find out is to try people out first on smaller and less important tasks and give them more scope when they demonstrate they can do them. You may start by supervising them fairly closely, but you can progressively let go until they are finally working mainly on their own with only periodical checks on progress. If they get on well, their sense of responsibility and powers of judgement will increase and improve and they will acquire the additional skills and confidence to justify your trust in their capacity to take on more demanding and responsible tasks.

Giving out the work

When you delegate you should ensure that the individuals or team concerned understand:

- why the work needs to be done;
- what they are expected to do;
- the date by which they are expected to do it;
- the end results they are expected to achieve;
- the authority they have to make decisions;
- the problems they must refer back;
- the progress or completion reports they should submit;
- any guidance and support that will be available to them.

You have to consider how much guidance will be required on how the work should be done. You don't want to give directions in such laborious detail that you run the risk of stifling initiative. Neither do you want to infuriate people by explaining everything needlessly. As long as you are reasonably certain that they will do the job to your satisfaction without embarrassing you or seriously upsetting people, exceeding the budget or breaking the law, let them get on with it. Follow Robert Heller's (1972) golden rule: 'If you can't do something yourself, find someone who can and then let them get on with it in their own sweet way'.

You can make a distinction between hard and soft delegation. Hard delegation takes place when you tell someone exactly what to do and how to do it. You spell it out, confirm it in writing and make a note in your diary of the date when you expect the job to be completed. And then you follow up regularly.

Soft delegation takes place when you agree generally what has to be done and leave the individual to get on with it. You still agree limits of authority, define the outcomes you expect, indicate how you will review progress and lay down when exception reports should be made. An exception report is one that only deals with events out of the ordinary. It is based on the principle of management by exception, which means focusing on the key events and measures that will show up good, bad or indifferent results – the exceptions to the norm – as a guide to taking action. This approach frees people to concentrate on the issues that matter.

You should always delegate by the results you expect. When you are dealing with an experienced and capable person you don't need to specify how the results should be achieved. In the case of less experienced people you have to exercise judgement on the amount of guidance required. Newcomers with little or no experience will need plenty of guidance. They are on a 'learning curve', ie they are gradually acquiring the knowledge and skills they need to reach the required level of performance. You are responsible for seeing that they progress steadily up the learning curve, bearing in mind that everyone will be starting from a different point and learning at a different rate. It is during this period that you act as a coach or an instructor, helping people to learn and develop. Even if you do not need to specify how the results should be achieved, it is a good idea when the delegation involves getting someone to solve a problem to ask them how they propose to solve it.

Monitoring performance

Delegation is not abdication. You are still accountable for the results obtained by the members of your team collectively and individually. The extent to which you need to monitor performance and how you do so depends on the individuals concerned and the nature of the task. If individuals or the team as a whole are inexperienced generally or are being specifically asked to undertake an unfamiliar task, you may at first have to monitor performance carefully. But the sooner you can relax and watch progress informally the better. The ideal situation is when you are confident that the individual or team will deliver the results you want with the minimum of supervision. In such cases you may only ask for periodical exception reports.

For a specific task or project, set target dates and keep a reminder of these in your diary so that you can check that they have been met. Don't allow people to become careless about meeting deadlines.

Without becoming oppressive, you should ensure that progress and exception reports are made when required so that you can agree any necessary corrective action. You should have indicated the extent to which people have the authority to act without reference to you. They must therefore expect to be criticized if they exceed their brief or fail to keep you informed. You don't want any surprises and your people must understand that keeping you in the dark is unacceptable.

Try to restrain yourself from interfering unnecessarily in the way the work is being done. After all, it is the results that count. Of course, you must step in if there is any danger of things going off the rails. Rash decisions, over-expenditure and ignoring defined and reasonable constraints must be prevented.

There is a delicate balance to be achieved between hedging people around with restrictions, which may appear petty, and allowing them licence to do what they like. There are no absolute rules as to where this balance should be struck. Managing people is an art, not a science. But you should at least have some notion of what is appropriate based on your knowledge of the people concerned and the situation you are in. It's a judgement call but the judgement is based on a full understanding of the facts. The best delegators are those who have a comprehensive knowledge of the strengths and weaknesses of their team members and of the circumstances in which they work.

Above all, avoid 'river banking'. This happens when a boss gives a subordinate a task that is more or less impossible to do. As the subordinate is going down for the third time, the boss can be observed in a remote and safe position on the river bank saying: 'It's easy, really; all you need to do is to try a bit harder.'

Facilitating

Facilitation is defined in the *Oxford English Dictionary* as to 'make easy, promote, help move forward'. Managers act as facilitators in relation to their team members when they make it easier for them to develop by promoting their skills and capabilities, thus helping them to move forward. Managers may also be involved in facilitating the work of groups of people assembled to carry out a task jointly.

Facilitating individual learning

The process of facilitating individual learning involves focusing on the learners and helping them to achieve agreed learning objectives. Facilitators work alongside learners – they do not act like 'trainers', delivering learning on a plate. Working with people means encouraging learners to participate in the learning process so that it becomes largely self-managed learning, with the manager as facilitator providing support, guidance and help, but only as required. Facilitators ask questions but do not provide ready-made answers to them. They help people to learn from their experience, listen to them and respond encouragingly. Facilitators may use coaching skills but always take account of the learner's views on what to learn and how best to learn it.

Facilitating groups

A group facilitator is there to help the group reach conclusions in the shape of ideas and solutions. Facilitators do not exist to 'chair' the meeting in the sense of controlling the discussion and pressurizing the group to agree to a course of action. The group is there to make up its own mind and the facilitator helps it to do so. The help is provided by asking questions that encourage the group members to think for themselves. These can be challenging and probing questions but the facilitator does not provide the answers – that is the role of the group. Neither do facilitators allow their own opinions to intrude – they are there to help the group marshal its opinions, not to enforce their own ideas. However, by using questioning techniques carefully, facilitators can ensure that the group does thoroughly discuss and analyse the issues and reaches conclusions by consensus, rather than allowing anyone to dominate the process.

Facilitators ensure that everyone has their say and that they are listened to. They step in quickly to defuse unproductive arguments. They see that the group defines and understands its objectives and any methodology they might use. They summarize from time to time the progress made in achieving the objectives without bringing their own views to bear. Facilitators are there to ensure that the group makes progress and does not get stuck in fruitless or disruptive argument. But they encourage the group rather than drive it forward.

Giving feedback

People need to be informed – to be provided with feedback – about how well they are doing in order to carry on doing it to good effect or to understand what they need to do to improve. They take action and then they learn through information that is fed back to them on how effective that action has been. Thus they complete the feedback loop by making any corrections to their behaviour on the basis of the information they have received.

Ideally, feedback should be built into the job. Individuals should be able to keep track of what they are doing so that they can initiate speedy corrective action. But that is not always feasible and then the manager has the responsibility of providing the feedback. This can and should be done regularly, and especially after a particular task has been carried out or a project has been completed. But it can also be provided in more formal performance review meetings.

Aim of feedback

The aim of feedback is to provide information to people that will enable them to understand how well they have been doing and how effective their behaviour has been. Feedback should promote this understanding so that appropriate action can be taken. This can be corrective action where the feedback has indicated that something has gone wrong or, more positively, action can be taken to make the best use of the opportunities the feedback has revealed. In the latter case, feedback acts as a reinforcement, and positive feedback can be a powerful motivator because it is a recognition of achievement.

Giving feedback

Feedback should be based on facts, not subjective judgements. The following are some guidelines on giving feedback:

- Build feedback into the job. Individuals or teams should be able to find out easily how they have done from the control information readily available to them. If it cannot be built into the job it should be provided as quickly as possible after the activity has taken place, ideally within a day or two.

- Provide feedback on actual events. Feedback should be provided on actual results or observed behaviour, not based on subjective opinion.

- Describe, don't judge. The feedback should be presented as a description of what has happened. It should not be accompanied by a judgement.

- Refer to specific behaviours. The feedback should be related to specific items of behaviour; it should not transmit general feelings or impressions.

- Ask questions rather than make statements: 'Why do you think this happened?', 'On reflection, is there any other way in which you think you could have handled the situation?', 'What are the factors that influenced you to make that decision?'

- Get people to work things out for themselves. Encourage people to come to their own conclusions about what they should do or how they should behave. Ask questions such as: 'How do you think you should tackle this sort of problem in the future?', 'How do you feel you could avoid getting into this situation again?'

- Select key issues and restrict the feedback to them. There is a limit to how much criticism anyone can take. If it is overdone, the shutters will go up and the discussion will get nowhere.

- Focus on aspects of performance that the individual can improve. It is a waste of time to concentrate on areas that they can do little or nothing about.

- Show understanding. If something has gone wrong, find out if this has happened because of circumstances beyond the individual's control and indicate that this is understood.

Receiving and acting on feedback

Managers both give and receive feedback. When they are on the receiving end they have to be prepared to take an objective view of what they are hearing. It is easy enough to take in positive feedback but negative feedback – however carefully or tactfully it is delivered – can easily provoke resentment and failure to act, even when it is pointing the way to an area for improvement. Receivers of feedback have the right to seek clarification about the basis on which it is given. This is why objective evidence is so important. But having obtained and accepted the evidence, it is necessary to discuss and agree with the manager what needs to be done to overcome the problem.

Networking

Increasingly in today's more fluid and flexible organizations, people get things done by networking. Networks are loosely organized connections between people with shared interests. Networking takes place within them when people exchange information, enlist support and create alliances – getting agreement with other people on a course of action and joining forces to make it happen. It occurs outside the usual formal communication channels. It is an essential way of getting things done in organizations – it ensures that the informal organization works.

Networks inside organizations are often fluid and informal. They exist to meet a need and can be dispersed if that need no longer exists, only to be reformed when it reappears. Networks may just consist of people with similar aims or interests who communicate with one another or get together as required. Networks are sometimes set up formally in organizations, for example the 'communities of interest' that are created to exchange and share knowledge and experience as part of a 'knowledge management' programme.

Networks can also exist outside the organization. Again, they may consist of like-minded individuals exchanging information and meeting informally, or they may be set up formally with regular meetings and newsletters.

Here are 10 steps you can take to network effectively:

1. Identify people who may be able to help.

2. Seize any opportunity that presents itself to get to know people who may be useful.

3. Have a clear idea of why you want to network – to share knowledge, to persuade people to accept your proposal or point of view, or to form an alliance.

4. Know what you can contribute – networking is not simply about enlisting support, it is just as much if not more concerned with developing knowledge and understanding and joining forces with like-minded people so that concerted effort can be deployed to get things done.

5. Show interest – if you engage with people and listen to them, they are more likely to want to network with you.

6. Ask people if you can help them as well as asking people to help you.

7. Put people in touch with one another.

8. Operate informally but be prepared to call formal meetings when necessary to reach agreement and plan action.

9. Make an effort to keep in touch with people.

10. Follow up – check with members of the network on progress in achieving something, refer back to conversations you have had, discuss with others how the network might be developed or extended to increase its effectiveness.

Problem-solving

Peter Drucker (1967) wrote that 'In every area of effectiveness within an organization, one feeds the opportunity and starves the problem'. It is indeed often said that 'there are no problems, only opportunities'. This is not universally true of course, but it does emphasize the point that a problem should lead to positive thinking about what is to be done now. It is not the time for recriminations. If a mistake has been made, the reasons for it should be analysed so that it does not happen again. The following are 10 steps for effective problem-solving:

1. Define the situation – establish what has gone wrong or is potentially going to go wrong.

2. Specify objectives – define what is to be achieved now or in the future to deal with an actual or potential problem or a change in circumstances.

3. Develop hypotheses – come up with theories about what has caused the problem.

4. Get the facts – find out what has actually happened and contrast this with an assessment of what ought to have happened. Obtain information about internal or external constraints that affect the situation. However, remember what Nietzsche (1883) wrote: 'There are no facts, only interpretations'. Try to understand the attitudes and motivation of those concerned. Remember that people will see what has happened in terms of their own position and feelings (their framework of reference).

5. Analyse the facts – determine what is relevant and what is irrelevant. Diagnose the likely cause or causes of the problem. Do not be tempted to focus on symptoms rather than root causes. Test any assumptions. Dig into what lies behind the problem.

6. Identify possible courses of action – spell out what each involves.

7. Evaluate alternative courses of action – assess the extent to which they are likely to achieve the objectives, the cost of implementation, any practical difficulties that might emerge and the possible reactions of stakeholders.

8. Weigh and decide – determine which alternative is likely to result in the most practical and acceptable solution to the problem. This is often a balanced judgement.

9. Plan implementation – timetable, project management, and resources required.

10. Implement – monitor progress and evaluate success. Remember that a problem has not been solved until the decision has been implemented. Always work out the solution to a problem with implementation in mind.

References

Drucker, P (1967) *The Effective Executive*, Heinemann, London
Gowers, Sir E (1987) *The Complete Plain Words*, Penguin, London
Heller, R (1972) *The Naked Manager*, Barrie & Jenkins, London
Nietzsche, F (1883) *Also Sprach Zarathustra: Ein Buch für Alle und Keinen*, Penguin Books (translated 1974), Harmondsworth

9

Managing Systems and Processes

'*Process and procedure are the last hiding place of people without the wit or wisdom to do their job properly.*'

The Office, BBC

This chapter deals with an important aspect of managerial activities, namely the management of the systems and processes that exist in organizations to get work done. A system consists of formally interconnected activities that are managed together to achieve certain defined ends. A process is a series of operations that are carried out in order to produce something, provide a service or carry out a complex task. In this chapter, the first two sections examine the approach to managing systems and processes. Examples are then given of system and process management. The chapter concludes with an assessment of the conflict and challenges that managing systems and processes presents. One word of warning: as the quotation at the head of this chapter implies, processes and procedures (which could be extended to systems) are only as effective as the people who operate them and do not replace good management and leadership.

Managing systems

Systems can be complex and when managing them it is necessary to know how each part of the system contributes to the whole result. It is then essential to see that the different parts of the system work smoothly together so that each contributes to satisfactory performance. Complications arise when the parts do not fit together. The design and development of systems has to be based on a thorough analysis of requirements, with close attention being paid to who will use it and how the system will perform in different circumstances.

Systems need to be maintained and updated to ensure that they continue to function effectively and deliver the required results. Their performance has to be monitored and corrective action taken as necessary. The purpose of the system has to be explained to those who use it and people will have to be trained in its operation.

Managing processes

The management of processes starts with process definition. This involves specifying what the process is, how it operates, and what results it is expected to achieve in terms of output levels or levels of service, speed of operation, quality standards and cost. The process specification defines the process and sets out its inputs and outputs and the internal and external customers it serves. It is necessary to clarify the inputs required at each stage. Flow charts are produced to represent diagrammatically the events and stages of the process with a view to defining how it functions and allocating responsibilities for its operation and management.

Managing the process involves ensuring that the resources (in the form of facilities and equipment) required are available and trained and capable people are there to operate the process. The technique of process capability analysis may be used to examine variables in the process to establish the extent to which it is doing the job properly, and if it is not, what should be done about it. Control information needs to be generated in order to monitor the performance of the process and the people who operate it. This will allow analysis of variations as a basis for further investigation.

Examples of systems and process management

The following examples of systems and process management are given in this section: information technology (IT), reward systems, and computer-integrated manufacturing.

Information technology

Managing an IT system involves in the first place planning the system, analysing and agreeing user requirements, and specifying how the system will meet them. Processors, operating systems and software have to be obtained and networks and databases developed, installed and maintained. Outsourcing to application service providers who run applications at their own data centres will need to be considered.

Managing an IT system within an organization means delivering to internal customers the information processing services they require. This involves managing support services which, as defined by the British Computer Society, means that the IT department must:

- establish the level of support that may reasonably be expected and provide the tools, documentation and suitably trained staff needed to meet this expectation;

- respond swiftly to support requests and satisfy internal customers that their needs are being met;

- identify to internal customers any changes to business procedures that will improve the efficiency of the service provided;

- keep internal customers informed of the steps being taken to maintain agreed service levels;

- maintain records of the services provided and take the actions needed to achieve target service levels.

Reward systems

A reward system is an example of a different type of system. It is designed and operated to achieve the reward management objectives of an organization. The elements and interrelationships in a reward system are illustrated in Figure 9.1. The task of reward management is to ensure that all these elements are properly provided for, that they operate effectively in relation to one another, and that the system achieves the reward objectives of the organization.

Computer-integrated manufacturing

A computer-integrated manufacturing (CIM) system uses information technology to integrate the various processes that together comprise the total manufacturing process. These processes can include design, production engineering, production planning and control, production scheduling, material requirement planning, manufacturing, material handling and inventory control. Such a system is illustrated in Figure 9.2.

The conflict and challenges of managing systems and processes

Conflict in managing systems and processes arises when they do not deliver to users what they are expected to deliver. Users expect an appropriate design and full support. If either of these are lacking they are rightly angry.

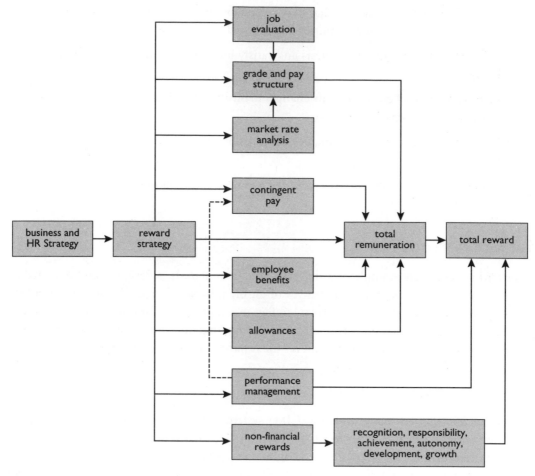

Figure 9.1   A reward management system

Problems with the management of systems and processes occur if:

- their design does not take sufficient account of user needs and is not user-friendly;
- they no longer serve their original purpose;
- their managers pay insufficient attention to developing them to meet new demands;
- support from technicians is inadequate;
- line managers find them difficult to use;
- they rely heavily on a computer system that is prone to failures;
- they are clumsy, time-consuming or wasteful.

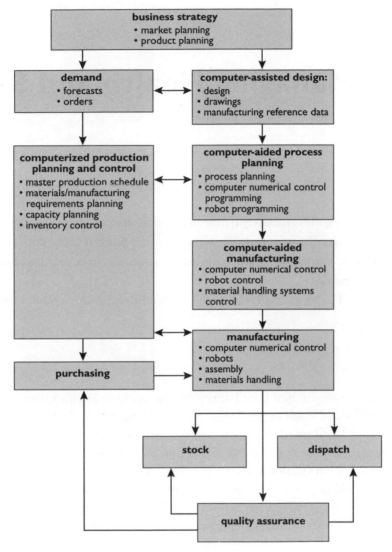

Figure 9.2   A computer-integrated manufacturing system

All of these problems can be resolved if sufficient care is taken over the design and maintenance of the system or process and if proper training and support is given to users.

10

Managing Health and Safety

'Managing health and safety is little different from managing any other aspect of your business. You need to do a risk assessment to find out about the risks in your workplace, put sensible measures in place to control them, and make sure they stay controlled.'

Health and Safety Executive (2006) *Introduction to Health and Safety*

The management of health and safety in the working environment is a corporate responsibility and many organizations have qualified staff to deal with it. But it is also very much the concern of individual managers who have to ensure that there is a healthy and safe system of work in their areas and that the people in their departments adhere to the organization's health and safety policies and procedures. This applies just as much for those working in offices, shops and laboratories as for those on the factory floor, in distribution centres or involved in transport. Health and safety policies and procedures are concerned with protecting employees – and other people affected by what the company produces and does – against the hazards arising from their employment or their links with the company.

Occupational health programmes deal with the prevention of ill health arising from working conditions. They consist of two elements:

- occupational medicine, which is a specialized branch of preventive medicine concerned with the diagnosis and prevention of health hazards at work, and dealing with any ill health or stress that has occurred in spite of preventive actions;

- occupational hygiene, which is the province of the chemist and the engineer or ergonomist engaged in the measurement and control of environmental hazards.

Safety programmes deal with the prevention of accidents and with minimizing the resulting loss and damage to persons and property. They relate more to systems of work than the working environment, but both health and safety programmes are concerned with protection against hazards, and their aims and methods are clearly interlinked.

The importance of health and safety in the workplace

It is estimated by the Royal Society for the Prevention of Accidents (2008) that every year in the United Kingdom we face the challenge of reducing about 350 fatalities at work and over 36 million days lost due to work-related accidents and ill health. It has also been estimated by the Health and Safety Executive (2002) that, apart from the pain and misery caused to those directly or indirectly concerned, the total cost to British employers of work-related injury and illness is £6.5 billion a year.

The response to this challenge must be to achieve and indeed go beyond the high standard in health and safety matters required by the legislation – the Health and Safety at Work etc Act 1974 and the various regulations laid down in the Codes of Practice. It cannot be emphasized too strongly that the prevention of accidents and elimination of health and safety hazards is a prime responsibility of management and managers in order to minimize suffering and loss.

As described in this chapter, managing health and safety at work is a matter of:

- developing health and safety policies;
- conducting risk assessments that identify hazards and assess the risks attached to them;
- carrying out health and safety audits and inspections;
- preventing accidents;
- implementing occupational health programmes;
- managing stress;
- determining the responsibility for health and safety.

Health and safety policies

Written health and safety policies are required to demonstrate that top management is concerned about the protection of the organization's employees from hazards at work and to indicate how this protection will be provided. Health and safety policies are first a declaration of intent, second, a definition of the means by which that intent will be realized, and third a statement of the guidelines that should be followed by everyone concerned – which means all employees – in implementing the policy.

The policy statement should consist of three parts:

- the general policy statement;
- a description of the organization for health and safety;
- details of arrangements for implementing the policy.

The general policy statement

The general policy statement should be a declaration of the intention of the employer to safeguard the health and safety of employees. It should emphasize four fundamental points:

- that the health and safety of employees and the public is of paramount importance;
- that health and safety takes precedence over expediency;
- that every effort will be made to involve all managers, team leaders and employees in the development and implementation of health and safety procedures;
- that health and safety legislation will be complied with in the spirit as well as the letter of the law.

Organization

This section of the policy statement should describe the health and safety organization of the business, through which high standards are set and achieved by people at all levels in the organization. This statement should underline the ultimate responsibility of top management for the health and safety performance of the organization. It should then indicate how key management personnel are held accountable for performance in their areas. The role of safety representatives and safety committees should be defined, and the duties of specialists such as the safety advisor and the medical officer should be summarized.

Conducting risk assessments

Risk assessments are concerned with the identification of hazards and the analysis of the risks attached to them. They may be carried out by specialists but managers and team leaders should be responsible for the continuous assessment of risks in their own departments and for initiating action as necessary.

A hazard is anything that can cause harm (eg working on roofs, lifting heavy objects, falls, chemicals, electricity, etc). A risk is the chance, large or small, of harm being actually done by the hazard. Risk assessments are concerned with looking for hazards and estimating the level of risk associated with them.

The purpose of risk assessments is to initiate preventive action. They enable control measures to be devised on the basis of an understanding of the relative importance of risks.

Looking for hazards

The following are typical activities where accidents happen or there are high risks:

- receipt of raw materials, eg lifting, carrying;
- stacking and storage, eg falling materials;
- movement of people and materials, eg falls, collisions;
- processing of raw materials, eg exposure to toxic substances;
- maintenance of buildings, eg roof work, gutter cleaning;
- maintenance of plant and machinery, eg lifting tackle, installation of equipment;
- using electricity, eg using hand tools, extension leads;
- operating machines, eg operating without sufficient clearance, or at an unsafe speed; not using safety devices;
- failure to wear protective equipment, eg hats, boots, clothing;
- distribution of products or materials, eg movement of vehicles;
- dealing with emergencies, eg spillages, fires, explosions;
- health hazards arising from the use of certain equipment or methods of working, eg VDUs, repetitive strain injuries from badly designed work stations or working practices.

Most accidents are caused by a few key activities. Risk assessments should concentrate initially on those that could cause serious harm. Operations such as roof work, maintenance and transport movement cause far more deaths and injuries each year than many mainstream activities.

When carrying out a risk assessment it is also necessary to consider who might be harmed, eg employees or visitors (including cleaners and contractors and the public when calling in to buy products or enlist services).

Assessing the risk

When the hazards have been identified it is necessary to assess how high the risks are. This involves answering three questions:

1.   What is the worst result?

2.   How likely is it to happen?

3.   How many people could be harmed if things go wrong?

A probability rating system can be used, such as:

1.   Probable – likely to occur immediately or shortly.

2.   Reasonably probable – probably will occur in time.

3.   Remote – may occur in time.

4.   Extremely remote – unlikely to occur.

Taking action

Risk assessment should lead to action. The type of action can be ranked in order of potential effectiveness in the form of a 'safety precedence sequence':

- Hazard elimination – use of alternatives, design improvements, change of process.

- Substitution – for example replacement of a chemical with one that is less risky.

- Use of barriers – removing the hazard from the worker or removing the worker from the hazard.

- Use of procedures – limitation of exposure, dilution of exposure, safe systems of work (these depend on human response).

- Use of warning systems – signs, instructions, labels (these also depend on human response).

- Use of personal protective clothing – this depends on human response and is used as a side measure only when all other options have been exhausted.

Monitoring and evaluation

Risk assessment is not completed when action has been initiated. It is essential to monitor the hazard and evaluate the effectiveness of the action in eliminating it or at least reducing it to an acceptable level.

Health and safety audits

Risk assessments identify specific hazards and quantify the risks attached to them. Health and safety audits provide for a much more comprehensive review of all aspects of health and safety policies, procedures, practices and programmes.

Health and safety audits can be conducted by safety advisors and/or HR specialists, but the more managers, employees and trade union representatives are involved the better. Audits are often carried out under the auspices of a health and safety committee, with its members taking an active part in conducting them.

Managers can also be held responsible for conducting audits within their departments and, even better, individual members of these departments can be trained to carry out audits in particular areas. The conduct of an audit will be facilitated if checklists are prepared and a simple form used to record results.

A health and safety audit should cover:

Policies

- Do health and safety policies meet legal requirements?
- Are senior managers committed to health and safety?
- How committed are other managers, team leaders and supervisors to health and safety?
- Is there a health and safety committee? If not, why not?
- How effective is the committee in getting things done?

Procedures

How effectively do the procedures:

- support the implementation of health and safety policies?
- communicate the need for good health and safety practices?
- provide for systematic risk assessments?
- ensure that accidents are investigated thoroughly?
- record data on health and safety that is used to evaluate performance and initiate action?
- ensure that health and safety considerations are given proper weight when designing systems of work or manufacturing and operational processes (including the design of equipment and work stations, the specification for products or services, and the use of materials)?

- provide safety training, especially induction training and training when jobs or working methods are changed?

Safety practices

- To what extent do health and safety practices in all areas of the organization conform to the general requirements of the Health and Safety at Work Act and the specific requirements of the various regulations and Codes of Practice?

- What risk assessments have been carried out? What were the findings? What actions were taken?

- What is the health and safety performance of the organization as shown by the performance indicators? Is the trend positive or negative? If the latter, what is being done about it?

- How thoroughly are accidents investigated? What steps have been taken to prevent their recurrence?

- What is the evidence that managers and supervisors are really concerned about health and safety?

What should be done with the audit?

The audit should cover the questions above but its purpose is to generate action. Those conducting the audit will have to assess priorities and costs and draw up action programmes for approval by the Board.

Health and safety inspections

Health and safety inspections are designed to examine a specific area of the organization – an operational department or a manufacturing process – in order to locate and define any faults in the system, equipment, plant or machines, or any operational errors that might cause an occupational health problem or be the source of accidents. Health and safety inspections should be carried out on a regular and systematic basis by line managers and supervisors with the advice and help of health and safety advisors. The steps to be taken in carrying out safety inspections are as follows:

- allocate the responsibility for conducting the inspection;

- define the points to be covered in the form of a checklist;

- divide the department or plant into areas and list the points to which attention needs to be given in each area;

- define the frequency with which inspections should be carried out – daily in critical areas;

- use the checklists as the basis for the inspection;

- carry out sample or spot checks on a random basis;

- carry out special investigations as necessary to deal with special problems such as operating machinery without guards to increase throughput;

- set up a reporting system (a form should be used for recording the results of inspections);

- set up a system to monitor whether health and safety inspections are being conducted properly and on schedule and whether corrective action is taken where necessary.

The distinction between risk assessments, audits and inspections

- Risk assessments focus on the identification of hazards and the analysis of the risks attached to them.

- Health and safety audits provide for a much more comprehensive review of all aspects of health and safety policies, procedures, practices and programmes.

- Health and safety inspections examine a specific area of the organization in order to locate and define any faults in the system, equipment, plant or machines, or any operational errors that might create a risk to health or be the source of accidents.

Accident prevention

The prevention of accidents is achieved by:

- identifying the causes of accidents and the conditions under which they are most likely to occur;

- taking account of safety factors at the design stage – building safety into the system;

- designing safety equipment and protective devices and providing protective clothing;

- carrying out regular risk assessments, audits, inspections and checks and taking action to eliminate risks;

- investigating all accidents resulting in damage to establish the cause and to initiate corrective action;

- maintaining good records and statistics in order to identify problem areas and unsatisfactory trends;

- conducting a continuous programme of education and training on safe working habits and methods of avoiding accidents.

Occupational health programmes

It is estimated by the Royal Society for the Prevention of Accidents (2008) that every year in the United Kingdom 30 million working days are lost because of work-related illness. Two million people say they suffer from an illness they believe was caused by their work. Muscular disorders, including repetitive strain injury (RSI) and back pain, are by far the most commonly reported work-related illnesses with 1.2 million affected, and the numbers are rising. The next biggest problem is stress, which 500,000 people say is so bad that it is making them ill. These are large and disturbing figures and they show that high priority must given to creating and maintaining programmes for the improvement of occupational health.

The control of occupational health and hygiene problems can be achieved by:

- eliminating the hazard at source through design and process engineering;

- isolating hazardous processes and substances so that workers do not come into contact with them;

- changing the processes or substances used, to promote better protection or eliminate the risk;

- providing protective equipment, but only if changes to the design, process or specification cannot completely remove the hazard;

- training workers to avoid risk;

- maintaining plant and equipment to eliminate the possibility of harmful emissions, controlling the use of toxic substances and eliminating radiation hazards;

- good housekeeping to keep premises and machinery clean and free from toxic substances;

- regular inspections to ensure that potential health risks are identified in good time;

- pre-employment medical examinations and regular checks on those exposed to risk;

- ensuring that ergonomic considerations (ie those concerning the design and use of equipment, machines, processes and work stations) are taken into account in design specifications, work routines and training – this is particularly important as a means of minimizing the incidence of repetitive strain injury;

- maintaining preventive medicine programmes that develop health standards for each job and involve regular audits of potential health hazards and regular examinations for anyone at risk.

Particular attention needs to be paid to the control of noise, fatigue and stress. The management and control of stress – a major health problem – should be regarded as a key part of any occupational health programme.

Managing stress

There are four main reasons why organizations should take account of stress and do something about it: first, because they have a social responsibility to provide a good quality of working life; second, because excessive stress causes illness; third, because it can result in inability to cope with the demands of the job, which creates more stress; and finally, because excessive stress can reduce employee effectiveness and therefore organizational performance.

The ways in which stress can be managed by an organization include:

- job design – clarifying roles, reducing the danger of role ambiguity and conflict, and giving people more autonomy within a defined structure to manage their responsibilities;

- targets and performance standards – setting reasonable and achievable targets that may stretch people but do not place impossible burdens on them;

- placement – taking care to place people in jobs that are within their capabilities;

- career development – planning careers and promoting staff in accordance with their capabilities, taking care not to over- or under-promote;

- performance management processes, which allow a dialogue to take place between managers and individuals about the latter's work problems and ambitions;

- counselling – giving individuals the opportunity to talk about their problems with a member of the HR department, or through an employee assistance programme;

- anti-bullying campaigns – bullying at work is a major cause of stress;

- management training in what managers can do to alleviate their own stress and reduce it in others.

The responsibility for health and safety

Health and safety concerns everyone in an establishment, although the main responsibility lies with management in general and individual managers in particular. Management develops and implements health and safety policies and ensures that procedures for carrying out risk assessments, safety audits and inspections are implemented. Importantly, management has the duty of monitoring and evaluating health and safety performance and taking corrective action as necessary. Managers can exert a greater influence on health and safety. They are in immediate control and it is up to them to keep a constant watch for unsafe conditions or practices and to take immediate action. They are also directly responsible for ensuring that employees are conscious of health and safety hazards and do not take risks.

References

Health and Safety Executive (2002) *Annual Report*, HSE, London
Royal Society for the Prevention of Accidents (2008) *Annual Report*, RoSPA, London

11

Self-development

'*Self-development of the effective executive is central to the development of the organization.*'

Peter Drucker (1967) *The Effective Executive*, Heinemann, London

As Peter Drucker (1955) also wisely said: 'Development is always self-development. Nothing could be more absurd than for the enterprise to assume responsibility for the development of a person. The responsibility rests with individuals, their abilities, their efforts.' This chapter expands on this statement by examining the processes of self-development and self-managed learning, discussing the use of personal development plans and examining the various ways in which organizations can help people to develop. The chapter concludes with comments on self-management strategies and the evaluation of one's own performance.

The process of self-development

The best way to get on is to rely on yourself while seeking and benefiting from any support you can get from your manager or the organization. As Drucker (1967) wrote: 'People grow according to the demands they make on themselves'. Self-development takes place through self-managed or self-directed learning. This means that you take responsibility for satisfying your own learning needs to develop skills, improve performance and progress your career. It is based on processes that enable you to identify what you need to learn by reflecting on your experience and analysing what you need to know and be able to do to increase your effectiveness now and in the future.

Self-managed learning

The case for self-managed or self-directed learning is that people learn and retain more if they find things out for themselves. But they may still need to be helped to identify what they should look for. Self-managed learning is about self-development and this will be furthered by self-assessment (evaluating the impact of your own performance), which leads to better self-understanding. Pedler and his co-writers (1986) recommend the following four-stage approach:

- Self-assessment based on analysis by individuals of their work and life situation.

- Diagnosis derived from the analysis of learning needs and priorities.

- Action planning to identify objectives, helps and hindrances, resources required (including people) and timescales.

- Monitoring and review to assess progress in achieving action plans.

Identifying learning and development needs

You can identify learning and development needs by ensuring that you understand what you are expected to do and the knowledge and skills you need to carry out your job effectively. Performance management processes can be used to identify self-development needs on your own or in discussion with your manager. These will include reviewing performance against agreed plans and assessing the levels of knowledge and skills or competence displayed in carrying out your work. If there are any gaps between the knowledge and skills you need and those you have, then this defines a development need. The analysis is always related to work and the capacity to carry it out effectively.

Defining the means of satisfying learning and development needs

When deciding how to satisfy learning and development needs you should remember that it is not just about selecting suitable training courses. These may form part of your development plan, but probably only a minor part; other learning activities are much more important. Examples include:

- planned use of internal learning and development processes including e-learning, coaching, mentoring and the use of learning libraries;

- distance learning – learning in your own time from material prepared elsewhere, eg correspondence courses;

- guided reading;

- coaching and mentoring others;

- seeing what others do (good practice);
- project work;
- networking – discussing management issues with other people and learning from them in the process. Organizations concerned with knowledge management (enhancing the availability and effective use of knowledge relevant to the organization) may set up 'communities of interest', which formalize networks by bringing people together to discuss ideas and enhance knowledge;
- involvement in other work areas;
- input to policy formulation;
- special assignments.

Personal development plans

A personal development plan sets out the actions you propose to take to learn and to develop yourself. You take responsibility for formulating and implementing the plan but you may receive support from the organization and your manager in doing so. Personal development planning aims to promote learning and to provide you with the knowledge and portfolio of transferable skills that will help to progress your career.

A personal development action plan sets out what needs to be done and how it will be done under headings such as:

- learning and development needs;
- outcomes expected (learning objectives);
- learning and development activities to meet these needs;
- responsibility for development – what individuals will do and what support they will require from their manager, the HR department or other people;
- timing – when the learning activity is expected to start and be completed;
- outcome – what development activities have taken place and how effective they were.

Other methods of management development

The other methods of management development discussed in the following section are coaching, mentoring and action learning. These can be used to complement and support self-development.

Coaching

Coaching, as described in detail in Chapter 8, is a person-to-person technique designed to develop individual skills, knowledge and attitudes. It can take place informally as part of the normal process of management or team leadership. This type of coaching consists of:

- helping people to become aware of how well they are doing and what they need to learn;
- controlled delegation;
- using whatever situations arise as learning opportunities;
- providing guidance on how to carry out specific tasks as necessary, but always on the basis of helping individuals to learn rather than force-feeding them with instructions on what to do and how to do it.

Executive coaching can be provided by specialist consultants. They usually concentrate on helping people to develop more productive ways of behaving and to change dysfunctional management styles. Coaching is often based on the information provided by personality questionnaires such as the Myers-Briggs Types Indicator.

Mentoring

Mentoring is the process of using specially selected and trained individuals to provide guidance and advice that will help to develop the careers of the people allocated to them (sometimes called 'protégés').

Mentoring is aimed at complementing learning on the job, which must always be the best way of acquiring the particular skills and knowledge the job holder needs. Mentoring also complements formal training by providing those who benefit from it with individual guidance from experienced managers who are 'wise in the ways of the organization'.

Mentors provide for the person or persons assigned to them:

- advice in drawing up self-development programmes or learning contracts;
- general help with learning programmes;
- guidance on how to acquire the necessary knowledge and skills to do a new job;
- advice on dealing with any administrative, technical or people problems individuals meet, especially in the early stages of their careers;
- information on 'the way things are done around here' – the corporate culture and its manifestations in the shape of core values and organizational behaviour (management style);

- coaching in specific skills;

- help in tackling projects – not by doing it for people but by pointing them in the right direction, that is, helping people to help themselves;

- a parental figure with whom the people they are dealing with can discuss their aspirations and concerns and who will lend a sympathetic ear to their problems.

There are no standard mentoring procedures. Typically, however, a mentor is allocated one or more people and given a very general brief to carry out the functions described above, having been carefully trained in mentoring techniques.

Action learning

Action learning, as developed by Revans (1989), is a method of helping managers develop their talents by exposing them to real problems. They are required to analyse the problems, formulate recommendations, and then take action. It accords with the belief that managers learn best by doing rather than being taught.

Revans produced the following formula to describe his concept:

L (learning) = P (programmed learning) + Q (questioning, insight)

He suggested that the concept is based on six assumptions:

1. Experienced managers have a huge curiosity to know how other managers work.

2. We don't learn as much when we are motivated to learn as when we are motivated to learn *something*.

3. Learning about oneself is threatening and is resisted if it tends to change one's self-image. However, it is possible to reduce the external threat to a level that no longer acts as a total barrier to learning about oneself.

4. People learn only when they do something, and they learn more the more responsible they feel the task to be.

5. Learning is deepest when it involves the whole person – mind, values, body, emotions.

6. The learner knows better than anyone else what they have learnt.

A typical action learning programme brings together a 'set' or group of four or five managers to solve a real problem. They help and learn from each other, but an external consultant, or 'set advisor', sits in with them regularly. The project may last several months, and the set meets frequently, possibly one day a week. The advisor helps the members of the set to learn from one another and clarifies the process of action learning. This process involves change embedded in the web of relationships called 'the client system'. The web comprises at least three separate networks: the power network; the information network; and the motivational network (this is what Revans refers to as 'who can, who knows, and who cares'). The forces for change are already there within the client system and it is the advisor's role to point out the dynamics of this system as the work of diagnosis and implementation proceeds.

The set has to manage the project like any other project, deciding on objectives, planning resources, initiating action and monitoring progress. But all the time, with the help of their advisor, they are learning about the management processes involved as they actually happen.

Self-management strategies

Self-management strategies should be based on self-assessment, which means assessing your own performance and identifying how you can improve. To assess your own performance you need to:

1.   Ensure that you are clear about what your job entails in terms of the main tasks or key result areas. If in doubt, ask your manager for clarification.

2.   Find out what you are expected to achieve for each of the key result areas. Expectations should be definable as objectives in the form of quantified targets or standards of performance (qualitative statements of what constitutes effective performance). Ideally they should have been discussed and agreed as part of the performance appraisal/management process, but if this has not happened, ask your manager to spell out what they expect you to achieve.

3.   Refer to the organization's competency framework. Discuss with your manager how they interpret this as far as you are concerned.

4.   At fairly regular intervals, say once a month, review your progress by reference to the objectives, standards and competency headings. Take note of your achievements and, if they exist, your failures. Ask yourself why you were successful or unsuccessful and what you can do to build on success or overcome failure. You may identify actions you can take or specific changes in behaviour you can try to achieve. Or you may identify a need for further coaching, training or experience.

5.   At the end of the review period and prior to the appraisal discussion with your manager, look back at each of your interim reviews and the actions you decided to take. Consider what more needs to be done in any specific area or generally. You will then be in a position to answer the following questions that might be posed by your manager before or during the appraisal discussion:

     −   How do you feel you have done?

- What are you best at doing?

- Are there any parts of your job that you find difficult?

- Are there any aspects of your work in which you would benefit from better guidance or further training?

Self-management strategies can be derived from this assessment, which should identify specific areas for development or improvement. The strategies can be based on the following 10 steps, which you can take to develop yourself:

1. Create a development log – record your plans and action.

2. State your objectives – the career path you want to follow and the skills you will need to proceed along that path.

3. Develop a personal profile – what sort of person you are, your likes and dislikes about work, your aspirations.

4. List your strengths and weaknesses – what you are good and not so good at doing.

5. List your achievements – what you have done well so far and why you believe these were worthwhile achievements.

6. List significant learning experiences – recall events where you have learnt something worthwhile (this can help you to understand your learning style).

7. Ask other people about your strengths and weaknesses and what you should do to develop yourself.

8. Focus on the present – what is happening to you now: your job, your current skills, your short-term development needs.

9. Focus on the future – where you want to be in the longer term and how you are going to get there (including a list of the skills and abilities you need to develop).

10. Plan your self-development strategy – how you are going to achieve your ambitions.

References

Drucker, P (1955) *The Practice of Management*, Heinemann, London

Drucker, P (1967) *The Effective Executive*, Heinemann, London

Pedler, M, Burgoyne J and Boydell, T (1986) *A Manager's Guide to Self Development*, McGraw-Hill, Maidenhead

Revans, R W (1989) *Action Learning*, Blond and Briggs, London

Part III
Organizations

Part III

12

Understanding Organizations

'*Organization structure is more than boxes on a chart; it is a pattern of interactions and coordination that links the technology, tasks and human components of the organization to ensure that the organization accomplishes its purpose.*'

Duncan, R B (1979) What is the right organization structure?
Organization Dynamics, 7 (3), p 429

Managers get results within the context of the organization in which they work. It is therefore necessary to understand how organizations function and the processes involved. This chapter covers:

- definitions of what an organization is and the process of organizing;

- how organizations function;

- organization structure;

- types of organization;

- the concept of organizational culture;

- the various processes that take place in organizations – group behaviour, interaction and networking, power, politics and conflict;

- the role of organizational policies.

Organizations and organizing

An organization is a group of people who exist to achieve a common purpose. Organizing is the process of making arrangements in the form of defined or understood responsibilities and relationships to enable those people to work cooperatively together.

Organizations may have formal structures with defined hierarchies (lines of command), but to varying degrees they can operate informally as well as formally by means of a network of roles and relationships that cut across formal organizational boundaries and lines of command. They also function through various other processes including group behaviour, the exercise of power, influence and authority and the use of politics.

How organizations function

The following schools of organization theory have evolved over the years:

- The classical school – the classical or scientific management school, as represented by Fayol (1916), Taylor (1911) and Urwick (1947), believed in control, order, formality and the need for organizations to minimize the opportunity for unfortunate and uncontrollable informal relations, leaving room only for the formal ones.

- The bureaucratic model – the bureaucratic model, as defined by Weber (1946), in some ways resembled the classical school. The features of a bureaucratic organization are maximum specialization, clear job definitions, vertical authority patterns, the maximum use of rules, and impersonal administration.

- The human relations school – the classical model was challenged by Barnard (1938). He emphasized the importance of the informal organization – the network of informal roles and relationships that, for better or worse, strongly influences the way the formal structure operates. The importance of informal groups and decent, humane leadership was emphasized by Elton Mayo (1933).

- The behavioural science school – in the 1950s and 1960s the focus shifted to the behaviour of people in organizations. Behavioural scientists such as Argyris (1957), Herzberg (1968), McGregor (1960) and Likert (1961) adopted a humanistic point of view that was concerned with what people can contribute and how they can best be motivated.

- The systems school – Miller and Rice (1967) stated that organizations should be treated as open systems that are continually dependent upon and influenced by their environment. The basic characteristic of the enterprise as an open system is that it transforms inputs into outputs within its environment.

- The socio-technical model – Emery (1959) and his Tavistock Institute colleagues proposed that in any system of organization, technical or task aspects are interrelated with the human or social aspects.

- The contingency school – in the 1960s Burns and Stalker (1961), Woodward (1965) and Lawrence and Lorsch (1969) analysed a variety of organizations and concluded that organization structures and methods of operation are a function of the circumstances in which they exist.

The post-modern school

The post-modern school emerged in the early 1990s and today dominates thinking about how organizations function. A number of commentators observed what was happening to organizations in their efforts to cope in a turbulent and highly competitive global environment. They noted that the emphasis was first on getting the process right and not bothering about rigid structures, and second on ensuring organizational agility – the ability to respond flexibly to new challenges. Organizations operate more flexibly without extended hierarchies, which resulted in the fashion for 'de-layering' – reducing the number of management tiers.

Post-modernism is about challenging assumptions, taking nothing for granted. It 'deconstructs' conventional wisdom about organizations so that previously unconsidered alternative approaches are revealed. As Huczynski and Buchanan (2007) commented, post-modernism represents a fundamental challenge to the ways in which we think about organizations and organizational behaviour.

Pascale (1990) described a 'new organizational paradigm', the features of which are:

- From the image of organizations as machines, with the emphasis on concrete strategy, structure and systems, to the idea of organizations as organisms, with the emphasis on the 'soft' dimensions – style, staff, and shared values.

- From a hierarchical model, with step-by-step problem-solving, to a network model, with parallel nodes of intelligence that surround problems until they are eliminated.

- From the status-driven view that managers think and workers do as they are told, to a view of managers as 'facilitators', with workers empowered to initiate improvements and change.

- From an emphasis on 'vertical tasks' within functional units to an emphasis on 'horizontal tasks' and collaboration across units.

- From a focus on 'content' and the prescribed use of specific tools and techniques to a focus on 'process' and a holistic synthesis of techniques.

- From the military model to a commitment model.

Ghoshal and Bartlett (1995) focused on process when they wrote:

> *Managers are beginning to deal with their organizations in different ways. Rather than seeing them as a hierarchy of static roles, they think of them as a portfolio of dynamic processes. They see core organizational processes that overlay and often dominate the vertical, authority-based processes of the hierarchical structure.*

Organization structure

All organizations have some form of structure – the framework for getting things done. As defined by Child (1977), organizations' structures consist of 'all the tangible and regularly occurring features which help to shape their members' behaviour'. Structures incorporate a network of roles and relationships and are there to help in the process of ensuring that collective effort is explicitly organized to achieve specified ends. Organizations vary in their complexity, but it is necessary to divide the overall management task into a variety of activities, to allocate these activities to the different parts of the organization and to establish means of controlling, coordinating and integrating them.

The formal structure of an organization consists of units, functions, divisions, departments and formally constituted work teams into which activities related to particular processes, projects, products, markets, customers, geographical areas or professional disciplines are grouped together. This structure indicates who is accountable for directing, coordinating and carrying out these activities and defines management hierarchies – the 'chain of command' – thus spelling out, broadly, who is responsible to whom and for what at each level in the organization. However, there are many different types of structures, as described later in this chapter.

Organization charts

Structures are usually described in the form of an organization chart (deplorably, sometimes called an 'organogram', especially in UK government circles). This places individuals in boxes that denote their job and their position in the hierarchy and traces the direct lines of authority (command and control) through the management hierarchies.

Organization charts are vertical in their nature and therefore misrepresent reality. They do not give any indication of the horizontal and diagonal relationships that exist within the framework between people in different units or departments, and do not recognize the fact that within any one hierarchy, commands and control information do not travel all the way down and up the structure as the chart implies. In practice, information jumps (especially computer-generated information) and managers or team leaders will interact with people at levels below those immediately beneath them.

Organization charts have their uses as a means of defining – simplistically – who does what and hierarchical lines of authority. But even if backed up by organization manuals (which no one reads and which are, in any case, out of date as soon as they are produced), they cannot convey how the organization really works. They may, for example, lead to definitions of jobs – what people are expected to do – but they cannot convey the roles these people carry out in the organization; the parts they play in interacting with others and the ways in which, like actors, they interpret the parts they are given.

Types of organization

Mintzberg (1983) produced an original analysis of organizations as:

1. Simple structures, which are dominated by the top of the organization, with centralized decision-making.

2. Machine bureaucracy, which is characterized by the standardization of work processes and extensive reliance on systems.

3. Professional bureaucracy, where the standardization of skills provides the prime coordinating mechanism.

4. Divisionalized structures, in which authority is drawn down from the top and activities are grouped together into units that are then managed according to their standardized outputs.

5. Adhocracies, where power is decentralized selectively to constellations of work that are free to coordinate within and between themselves by mutual adjustments.

Organizations can also be categorized as follows.

Line and staff

The line and staff organization was the type favoured by the classical theorists, based on a military model. Although the term is not so much used today, except when referring to line managers, it still describes many structures. The line hierarchy in the structure consists of functions and managers who are directly concerned with achieving the primary purposes of the organization, for example manufacturing and selling or directing the organization as a whole. 'Staff' in functions such as finance, HR and engineering provide services to the line to enable them to get on with their job.

Unitary structures

Unitary structures are those that exist as single and separate units that have not been subdivided into divisions. In such structures the heads of each major function usually report directly to the top, although organizations may differ in defining what these key functions are. A unitary structure is illustrated in Figure 12.1.

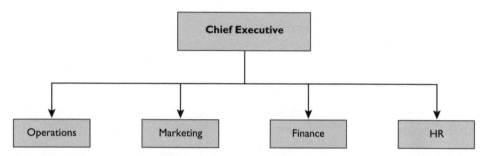

Figure 12.1 A unitary organization structure

This is the most common structure. It is simple and relationships are clearly defined. However, there is an ever-present risk of lack of cooperation between functions or departments, and to avoid this, the chief executive has a key role in coordinating as well as directing activities.

Centralized structures

A centralized structure is one where authority is located at the centre, which exercises total control over the activities and decisions of any divisions, subsidiaries or regionalized units. This control is exercised by authority emanating from headquarters. This defines policies, procedures, targets and budgets, which have to be followed and achieved. A centralized structure is illustrated in Figure 12.2.

In a centralized structure close control is maintained over divisional activities, standardized procedures and systems are used, and guidance is provided by functional specialists at headquarters. The disadvantage is that centralization restricts the scope of divisional management to handle their own affairs in the light of local knowledge, and the lack of autonomy in divisions can constrain initiative and entrepreneurship.

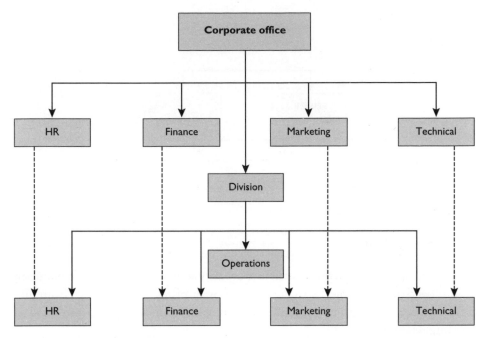

Figure 12.2   A centralized organization structure

Divisionalized or decentralized organizations

The process of divisionalization, as first described by Sloan (1986) on the basis of his experience in running General Motors, involves structuring the organization into separate divisions, each concerned with discrete manufacturing, sales, distribution or service functions, or with serving a particular market. These may operate as strategic business units (SBUs) largely responsible for generating their own profits in order to achieve targets set by the centre. At group headquarters functional departments may exist in such areas as finance, planning, HR, legal and engineering to provide services to the divisions or SBUs and, importantly, to exercise a degree of functional control over their activities. The amount of control exercised will depend on the extent to which the organization has decided to decentralize authority to strategic business units that are positioned close to the markets they serve. A divisionalized organization is illustrated in Figure 12.3.

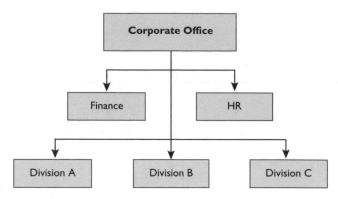

Figure 12.3   A divisionalized organization

Matrix organizations

A matrix organization is a functional structure consisting of a number of different disciplines or functions overlaid by a project structure consisting of project teams drawn from the disciplines. Thus an employee can be a member of a discipline and of a project team and so have two reporting relationships.

Matrix organizations are project-based. Development, design or construction projects will be controlled by project directors or managers or, in the case of a consultancy, assignments will be conducted by project leaders. Project managers will have no permanent staff except, possibly, some administrative support. They will draw the members of their project teams from discipline groups, each of which will be headed up by a director or manager who is responsible on a continuing basis for resourcing the group, developing and managing its members and ensuring that they are assigned as fully as possible to project teams. These individuals are assigned to a project team and they will be responsible to the team leader for delivering the required results, but they will continue to be accountable generally to the head of their discipline for their overall performance and contribution. The most typical form of matrix organization is a large multi-discipline consultancy. A matrix organization is illustrated in Figure 12.4.

		Disciplines			
		A	B	C	D
Project teams	1	◯		◯	
	2		◯		◯
	3	◯	◯	◯	
	4		◯	◯	◯

Figure 12.4   A matrix organization

Flexible organizations

Flexible organizations may conform broadly to the Mintzberg (1983) category of an adhocracy in the sense that they are capable of quickly adapting to new demands and operate fluidly. The flexible firm is one in which there is structural, functional and numerical flexibility. The concept originated in the work of Doeringer and Priore (1971) and Loveridge and Mok (1979) but was popularized by Atkinson (1984).

Structural flexibility is present when the core of permanent employees is supplemented by a peripheral group of part-time employees, employees on short- or fixed-term contracts (for example interim managers who are appointed to fill in for a manager over a limited period of time) or subcontracted workers. This is often called a core-periphery organization.

Functional flexibility exists when employees can be redeployed quickly and smoothly between activities and tasks. It may require multi-skilling (workers who possess and can apply a number of skills, for example both mechanical and electrical engineering) or multi-tasking (workers who carry out a number of different tasks, for example in a work team).

Numerical flexibility happens when the numbers of employees can be quickly and easily increased or decreased in line with even short-term changes in the level of demand for labour.

The 'shamrock' organization was the term used by Charles Handy (1985) for a core-periphery structure. As he put it: 'The core will be composed of well-qualified people, professionals, technicians or managers. They get most of their identity and purpose from their work. They are the organization and are likely to be both committed to it and dependent on it.' In contrast, what Handy calls the 'contractual fringe' will be made up of both individuals and organizations. The individuals will be self-employed professionals or technicians, many of them past employees of the central organization who preferred the freedom of self-employment. The core and the contractual fringe compose two leaves of the shamrock; the third leaf consists of the flexible labour force who carry out part-time or temporary work.

Atkinson (1984) suggested that the growth of the flexible firm has involved the break-up of the labour force into increasingly peripheral (and therefore numerically flexible) groups of workers clustered around a numerically stable core group that will conduct the organization's key, firm-specific activities. At the core, the focus is on functional flexibility. Shifting to the periphery, numerical flexibility becomes more important. As the market grows, the periphery expands to take up slack; as growth slows, the periphery contracts. At the core, only tasks and responsibilities change; the workers here are insulated from medium-term fluctuations in the market and can therefore enjoy a measure of job security, whereas those in the periphery are exposed to them.

The lean organization

A lean organization is one in which 'lean production' methods are practised. The term was popularized by Womack and Jones (1970) in *The Machine that Changed the World*. But the drive for leaner methods of working was confined initially to the car industry, as in Toyota, one of the pioneers of lean production, or more loosely, 'world-class manufacturing'.

Lean production aims to add value by minimizing waste in terms of materials, time, space and people. Production systems associated with leanness include just-in-time, supply chain management, material resources planning and zero defects/right first time.

The concept of 'leanness' has since been extended to non-manufacturing organizations. This can often be number-driven and is implemented by means of a reduction in headcounts (downsizing) and a reduction in the number of levels of management and supervision (de-layering). But there is no standard model of what a lean organization looks like. According to research conducted by Kinnie *et al* (1996), firms select from a menu the methods that meet their business needs. These include, other than de-layering or the negative approach of downsizing, positive steps such as team-based work organizations, cross-functional management and development teams, emphasis on horizontal business processes rather than vertical structures, and HRM (human resource management) policies aimed at high performance and commitment including communication programmes and participation in decision-making.

The process-based organization

A process-based organization conforms broadly to the post-modern model. The focus is on horizontal processes that cut across organizational boundaries and it is sometimes called a 'boundary-less organization'.

Traditional organization structures consisted of a range of functions operating semi-independently, each with its own, usually extended, management hierarchy. Functions acted as vertical 'chimneys' with boundaries between what they did and what happened next door. Continuity of work between functions and the coordination of activities was prejudiced. Attention was focused on vertical relationships and authority-based management – the 'command and control' structure.

Horizontal processes received relatively little attention. It was not recognized, for example, that meeting the needs of customers by systems of order processing could only be carried out satisfactorily if the flow of work from sales through manufacturing to distribution were treated as a continuous process and not as three distinct parcels of activity. Another horizontal process that drew attention to the need to reconsider how organizations should be structured was total quality. This is not a top-down system. It cuts across the boundaries separating organizational units to ensure that quality is built into the organization's products and services.

In a process-based organization there may still be designated functions for, say, manufacturing, sales and distribution. But the emphasis will be on how these areas work together on multi-functional projects to deal with new demands such as product/market development. Teams will jointly consider ways of responding to customer requirements. Quality and continuous improvement will be regarded as a common responsibility shared between managers and staff from each function. The overriding objective will be to maintain a smooth flow of work between functions and to achieve synergy by pooling resources from different functions in task forces or project teams.

Organizational culture

Organizational or corporate culture is the pattern of values, norms, beliefs, attitudes and assumptions that may not have been articulated but that shape the ways in which people in organizations behave and things get done. It can be expressed through the medium of a prevailing management style in the organization. It is often described as 'the way we do things around here'.

As Furnham and Gunter (1993) point out:

> *Culture represents the 'social glue' and generates a 'we-feeling', thus counteracting processes of differentiation which are an unavoidable part of organizational life. Organizational culture offers a shared system of meanings which is the basis for communications and mutual understanding. If these functions are not fulfilled in a satisfactory way, culture may significantly reduce the efficiency of an organization.*

The components of culture

Organizational culture can be described in terms of values, norms, artefacts and management style.

Values

Values are beliefs in what is best or good for the organization and what should or ought to happen. The 'value set' of an organization may only be recognized at top level, or it may be shared throughout the business, in which case it could be described as value driven.

The stronger the values, the more they will influence behaviour. This does not depend upon their having been articulated. Implicit values that are deeply embedded in the culture of an organization and are reinforced by the behaviour of management can be highly influential, while espoused values that are idealistic and are not reflected in managerial behaviour may have little or no effect. When values are acted on they are called 'values in use'.

Some of the most typical areas in which values can be expressed, implicitly or explicitly, are:

- performance;
- competence;
- competitiveness;
- innovation;
- quality;
- customer service;
- teamwork;
- care and consideration for people.

Values are translated into reality through norms and artefacts as described in the following sections. They may also be expressed through the media of language (organizational jargon), rituals, stories and myths.

Norms

Norms are the unwritten rules of behaviour, the 'rules of the game', which provide informal guidelines on how to behave. Norms tell people what they are supposed to be doing, saying, believing, even wearing. They are never expressed in writing – if they were, they would be policies or procedures. They are passed on by word of mouth or behaviour and can be enforced by the reactions of people if they are violated. They can exert very powerful pressure on behaviour because of these reactions – we control others by the way we react to them.

Norms refer to such aspects of behaviour as:

- how managers treat the members of their teams (management style) and how the latter relate to their managers;
- the prevailing work ethic, eg 'work hard, play hard', 'come in early, stay late', 'if you cannot finish your work during business hours you are obviously inefficient', 'look busy at all times', 'look relaxed at all times';
- status – how much importance is attached to it; the existence or lack of obvious status symbols;
- ambition – naked ambition is expected and approved of, or a more subtle approach is the norm;
- performance – exacting performance standards are general; the highest praise that can be given in the organization is to be referred to as very professional.

Artefacts

Artefacts are the visible and tangible aspects of an organization that people hear, see or feel and that contribute to their understanding of the organization's culture. Artefacts can include such things as the working environment, the tone and language used in e-mails, letters or memoranda, the manner in which people address each other at meetings or over the telephone, the welcome (or lack of welcome) given to visitors, and the way in which telephonists deal with outside calls. Artefacts can be very revealing.

Management style

Management style is the approach used by managers to manage other people. The concept of management style is associated with that of leadership style as described in Chapter 3. To varying degrees management style can be autocratic or democratic, enabling or controlling, transactional or transformational. Although individual managers have their own management style, the organizational culture may foster a prevailing management style that is widely adopted.

Classifying organizational culture

There have been many attempts to classify or categorize organizational culture as a basis for the analysis of cultures in organizations and for taking action to support or change them. Two of the best-known ones are summarized in the following section.

Harrison

Harrison (1972) categorized what he called 'organization ideologies'. These are:

- Power-orientated – competitive, responsive to personality rather than expertise.
- People-orientated – consensual, management control rejected.
- Task-orientated – focus on competency, dynamic.
- Role-orientated – focus on legality, legitimacy and bureaucracy.

Handy

Handy (1976) based his typology on Harrison's classification, although Handy preferred the word 'culture' to 'ideology' as culture conveyed more of the feeling of a pervasive way of life or set of norms. His four types of culture were:

1. The power culture, in which a central power source exercises control. There are few rules or procedures and the atmosphere is competitive, power-orientated and political.

2. The role culture, in which work is controlled by procedures and rules and the role, or job description, is more important than the person who fills it. Power is associated with positions not people.

3. The task culture, in which the aim is to bring together the right people and let them get on with it. Influence is based more on expert power than position or personal power. The culture is adaptable and teamwork is important.

4. The person culture, in which the individual is the central point. The organization exists only to serve and assist the individuals in it.

Appropriate cultures

As described by Furnham and Gunter (1993), 'a good culture is consistent in its components and shared amongst organizational members, and it makes the organization unique, thus differentiating it from other organizations.' It is said that such a culture exerts a positive influence on organizational behaviour and helps to create a 'high-performance' culture, one that will produce a high level of business performance.

However, a high-performance culture simply means any culture that will produce a high level of business performance. The attributes of cultures vary tremendously by context. The qualities of a high-performance culture for an established retail chain, a growing service business and a consumer products company that is losing market share may be very different. Cultures may vary in different organizational functions, for example manufacturing and marketing. Furthermore, in addition to context differences, all cultures evolve over time. Cultures that are 'good' in one set of circumstances or period of time may be dysfunctional in different circumstances or different times.

Because culture is developed and manifests itself in different ways in different organizations, it is not possible to say that one culture is better than another, only that it is dissimilar in certain ways. There is no such thing as an ideal culture, only an appropriate culture. This means that there can be no universal prescription for managing culture, though there are certain approaches that can be helpful, as described in the next section.

Supporting and changing cultures

While it may not be possible to define an ideal structure or to prescribe how it can be developed, it can at least be stated with confidence that embedded cultures exert considerable influence on organizational behaviour and therefore performance. If there is an appropriate and effective culture it would be desirable to take steps to support or reinforce it. If the culture is inappropriate, attempts should be made to determine what needs to be changed and to develop and implement plans for change.

Organizational processes

The ways in which organizations function are expressed through their cultures and through the various associated processes described in this section.

Group behaviour

Organizations consist of groups of people working together. Groups or teams may be set up as part of the structure or they may be informal gatherings. Interactions take place within and between groups and the degree to which these processes are formalized varies according to the organizational context.

Formal groups

Formal groups are groups of people who are set up as formally constituted teams to carry out defined tasks. A system exists for directing, coordinating and controlling the group's activities. The structure, composition and size of the group will depend largely on the nature of the task; although tradition, organizational culture and management style may exert considerable influence.

The more routine or clearly defined the task is, the more structured the group will be. In a highly structured group the leader will have a positive role and may well adopt an authoritarian style. The role of each member of the group will be precise and a hierarchy of authority is likely to exist.

The more ambiguous the task, the more difficult it will be to structure the group. The leader's role is then more likely to be supportive – they will tend to concentrate on encouragement and coordination rather than on issuing orders. The group will operate in a more democratic way and individual roles will be fluid and less clearly defined.

Informal groups

Informal groups are set up by people in organizations who have some affinity for one another. It could be said that formal groups satisfy the needs of the organization, while informal groups satisfy the needs of its members.

Group processes

Group processes include:

- the ways in which people in groups interact and behave with each other and with people outside the group;
- ideology of the group – its values and norms, which affect the behaviour of its members;

- cohesion – a cohesive group will share a common ideology and its members will identify closely with it because they, like the other members, approve of the purpose and work of the group and wish to be associated with the standing of the group in the organization.

Interaction and networking

Interactions between people criss-cross the organization, creating networks for getting things done and exchanging information that are not catered for in the formal structure. 'Networking' is an increasingly important process in flexible and de-layered organizations where more fluid interactions across the structure are required between individuals and teams. Individuals can often get much more done by networking than by going through formal channels. They can canvass opinion and enlist support to promote their projects or ideas.

People also get things done in organizations by creating alliances – getting agreement from other people on a course of action and joining forces to get things done.

Power

Organizations exist to get things done, and in the process of doing this, people or groups exercise power. Directly or indirectly, the use of power in influencing behaviour is a pervading feature of organizations, whether it is exerted by managers, specialists, informal groups or trade union officials. According to Nietzsche (1883) 'power has crooked legs', and Marks *et al* (2006) propose that power is 'the central concept in management, as the disinclination to talk about it suggests'.

Power is the capacity to secure the dominance of one's goals or values on others and thus obtain compliance. It can, of course, be misused but it is a fact of life in all organizations and its role needs to be understood. Four different types of power have been identified by French and Raven (1959):

1. Reward power – derived from the belief of individuals that compliance brings rewards; the ability to distribute rewards contributes considerably to an executive's power.

2. Coercive power – making it plain that non-compliance will bring punishment.

3. Expert power – exercised by people who are popular or admired and with whom the less powerful can identify.

4. Legitimized power – power conferred by the position in an organization held by an executive.

John Kotter (1977) interviewed over 250 managers who were in a position to use power. He found that the successful ones had the following characteristics:

1. They use power openly and legitimately. They are seen as genuine experts in their field and constantly live up to the leadership images they build for themselves.

2. They are sensitive to what types of power are most effective with different kinds of people. For example, experts respect expertise.

3. They develop all their sources of power and do not rely on any particular technique.

4. They seek jobs and tasks that will give them the opportunity to acquire and use power. They constantly seek ways to invest the power they already have to secure an even higher positive return.

5. They use their power in a mature and self-controlled way. They seldom if ever use power impulsively or for their own aggrandizement.

6. They get satisfaction from influencing others.

Influence and persuasion

Exerting influence and persuading others to do things are important parts of the role managers play. They may be given power and authority but this will not necessarily ensure that they will be able to get things done the way they want them done, especially when it involves their own managers and their colleagues. And although managers are in a position of authority over their own staff, the extent to which that authority will force people to do something may be limited. They, like other people in the organization, may only move in the direction they want to if they are effective persuaders.

The 10 rules for effective persuasion are:

1. Define the problem. Determine whether the problem is a misunderstanding (a failure to understand each other accurately) or a true disagreement (a failure to agree even when both parties understand one another). It is not necessarily possible to resolve a true disagreement by understanding each other better. People generally believe that an argument is a battle to understand who is correct. More often, it is a battle to decide who is more stubborn.

2. Define your objective and get the facts. Decide what you want to achieve and why. Assemble all the facts you need to support your case. Eliminate emotional arguments so that you and others can judge the proposition on the facts alone.

3. Find out what the other party wants. The key to all persuasion is to see your proposition from the other person's point of view. Find out how they look at things. Establish what they need and want.

4. Accentuate the benefits. Present your case in a way that highlights the benefits to the other party or at least reduces any objections or fears.

5. Predict the other person's response. Everything you say should be focused on that likely response. Anticipate objections by asking yourself how the other party might react negatively to your proposition and thinking up ways of responding to them.

6. Create the other person's next move. It is not a question of deciding what you want to do but what you want the other person to do. Your goal is to get results.

7. Convince people by reference to their own perceptions. People decide what to do on the basis of their own perceptions, not yours.

8. Prepare a simple and attractive proposition. Make it as straightforward as possible. Present the case 'sunny side up', emphasizing its benefits. Break the problem into manageable pieces and deal with them one step at a time.

9. Make the person a party to your ideas. Get them to contribute. Find some common ground so that you can start with agreement. Don't try to defeat them in an argument – you will only antagonize them.

10. Clinch and take action. Choose the right moment to clinch the proposal – don't prolong the discussion and risk losing it. But follow up promptly.

Authority

Authority is exercised when someone gets someone else to do something. Managers are given the authority to get things done. They are expected to ensure that their teams follow their leadership, although this should not necessarily mean telling them what to do. It can involve motivating, empowering and persuading. Effective managers give the lead and their teams follow, without being forced to do so by the use of authority in a 'command and control' mode.

Charles Handy (1994) advocates the development of a 'culture of consent' where the emphasis is on the virtues of decentralization, empowerment and self-managed teams. Authority is best exercised in the form of management by agreement rather than management by control. Managers who rely entirely on what is called authority based on position are less likely to succeed than those whose authority rests on the respect they have earned from their team on the basis of their ability to lead and get results and their expertise.

However, managers still have to be authoritative. As such, they are listened to. They get things done and others take note of what they say and act on it. Good managers demonstrate that they are authoritative by the way they behave. They rely on the authority of expertise and wisdom rather than the authority of power. Managers may be 'drest in a little brief authority' but they have to earn respect for that authority and keep on earning it.

To be authoritative you have to:

- Be good at what you are doing as a leader, a manager, an expert or all three.

- Be able to define what you expect people to do clearly, concisely and persuasively.

- Demonstrate that you know where you are going, what you are doing and why you are doing it.

- As necessary, explain the course of action you are taking.

- Lead by example.

- Accept that your authority is not absolute – it only exists if others recognize it.

- Be decisive but avoid rushing into decisions without careful thought.

- Get people to accept that there will be occasions when what you say goes – you are accountable and the final decision is always yours.

- Be self-confident and convey that to everyone concerned.

- Be a good communicator, ensuring that people know exactly what is expected of them.

Politics

Power and politics are inextricably mixed, and in any organization there will inevitably be people who want to achieve their satisfaction by acquiring power, legitimately or illegitimately. Kakabadse (1983) defines politics as 'a process, that of influencing individuals and groups of people to your point of view, where you cannot rely on authority.' People who 'play politics' in organizations get their way by machinations, manipulations, wire-pulling, exerting more or less subtle pressure, influencing people and events 'behind the scenes', and generally adopting a Machiavellian approach that includes the belief that the end justifies the means.

Politics play an inevitable part in organizations that contain individuals who, while they are ostensibly there to achieve a common purpose, are, at the same time, driven by their own needs to achieve their own goals. Some individuals genuinely believe that using political means to achieve their goals is the only way to get things done and will benefit the organization as well as themselves. Others rationalize this belief. Yet others unashamedly pursue their own ends.

Conflict

Conflict happens in organizations because they function by means of adjustments and compromises among competitive elements in their structure and membership. Conflict also arises when there is change, because it may be seen as a threat to be challenged or resisted, or when there is frustration – this may produce an aggressive reaction; fight rather than flight. Conflict is not to be deplored. It is an inevitable result of progress and change and it can and should be used constructively.

Conflict between individuals raises fewer problems than conflict between groups. Individuals can act independently and resolve their differences. Members of groups may have to accept the norms, goals and values of their group. The individual's loyalty will usually be to their own group if it is in conflict with others.

Understanding organizational policies

Policies exist to provide guides to action and set limits to decision-making – what should be done in certain circumstances, how particular requirements or issues should be dealt with. Organizational policies can be set up in such areas as marketing (eg what products should be sold, what markets should be developed, what price levels should be set, what levels of service should be provided for customers), operations (eg make or buy products, how to achieve high quality, what stock levels should be maintained, outsourcing), finance (eg treatment of depreciation, inflation accounting, capital budgeting, cash flow) and human resources (eg pay levels compared with market rates, equal opportunity, promote from within or external recruitment, work–life balance, security of employment).

Organizational policies may be expressed formally in manuals, and it is clearly necessary for managers to familiarize themselves with relevant policies and how they should be interpreted (however carefully expressed, policies almost always leave room for interpretation). Policies may also be informal and have grown by custom and practice over the years. Not knowing what is expected of them in the areas covered by such policies can make the life of managers more difficult. It is up to more senior managers to communicate policies if they have not been set out in writing, but it is the job of all managers to find out what policies do impinge on their work, even when they are not recorded in a manual, and act accordingly.

References

Argyris, C (1957) *Personality and Organization*, Harper & Row, New York

Atkinson, J (1984) Manpower strategies for flexible organizations, *Personnel Management*, August, pp 28–31

Barnard, C (1938) *The Functions of an Executive*, Harvard University Press, Boston, MA

Burns, T and Stalker, G (1961) *The Management of Innovation*, Tavistock, London

Child, J (1977) *Organization: A guide to problems and practice*, Harper & Row, London

Doeringer, P and Piore, M (1971) *Internal Labor Markets and Labor Market Analysis*, Heath, Lexington, DC

Emery, F E (1959) *Characteristics of Socio-Technical Systems*, Tavistock Publications, London

Fayol, H (1916) *Administration Industrielle et General*, translated by C Storrs (1949) as *General and Industrial Management*, Pitman, London

French, J R and Raven, B (1959) The basis of social power, in *Studies in Social Power*, ed D Cartwright, pp 150–67, Institute for Social Research, Ann Arbor, MI

Furnham, A and Gunter, B (1993) *Corporate Assessment*, Routledge, London

Ghoshal, S and Bartlett, C A (1995) Changing the role of top management: beyond structure to process, *Harvard Business Review*, January–February, pp 86–96

Handy, C (1985) *Understanding Organizations*, Penguin, Harmondsworth

Handy, C (1994) *The Empty Raincoat*, Hutchinson, London

Harrison, R (1972) Understanding your organization's character, *Harvard Business Review*, **5**, pp 119–28

Herzberg, F (1968) One more time: how do you motivate employees? *Harvard Business Review*, January–February, pp 109–20

Huczynski, A A and Buchanan, D A (2007) *Organizational Behaviour*, 6th edn, FT Prentice Hall, Harlow

Kakabadse, A (1983) *The Politics of Management*, Gower, Aldershot

Kinnie, N *et al* (1996) *The People Management Implications of Leaner Methods of Working*, IPD, London

Kotter, J (1977) Power, dependence and effective management, *Harvard Business Review*, July–August, pp 125–36

Lawrence, P R and Lorsch, J W (1969) *Developing Organizations*, Addison-Wesley, Reading, MA

Likert, R (1961) *New Patterns of Management*, Harper & Row, New York

Loveridge, R and Mok, A (1979) *Theories of Labour Market Segmentation: A critique*, Martinus Nijhoff, The Hague

Marks, B, Marks, R and Spillane, R (2006) *The Management Contradictionary*, Michelle Anderson Publishing, South Yarra, Vic

Mayo, E (1933) *Human Problems of an Industrial Civilisation*, Macmillan, London

McGregor, D (1960) *The Human Side of Enterprise*, McGraw-Hill, New York

Miller, E and Rice, A (1967) *Systems of Organization*, Tavistock, London

Mintzberg, H (1983) *Structure in Fives*, Prentice-Hall, Englewood Cliffs, NJ

Nietzsche, F (1883) *Also Sprach Zarathustra: Ein Buch für Alle und Keinen*, Penguin Books (translated 1974), Harmondsworth

Pascale, R (1990) *Managing on the Edge*, Viking, London

Sloan, A P (1986) *My Years With General Motors*, Sidgwick & Jackson, London

Taylor, F W (1911) *Principles of Scientific Management*, Harper, New York

Urwick, L F (1947) *Dynamic Administration*, Pitman, London

Weber, M (1946) *From Max Weber: Essays in sociology*, ed H H Gerth and C W Mills, Oxford University Press, Oxford

Womack, J and Jones, D (1970) *The Machine that Changed the World*, Rawson, New York

Woodward, J (1965) *Industrial Organization*, Oxford University Press, Oxford

13
Designing Organizations

'Most organizations are not designed, they grow.'
Charles Handy (1976) *Understanding Organizations*, **Penguin Books, Harmondsworth**

The management of people in organizations constantly raises questions such as:

- Who does what?

- How should activities be grouped together?

- What lines and means of communication need to be established?

- How should people be helped to understand their roles in relation to the objectives of the organization and the roles of their colleagues?

- Are we doing everything that we ought to be doing and nothing that we ought not to be doing?

- How can we achieve a reasonable degree of flexibility?

- Have we got too many unnecessary layers of management in the organization?

- How can we overcome the organizational dilemma of reconciling the potential inconsistency between individual needs and aspirations on the one hand, and the collective purpose of the organization on the other?

- How can we design jobs to provide for motivation and engagement?

These are questions involving people that must concern managers who are leading and therefore organizing the efforts of people to get results.

This chapter covers: (1) the process of organizing; (2) the aims of organizational design; (3) conducting organization reviews; (4) organizational analysis; (5) organizational diagnosis; and (6) job design.

The process of organizing

Organizations exist to achieve a purpose. They do this through the collective efforts of the members of the organization. The process of organizing can be described as the design, development and maintenance of a system of coordinated activities in which individuals and groups of people work cooperatively under leadership towards commonly understood and accepted goals. The key word in that definition is 'system'. Organizations are systems that, as affected by their environment, have a structure that has both formal and informal elements. The process of organizing may involve the redesign of the total structure, but most frequently it is concerned with the organization of particular functions and activities and the basis upon which the relationships between them are managed.

Charles Handy's point at the head of this chapter should be remembered. Organizations tend to grow haphazardly rather than being totally renewed through a grand design process. Organizations are not static things. Changes are constantly taking place in the business itself, in the environment in which the business operates, and in the people who work in the business. There is no such thing as an 'ideal' organization. The most that can be done is to optimize the processes involved, remembering that whatever structure evolves, it will be contingent on the circumstances of the organization. An important aim of organizational design is to achieve the 'best fit' between the structure and these circumstances. An attempt has to be made to ensure that the growth of the organization does not produce unwieldy, unmanageable or inappropriate structures.

Another important point to bear in mind is that organizations consist of people working more or less cooperatively together. Inevitably, and especially at managerial levels, the organization may have to be adjusted to fit the particular strengths and attributes of the people available. The result may not conform to the ideal, but it is more likely to work than a structure that ignores the human element. It is always desirable to have an ideal structure in mind, but it is equally desirable to modify it to meet particular circumstances, as long as there is awareness of the potential problems that may arise. This may seem an obvious point, but it is frequently ignored by management consultants and others who adopt a doctrinaire approach to organization, often with disastrous results.

Aim of organizational design

Bearing in mind the need to take an empirical and contingent approach to organizing as suggested in the last section, the aim of organizational design could be defined as being to optimize the arrangements for conducting the affairs of the business or a unit in the business. To do this it is necessary, as far as circumstances allow, to:

- clarify the overall purposes of the organization – the strategic goals that govern what it does and how it functions;

- define how work should be organized to achieve that purpose, including the use of technology and other work processes;

- define as precisely as possible the key activities involved in carrying out the work;

- group these activities logically together to avoid unnecessary overlap or duplication;

- provide for the integration of activities and the achievement of cooperative effort and teamwork;

- build flexibility into the system so that organizational arrangements can adapt quickly to new situations and challenges;

- provide for the rapid communication of information throughout the organization;

- define the role and function of each organizational unit so that all concerned know how it plays its part in achieving the overall purpose;

- clarify individual roles, accountabilities and authorities;

- take account of individual needs and aspirations;

- design jobs to make the best use of the skills and capacities of the job holders and to provide them with high levels of intrinsic motivation;

- plan and implement organization development activities to ensure that the various processes within the organization operate in a manner that contributes to organizational effectiveness (see Chapter 14);

- set up teams and project groups as required to be responsible for specific processing, development, professional or administrative activities or for the conduct of projects.

Conducting organization reviews

Organization reviews are conducted in the following stages:

1. An analysis, as described in the next section, of the existing arrangements and the factors that may affect the organization now and in the future.

2. A diagnosis, also described later in this chapter, of the problems and issues facing the organization and of what therefore needs to be done to improve the way in which the organization is structured and functions.

3. A plan to implement any revisions to the structure emerging from the diagnosis, possibly in phases. The plan may include longer-term considerations about the structure and the type of managers and employees who will be required to operate within it.

4. Implementation of the plan.

Organizational analysis

Organizational analysis starts with an examination of the activities carried out to establish what work is done and what needs to be done to achieve the objectives of the organization or organizational unit. The analysis should cover what is and is not being done, who is doing it and where, and how much is being done. An answer is necessary to the key questions: 'Are all the activities required properly catered for?' and 'Are there any unnecessary activities being carried out, ie those that do not need to be done at all or those that could be conducted more economically and efficiently by outsourcing to external contractors or providers?'.

Next, the structure is analysed to determine how activities are grouped together and the number of levels in the hierarchy. Attention would be paid to such issues as the logic of the way in which activities are grouped and decentralized, the span of control of managers (the number of separate functions or people they are directly responsible for), any overlap between functions or gaps leading to the neglect of certain activities, the existence of unnecessary activities or layers of management, and the extent to which jobs are designed in ways that will maximize motivation and engagement.

There are no absolute standards against which an organization structure can be judged. Every organization is and should be different. There is never one right way of organizing anything and there are no absolute principles that govern organizational choice. Never follow fashion. Always do what is right in the context in which the organization exists. The fashion for de-layering organizations had much to commend it but it could go too far, leaving units and individuals adrift without any clear guidance on where they fit into the structure and how they should work with one another, and denuding the organization of key middle managers.

Organizational diagnosis

The aim of the diagnosis is to establish the reasons for any structural problems. The diagnosis should be made on the basis of the initial analysis. The organizational guidelines set out in the following section can be used to identify causes and therefore indicate possible solutions.

Organizational guidelines

There are a number of organizational guidelines that are worth bearing in mind. But they are not absolutes. Their relevance is contingent on the circumstances. The days have long gone when the classical principles of organization (line of command, span of control, etc) as formulated by Urwick (1947) and others were seen as the only basis for organizational design. These principles do, however, persist in the minds of many managers. Some time ago, Tom Lupton (1975) pointed out that: 'The attraction of the classical design from the point of view of top management is that it seems to offer control'. Managers like to think they are rational and this has all the appearance of a rational approach. But without falling into the trap of believing that classical design works as it is supposed to do, the following guidelines are worth bearing in mind at all stages in an organization study and can help in the diagnosis of problems.

- Allocation of work. The work that has to be done should be defined and allocated to functions, units, departments, work teams, project groups and individual positions. Related activities should be grouped together. There will be a choice between dividing work by product, process, market or geographical area.

- Differentiation and integration. As Lawrence and Lorsch (1969) emphasized, it is necessary to differentiate between the different activities that have to be carried out, but it is equally necessary to ensure that these activities are integrated so that everyone in the organization is working towards the same goals.

- Teamwork. Jobs should be defined and roles described in ways that facilitate and underline the importance of teamwork. Areas where cooperation is required should be highlighted. The organization should be designed and operated in such a way as to facilitate cooperation across departmental or functional boundaries. Wherever possible, self-managing teams and autonomous work groups should be set up and given the maximum amount of responsibility to run their own affairs, including planning, budgeting and exercising quality control. Networking should be encouraged in the sense of people communicating openly and informally with one another as the need arises. It is recognized that these informal processes can be more productive than rigidly 'working through channels' as set out in the organization chart. As the highly original and influential thinker about management Mary Parker Follett (1924) stressed, the primary task of management is to arrange the situation so that people cooperate of their own accord.

- Flexibility. The organization structure should be flexible enough to respond quickly to change, challenge and uncertainty. Flexibility should be enhanced by the creation of core groups and by using part-time, temporary and contract workers to handle extra demands. At top management level and elsewhere, a 'collegiate' approach to team operation should be considered in which people share responsibility and are expected to work with their colleagues in areas outside their primary function or skill.

- Role clarification. People should be clear about their roles as individuals and as members of a team. They should know what they will be held accountable for and be given every opportunity to use their abilities in achieving objectives that they have agreed and are committed to. Role profiles should be used to define key result areas but should not act as straitjackets, restricting initiative and unduly limiting responsibility.

- Decentralization. Authority to make decisions should be delegated as close to the scene of action as possible. Profit centres should be set up as strategic business units that operate close to their markets and with a considerable degree of autonomy. A multi-product or multi-market business should develop a federal organization with each federated entity running its own affairs, although they will be linked together by the overall business strategy.

- De-layering. Organizations should be 'flattened' by stripping out superfluous layers of management and supervision in order to promote flexibility, facilitate swifter communication, increase responsiveness, enable people to be given more responsibility as individuals or teams, and reduce costs.

Job design

The aim of job design is to ensure so far as possible that motivation is achieved through the work itself, ie intrinsic motivation. Three characteristics have been distinguished by Lawler (1969) as being required in jobs if they are to be intrinsically motivating:

1. Feedback – individuals must receive meaningful feedback about their performance, preferably by evaluating their own performance and defining the feedback. This implies that they should ideally work on a complete product, or a significant part of it that can be seen as a whole.

2. Use of abilities – the job must be perceived by individuals as requiring them to use abilities they value in order to perform the job effectively.

3. Self-control – individuals must feel that they have a high degree of self-control over setting their own goals and over defining the paths to these goals.

A useful perspective on the factors affecting job design and motivation is provided by Hackman and Oldham's (1974) job characteristics model. They suggest that the 'critical psychological states' of 'experienced meaningfulness of work, experienced responsibility for outcomes of work and knowledge of the actual outcomes of work' strongly influence motivation, job satisfaction and performance. The six characteristics identified by their research were: variety, autonomy, required interaction, optional interaction, knowledge and skill required, and responsibility.

References

Follett, M P (1924) *Creative Experience*, Longmans Green, New York

Hackman, J R and Oldham, G R (1974) Motivation through the design of work: test of a theory, *Organizational Behaviour and Human Performance*, **16** (2), pp 250–79

Lawler, E E (1969) Job design and employee motivation, *Personnel Psychology*, **22**, pp 426–35

Lawrence, P R and Lorsch, J W (1969) *Developing Organizations*, Addison-Wesley, Reading, MA

Lupton, T (1975) Best fit in the design of organizations, *Personnel Review*, **4** (1), pp 15–22

Urwick, L F (1947) *Dynamic Administration*, Pitman, London

14

Organization Development

'For a large organization to be effective, it must be simple. For a large organiza-
tion to be simple, its people must have self-confidence and intellectual self-
assurance.'

Jack Welch, as reported by N Tichy and R Charan (1991) in *Managing People*
and Organizations, Harvard Business School, Boston, MA

Organization development (OD) is about taking systematic steps to improve organizational capability. It is concerned with process and people – how things get done by those
who work in the organization. In this chapter: (1) organization development is defined;
(2) organization development strategies are examined; (3) consideration is given to the
assumptions and values of OD; and (4) OD activities are described. Processes associated with OD for managing change and organizational transformation are dealt with in
Chapter 16.

Organization development defined

Organization development is defined by Cummins and Worley (2005) as: 'The system-
wide application and transfer of behavioural science knowledge to the planned development, improvement and refinement of the strategies, structures and processes that
lead to organizational effectiveness'. Organization development aims to help people
work better together, improve organizational processes such as the formulation and
implementation of strategy, and facilitate the transformation of the organization and
the management of change. As expressed by Beer (1980), OD operates as 'A system-wide
process of data collection, diagnosis, action planning, intervention and evaluation'.

OD is based on behavioural science concepts, but during the 1980s and 1990s the focus shifted to a number of other approaches. Some of these, such as organizational transformation, resemble OD. Others, such as change management, are built on some of the basic ideas developed by writers on organization development and OD practitioners. Yet other approaches, such as high-performance work systems, total quality management and performance management, can be described as holistic processes that attempt to improve overall organizational effectiveness from a particular perspective. More recently, as noted by Cummins and Worley (2005), the practice of OD has gone 'far beyond its humanistic origins by incorporating concepts from organization strategy that complement the early emphasis on social processes'.

Organization development strategies

OD strategies concentrate on how things are done as well as what is done. They are concerned with system-wide change and are developed as programmes with the following features:

- They are managed (or at least strongly supported) from the top, but may make use of third parties or 'change agents' to diagnose problems and to manage change by various kinds of planned activity or 'intervention'.

- The plans for organization development are based upon a systematic analysis and diagnosis of the strategies and circumstances of the organization and the changes and problems affecting it.

- They use behavioural science knowledge and aim to improve the way the organization copes in times of change through such processes as interaction, communications, participation, planning and conflict management.

- They focus on ways of ensuring that business and HR strategies are implemented and change is managed effectively.

- In accordance with the views of Jack Welch quoted at the head of this chapter, they avoid complexity and aim to build confidence.

Assumptions and values of organization development

OD is based upon the following assumptions and values:

- Most individuals are driven by the need for personal growth and development as long as their environment is both supportive and challenging.

- The work team, especially at the informal level, has great significance for feelings of satisfaction and the dynamics of such teams have a powerful effect on the behaviour of their members.

- OD programmes aim to improve the quality of working life of all members of the organization.

- Organizations can be more effective if they learn to diagnose their own strengths and weaknesses.

- However, managers often do not know what is wrong and need special help in diagnosing problems, although the outside 'process consultant' ensures that decision-making remains in the hands of the client.

- The implementation of strategy involves paying close attention to the people processes involved and the management of change.

Organization development activities

Action research

This is an approach developed by Lewin (1951), which takes the form of systematically collecting data from people about process issues and feeding it back in order to identify problems and their likely causes. This provides the basis for an action plan to deal with the problem, which can be implemented cooperatively by the people involved. The essential elements of action research are data collection, diagnosis, feedback, action planning, action and evaluation.

Survey feedback

This is a variety of action research in which data are collected about the system and then fed back to groups to analyse and interpret as the basis for preparing action plans. The techniques of survey feedback include the use of attitude surveys and workshops to feed back results and discuss implications.

Interventions

The term 'intervention' in OD refers to core structured activities involving clients and consultants. The activities can take the form of action research, survey feedback or any of those mentioned in the following sections.

Process consultation

As described by Schein (1969), this involves helping clients to generate and analyse information that they can understand and, following a diagnosis, act upon. The information will relate to organizational processes such as inter-group relations, interpersonal relations and communications. The job of the process consultant was defined by Schein as being to 'help the organization to solve its own problems by making it aware of organizational processes, of the consequences of these processes, and of the mechanisms by which they can be changed'.

Group dynamics

Group dynamics (a term coined by Lewin, 1951) are the processes that take place in groups that determine how they act and react in different circumstances. Team-building interventions can deal with permanent work teams or those set up to deal with projects or to solve particular problems. Interventions are directed towards an analysis of the effectiveness of team processes such as problem-solving, decision-making and interpersonal relationships, a diagnosis and discussion of the issues, and joint consideration of the actions required to improve effectiveness.

Inter-group conflict interventions

As developed by Blake *et al* (1964), these aim to improve inter-group relations by getting groups to share their perceptions of one another and to analyse what they have learnt about themselves and the other group. The groups involved meet each other to share what they have learnt and to agree on the issues to be resolved and the actions required.

Integrated strategic change

Integrated strategic change methodology is a highly participative process conceived by Worley *et al* (1996). The aim is to facilitate the implementation of strategic plans. The steps required are:

1. Carry out strategic analysis – a review of the organization's strategic orientation (its strategic intentions within its competitive environment) and a diagnosis of the organization's readiness for change.

2. Develop strategic capability – the ability to implement the strategic plan quickly and effectively.

3. Integrate individuals and groups throughout the organization into the processes of analysis, planning and implementation to maintain the firm's strategic focus, direct attention and resources to the organization's key competencies, improve coordination and integration within the organization, and create higher levels of shared ownership and commitment.

4. Create the strategy, gain commitment and support for it and plan its implementation.

5. Implement the strategic change plan, drawing on knowledge of motivation, group dynamics and change processes, dealing with issues such as alignment, adaptability, teamwork and organizational and individual learning.

6. Allocate resources, provide feedback and solve problems as they arise.

References

Beer, M (1980) *Organization Change and Development: A systems view*, Goodyear, Santa Monica, CA

Blake, R, Shepart, H and Mouton, J (1964) Breakthrough in Organizational Development, *Harvard Business Review*, **42**, pp 237–58

Cummins, T G and Worley, C G (2005) *Organization Development and Change*, South Western, Mason, Ohio

Lewin, K (1951) *Field Theory in Social Science*, Harper & Row, New York

Schein, E H (1969) *Process Consultation: Its role in organizational development*, Addison-Wesley, Reading, MA

Worley, C G, Hitchin, D and Ross, W (1996) *Integrated Strategic Change: How organization development builds competitive advantage*, Addison-Wesley, Reading, MA

Part IV

Delivering Change

15

The Process of Change

'Everything flows and nothing abides; everything gives way and nothing is fixed.'
Heraclitus, 513 BC

Change, it is often said, is the only thing that remains constant in organizations. As A P Sloan wrote in *My Years with General Motors* (1967): 'The circumstances of an ever-changing market and an ever-changing product are capable of breaking any business organization if that organization is unprepared for change'. This chapter is concerned with an initial analysis of the process of change, covering the types of change, how change happens, the concepts of equilibrium, stability and disequilibrium and how organizations grow and change (organizational dynamics). Approaches to managing change and models of change are covered in Chapter 16.

Types of change

There are seven types of change: incremental, transformational, strategic, organizational, systems and processes, cultural, and behavioural.

Incremental change

Incremental change is gradual change. It takes place in small steps. At the strategic level James Quinn (1980) coined the phrase 'logical incrementalism' to describe how organizations develop their change strategies. He suggested that organizations go through an iterative process that leads to incremental commitments that enable the enterprise to experiment with, and learn about, an otherwise unknowable future. He observed that:

Top managers seeking change often consciously create forums and allow slack time for their organizations to talk though threatening issues, work out the implications of new solutions, or gain an improved information base that will permit new options to be evaluated objectively in comparison with more familiar alternatives. In many cases strategic concepts which are strongly resisted gain acceptance and support simply by the passage of time.

Incremental change takes place at the operational as distinct from the strategic level. Continuous improvement as discussed in Chapter 19 is not about making sudden quantum leaps in response to crisis situations; it is about adopting a steady, step-by-step approach to improving the ways in which the organization goes about doing things. Innovations can be tried and tested and the people affected by them can progressively get used to new processes, systems or procedures without being startled and upset by a sudden, unexpected and dramatic change.

Transformational change

Transformation, according to *Webster's Dictionary*, is: 'A change in the shape, structure, nature of something'. Transformational change is the process of ensuring that an organization can develop and implement major change programmes so that it responds strategically to new demands and continues to function effectively in the dynamic environment in which it operates. Organizational transformation may involve radical changes to the structure, culture and processes of the organization. This may be in response to competitive pressures, mergers, acquisitions, investments, disinvestments, changes in technology, product lines, markets, cost reduction exercises and decisions to downsize or outsource work. Transformational change may be forced on an organization by investors or government decisions. It may be initiated by a new chief executive and top management team with a remit to 'turn round' the business.

As Jack Welch said when CEO of General Electric: 'Shun the incremental: go for the leap'. He also stated that: 'We want to be a company that is constantly renewing itself, shedding the past, adapting to change'.

A distinction can be made between first-order and second-order transformational development. First-order development is concerned with changes to the ways in which particular parts of the organization function. Second-order change aims to make an impact on the whole organization.

Strategic change

Strategic change is concerned with broad, long-term and organization-wide issues. It is about moving to a future state that has been defined generally in terms of strategic vision and scope. It will cover the purpose and mission of the organization, its corporate philosophy on such matters as growth, quality, innovation and values concerning people (employees and customers), and the technologies employed. This overall definition leads to specifications of competitive positioning and strategic goals for achieving competitive advantage and for product-market development. These goals are supported by policies concerning marketing, sales, customer service, product and process development, and human resource management.

Strategic change takes place within the contexts of the external competitive, economic and social environment and the organization's internal resources, capabilities, culture, structure and systems. Its successful implementation requires thorough analysis of these factors in the formulation and planning stages.

Organizational change

Organizational change deals with how organizations are structured and, in broad terms, how they function. It involves identifying the need to reconsider the formal structure of organizations, which Child (1977) has defined as comprising 'all the tangible and regularly occurring features which help to shape their members' behaviour'. Organizational change programmes address issues of centralization and decentralization, how the overall management task should be divided into separate activities, how these activities should be allocated to different parts of the organization, and how they should be directed, controlled, coordinated and integrated. They will be concerned with 'organizational process' – how the organization should function. This may mean trying to free up the ways things are done to ensure that there is more flexibility in the system to enable the organization to respond and adapt to change.

Systems and processes

Changes to systems and processes affect operations and impact on working arrangements and practices in the whole or part of an organization. They take place when operating methods are revised, new technology is introduced or existing technology is modified. The technology may consist of computer systems (information technology) that are concerned with such activities as electronic data interchange, enterprise resource planning, customer relationship management (CRM), computer-based supply chain automation, mechanized manufacturing processes, automated manufacturing processes (eg computer-integrated manufacturing), and distribution systems.

New or changed systems may be concerned with various aspects of administration such as financial and management accounting, material requirements planning, scheduling, procurement, order processing and distribution. Changes affecting individuals may also be made to terms and conditions of employment, working arrangements, the content of their job, employment procedures and the reward system.

Changes to systems and processes affect the daily lives of people in the organization – the jobs they do, how they are required to do them and how they are treated. Their immediate impact may therefore be as high if not higher than strategic or organizational change, and they have to be handled just as carefully. This is an area where getting change management processes right, as described in Chapter 16, is vital.

Cultural change

Cultural change aims to change the existing culture of an organization. Organizational or corporate culture is the system of values (what is regarded as important in organizational and individual behaviour) and accepted ways of behaviour (norms) that strongly influence 'the way things are done around here'. It is founded on well-established beliefs and assumptions.

Organizational culture is significant because it conveys a sense of identity and unity of purpose to members of an organization, facilitates the generation of commitment and helps to shape behaviour by providing guidance on what is expected. It can work for an organization by creating an environment that is conducive to high performance. It can work against an organization by encouraging unproductive behaviour. Strong cultures have more widely shared and more deeply held beliefs than weak ones. These will have been formed over a considerable period of time. Strong cultures are only appropriate if they promote desirable behaviour. If they don't, they are inappropriate and must be changed.

A deeply rooted culture may be difficult to change – old habits die hard. Deal and Kennedy (1982) said that there are only five reasons to justify large-scale cultural change:

1. If the organization has strong values that do not fit a changing environment.
2. If the industry is very competitive and moves with lightning speed.
3. If the organization is mediocre or worse.
4. If the company is about to join the ranks of the very largest companies.
5. If the company is small but growing rapidly.

They say that if none of these reasons apply, don't do it. Their analysis of 10 cases of attempted cultural change indicated that it will cost between 5 and 10 per cent of what you already spend on the people whose behaviour is supposed to change, and even then you are likely to get only half the improvement you want. They warn that it costs a lot in effort and money and takes a long time.

Cultural change may mean ensuring that the organization has what John Purcell and his colleagues at Bath University (2003) called 'the big idea'. Their research established that this is what the most successful companies possess. They had a clear vision and a set of integrated values that were embedded, enduring, collective, measured and managed. They were concerned with sustaining performance and flexibility.

Cultural change involves developing a more appropriate set of the values that influence behaviour and ensuring that people 'live the values'. The problem is that there may be a large difference between the values espoused by an organization and the ways in which they are or are not applied – values in use. Gratton and Hailey (1999) found through their research that there was generally a wide divergence between the rhetoric of managements about core values and the reality of their application – the 'rhetoric–reality gap'. Managements may start off with good intentions but the realization of them – theory in use – is often very difficult. This arises because of contextual and process problems: other business priorities, short-termism, lack of support from line managers, an inadequate infrastructure of supporting processes, lack of resources, resistance to change, and a climate in which employees do not trust management, whatever they say. It is therefore advisable to be cautious about 'big bang' cultural change projects. An incremental, gradualist approach that focuses on behavioural change (see the next section) may be more realistic. The aim is to close or at least reduce the rhetoric–reality gap.

If it is believed that a major cultural change programme is required it should not be too ambitious. However, it can be conducted systematically in the following sequence of activities:

1.   Analysis of the current situation in terms of environment, strategy, performance, culture, structure, systems and processes, and the availability and quality of resources – human, financial and material.

2.   Diagnosis of the causes of any problems identified by the analysis that will need to be overcome.

3.   Action planning – the preparation of plans to change or reinforce the culture and deal with the requirements and problems. Plans may deal with specifically cultural matters such as creating and disseminating mission and value statements and ensuring that they are acted upon. Or they may be concerned with human capital factors such as the skills, behaviour, motivation and commitment of people. Alternatively, action plans may address issues concerning organizational processes such as the development of continuous improvement and total quality programmes, provisions for achieving higher standards of customer service, or performance management.

4.   Implementation – delivering the results required by the action plan.

Behavioural change

Behavioural change involves taking steps to encourage people to be more effective by shaping or modifying the ways in which they carry out their work. Organizations depend on people behaving in ways that will contribute to high performance and support core values. They must recognize that people at work often have discretion on the way they do their work and the amount of effort, care, innovation and productive behaviour they display. Expectations of what sort of discretionary behaviour is considered desirable need to be defined and encouraged to attain behavioural commitment – people directing their efforts to achieving organizational and role objectives.

Behavioural expectations can be defined in the form of a set of values such as the core values of the Scottish Parliament:

- Integrity: We demonstrate high standards of honesty and reliability.

- Impartiality: We are fair and even-handed in dealing with members of the public and each other.

- Professionalism: We provide high-quality professional advice and support services.

- Client focus: We are responsive to the needs of members, the public and one another.

- Efficiency: We use resources responsibly and cost-effectively.

- Mutual respect: We treat everyone with respect and courtesy and take full account of equal opportunities issues at all times.

Competency frameworks can also be developed, which define behavioural requirements under such headings as:

- team working;

- leadership;

- developing others;

- quality focus;

- customer focus;

- results orientation;

- initiative;

- business awareness.

Behavioural change can be achieved by getting people involved in setting objectives, giving them more responsibility to manage their own jobs as individuals or as teams (empowerment), and providing for rewards to be clearly related to success in achieving agreed goals. The following sequence of behavioural modification steps as defined by Luthans and Kreitner (1975) can be adopted:

1. Identify the critical behaviour – what people do or do not do that needs to be changed.

2. Measure the frequency – obtain hard evidence that a real problem exists.

3. Carry out a functional analysis – identify the stimuli that precede the behaviour and the consequences in the shape of reward or punishment that influence the behaviour.

4. Develop and implement an intervention strategy – this may involve the use of positive or negative reinforcement to influence behaviour (ie providing or withholding financial or non-financial rewards).

5. Evaluate the effects of the intervention – what improvements, if any, happened, and if the interventions were unsuccessful, what needs to be done next?

Organization development (OD) processes can also be used. These involve the planning and implementation of programmes designed to improve the effectiveness with which an organization functions and responds to change. Organization development is concerned with process, not structure or systems – with the way things are done rather than what is done. Process refers to the ways in which people act and interact. It is about the roles they play on a continuing basis to deal with events and situations involving other people and to adapt to changing circumstances.

How change happens

Change management, as Rosabeth Moss Kanter (1984) puts it, is the process of analysing 'the past to elicit the present actions required for the future'. It involves moving from a present state through a transitional state to a future state. There are four stages:

1. Analysis of the here and now – an assessment of strengths and weaknesses that will be based on an understanding of what is happening, how it is happening and what effect it has. A diagnosis of the causes of any problems follows the analysis. The desirable outcome of any change – the future state – can then be specified. This forms the basis for defining the objectives of the change programme. Options – alternative courses of action – can then be considered and a choice made of the action that, usually on balance, seems to provide the best chance of achieving the objectives of change.

2. Getting from here to there – managing the transition, which is the most challenging stage in introducing change. It is here that the problems emerge and have to be managed. These problems can include resistance to change, low stability, high levels of stress, misdirected energy, conflict and loss of momentum.

3. Implementation – the transitional stage leads to implementation, which, as described by Pettigrew and Whipp (1991), is an 'iterative, cumulative and reformulation-in-use process'.

4. Consolidation (holding the gains) – ensuring that the benefits resulting from the change are maintained by monitoring the impact of the change and making further amendments as necessary.

Organizational dynamics – how organizations grow and change

Equilibrium and stability are desirable qualities in organizations. But they are difficult to achieve and maintain. Organizations are in a constant state of motion. They do not stand still. Disequilibrium and instability are frequently present in rapidly growing and changing organizations and have to be managed.

Equilibrium, stability and disequilibrium

Equilibrium exists in organizations when a balance is achieved between the competing claims of growth and stability. There is a constant battle to promote growth while at the same time consolidating advances so that they can be 'operationalized', that is, become a stable part of the normal operating processes of the organization. As a result, continuity is attained and people become familiar with the requirements of the changed situation, having acquired the necessary expertise in coping with them. Disequilibrium sets in when operational processes are no longer in balance and when new situations arise that cannot be managed effectively through the use of tried and tested techniques. To achieve stability while still maintaining growth requires the successful use of the change management approaches described in Chapter 16.

Stages in the development of organizations

The pursuit of equilibrium and stability has to be carried out in dynamic organizations that inevitably go through successive stages of development. It is necessary to understand the stage that has been reached by an organization to determine how the changes can be managed without causing disruption in the shape of instability or disequilibrium. There are typically four stages of development:

1. Start-up – this is the stage at which a new organization is born. It may be a new venture launched by someone with a bright idea, a 'stand-alone' business resulting from diversification, or a business formed by a group of executives fired with the desire to create something new and leave behind the strictures of their old organization. This stage may last for several years and can involve rapid growth until the curve begins to flatten.

2. Maturity – a mature organization is one that has reached a fairly stable stage. Management, however, may still be responsive and flexible, reacting effectively to competitive pressure, proactively seeking new markets and products and developing its management processes and systems to grow and improve performance.

3. Stagnation – this is the stage organizations reach if they have grown too large or set in their ways to do anything other than maintain their market share and influence. Hierarchy and bureaucracy may have become a way of life and the organization becomes

progressively more traditionalist in its management style and culture. Such organizations are often characterized by management teams that have grown up and matured together and have not sought actively to bring in new blood or to challenge their established assumptions and practices. In the United Kingdom many older, larger organizations and much of the public sector have been through this stage and are emerging from it in varying ways.

4. Regeneration – this stage follows the collapse of the 'old age' organization. It may start with a merger or a management buyout or the replacement of most of the top managers. This enables it to pull together what is left, reorganize and head off in a new direction with renewed vigour. Organizations in this phase often have to operate in a constrained economic environment in the first years. The phase has much in common with the start-up stage except that the organization is not operating in a green field situation and may still have to tackle the remains of the past as well as the future. If regeneration fails the organization will not survive – it will be taken over or wound up.

References

Child, J (1977) *Organization: A guide to problems and practice*, Harper & Row, London

Deal, T and Kennedy, A (1982) *Corporate Cultures*, Addison-Wesley, Reading, MA

Gratton, L A and Hailey, V H (1999) The rhetoric and reality of new careers, in *Strategic Human Resource Management*, eds L Gratton *et al*, pp 79–100, Oxford University Press, Oxford

Kanter, R M (1984) *The Change Masters*, Allen & Unwin, London

Luthans, F and Kreitner, R (1975) *Organizational Behaviour Modification*, Scott-Foresman, Glenview, Ill

Pettigrew, A and Whipp, R (1991) *Managing Change for Competitive Success*, Blackwell, Oxford

Purcell, J *et al* (2003) *Understanding the People and Performance Link: Unlocking the black box*, CIPD, London

Quinn, J B (1980) Managing strategic change, *Sloane Management Review*, **11** (4/5), pp 3–30

Sloane, A P (1967) *My Years with General Motors*, Pan Books, London

16

Change Management

'See change as an opportunity. Remember that change is a necessary thread in the fabric of life.'

Jack Welch (2004) *The Welch Way*, McGraw-Hill, London

Change management is the process of ensuring that an organization is ready for change and takes action to ensure that change is accepted and implemented smoothly. This chapter covers:

- the various models for change;
- the steps to effective change;
- how people change;
- resistance to change;
- developing and embracing a change culture;
- identifying the need for change;
- the benefits and risks of change;
- planning the change programme;
- requirements for success in managing change;
- transformational change;
- holding the gains.

Change models

A number of models have been developed to explain the process of change management and these are described and evaluated in the following section.

Kurt Lewin

The basic mechanisms for managing change as described by Kurt Lewin (1951) are as follows:

- Unfreezing – altering the present stable equilibrium, which supports existing behaviours and attitudes. This process must take account of the inherent threats change presents to people and the need to motivate those affected to attain the natural state of equilibrium by accepting change.

- Changing – developing new responses based on new information.

- Re-freezing – stabilizing the change by introducing the new responses into the personalities of those concerned.

Richard Beckhard

Richard Beckhard (1969) explained that a change programme should incorporate the following processes:

- Setting goals and defining the future state or organizational conditions desired after the change.

- Diagnosing the present condition in relation to these goals.

- Defining the transition state activities and commitments required to meet the future state.

- Developing strategies and action plans for managing this transition in the light of an analysis of the factors likely to affect the introduction of change.

Keith Thurley

Keith Thurley (1979) described the following five approaches to managing change:

1. Directive – the imposition of change in crisis situations or when other methods have failed. This is done by the exercise of managerial power without consultation.

2. Bargained – this approach recognizes that power is shared between the employer and the employed and that change requires negotiation, compromise and agreement before being implemented.

3. 'Hearts and minds' – an all-embracing thrust to change the attitudes, values and beliefs of the whole workforce. This 'normative' approach (ie one that starts from a definition of what management thinks is right or 'normal') seeks 'commitment' and 'shared vision' but does not necessarily include involvement or participation.

4. Analytical – a theoretical approach to the change process using models of change such as those described previously. It proceeds sequentially from the analysis and diagnosis of the situation, through the setting of objectives, the design of the change process, the evaluation of the results and, finally, the determination of the objectives for the next stage in the change process. This is the rational and logical approach much favoured by consultants – external and internal. But change seldom proceeds as smoothly as this model would suggest. Emotions, power politics and external pressures mean that the rational approach, although it might be the right way to start, is difficult to sustain.

5. Action-based – this recognizes that the way managers behave in real life bears little resemblance to the analytical, theoretical model. The distinction between managerial thought and managerial action blurs in practice to the point of invisibility. What managers think is what they do. Real life therefore often results in a 'ready, aim, fire' approach to change management. This typical approach to change starts with a broad belief that some sort of problem exists, although it may not be well defined. The identification of possible solutions, often on a trial and error basis, leads to a clarification of the nature of the problem and a shared understanding of a possible optimal solution, or at least a framework within which solutions can be discovered.

Commentary

The least known of these models – that produced by Professor Keith Thurley of the London School of Economics – provides the best practical and realistic guidance on what change management is about. It is descriptive rather than analytical, as is the case with the Lewin and Beckhard models.

The steps to effective change

Michael Beer and colleagues (1990) suggested that most change programmes are guided by a theory of change that is fundamentally flawed. This theory states that changes in attitudes lead to changes in behaviour. 'According to this model, change is like a conversion experience. Once people "get religion", changes in their behaviour will surely follow'. They believe that this theory gets the change process exactly backwards.

In fact, individual behaviour is powerfully shaped by the organizational roles people play. The most effective way to change behaviour, therefore, is to put people into a new organizational context, which imposes new roles, responsibilities and relationships on them. This creates a situation that in a sense 'forces' new attitudes and behaviour on people.

They prescribe six steps to effective change, which concentrate on what they call 'task alignment' – reorganizing employees' roles, responsibilities and relationships to solve specific business problems in small units where goals and tasks can be clearly defined. The aim of following the overlapping steps is to build a self-reinforcing cycle of commitment, coordination and competence. The steps are:

1. Mobilize commitment to change through the joint analysis of problems.

2. Develop a shared vision of how to organize and manage to achieve goals such as competitiveness.

3. Foster consensus for the new vision, competence to enact it, and cohesion to move it along.

4. Spread revitalization to all departments without pushing it from the top – don't force the issue, let each department find its own way to the new organization.

5. Institutionalize revitalization through formal policies, systems and structures.

6. Monitor and adjust strategies in response to problems in the revitalization process.

According to Beer and colleagues (1990), this approach is fundamental to the effective management of change. But account should be taken of the likelihood of resistance to change and what can be done about it.

How people change

A helpful analysis of the ways in which people change was made by Bandura (1977). He stated that:

1. People make conscious choices about their behaviours.

2. The information people use to make their choices comes from their environment.

3. Their choices are based upon the things that are important to them, the views they have about their own abilities to behave in certain ways, and the consequences they think will accrue to whatever behaviour they decide to engage in.

In essence, this explanation of how people change suggests that change management approaches should spend time explaining the benefits of change to individuals on the grounds that people are more likely to behave in certain ways if they believe that they can alter their behaviour and that the outcome of that behaviour will produce a desirable outcome for them.

Resistance to change

Change management programmes have to take account of the fact that many people resist change. There are those who are stimulated by change and see it as a challenge and an opportunity. But they are in the minority. It is always easy for people to select any of the following 10 reasons for doing nothing:

1. It won't work.

2. We're already doing it.

3. It's been tried before without success.

4. It's not practical.

5. It won't solve the problem.

6. It's too risky.

7. It's based purely on theory.

8. It will cost too much.

9. It will antagonize the customers/management/union/workers/shareholders.

10. It will create more problems than it solves.

Reasons for resistance to change

People resist change when they see it as a threat to their established and familiar life at work. They are used to their routines and patterns of behaviour and may be concerned about their ability to cope with new demands. They may believe that the change will affect their status, security or earnings. They may not believe statements by management that the change is for their benefit as well as that of the organization – sometimes with good reason. They may feel that management has ulterior motives, and sometimes the louder the protestations of managements, the less they will be believed.

Joan Woodward (1968) looked at change from the viewpoint of employees and wrote:

> When we talk about resistance to change we tend to imply that management is always rational in changing its direction, and that employees are stupid, emotional or irrational in not responding in the way they should. But if an individual is going to be worse off, explicitly or implicitly, when the proposed changes have been made, any resistance is entirely rational in terms of his best interest. The interests of the organisation and the individual do not always coincide.

Overcoming resistance to change

Because resistance to change is natural and even inevitable, it is difficult to overcome. But the attempt must be made. This starts with an analysis of the likely effect of change and the extent to which it might be resisted, by whom and why. Derek Pugh (1993) points out that: 'It is not enough to think out what the change will be and calculate the benefits and costs from the proposer's point of view. The others involved will almost inevitably see the benefits as less and the costs as greater.' He recommends 'thinking through' the change and systematically obtaining answers to the following questions:

- Will the change alter job content?

- Will it introduce new and unknown tasks?

- Will it disrupt established methods of working?

- Will it rearrange group relationships?

- Will it reduce autonomy or authority?

- Will it be perceived to lower status?

- Will it be established without full explanation and discussion?

On the other side, it is necessary to answer the question: 'What are the benefits in pay, status, job satisfaction and career prospects that are generated by the change, as well as the increase in performance?'

Resistance to change may never be overcome completely but it can be reduced through involvement and communications.

Involvement

Involvement in the change process gives people the chance to raise and resolve their concerns and make suggestions about the form of the change and how it should be introduced. The aim is to get 'ownership' – a feeling amongst people that the change is something that they are happy to live with because they have been involved in its planning and introduction – it has become their change. Involvement is important because people are more likely to own something they helped to create.

Communicating plans for change

Nadler (1993) suggests that the first and most critical step for managing change is 'to develop and communicate a clear image of the future'. He believes that: 'Resistance and confusion frequently develop in an organizational change because people are unclear about what the future state will be like. Thus the goals and purposes of the change become blurred, and individual expectancies get formed on the basis of information that is frequently erroneous.'

Communications should describe why change is necessary, what the changes will look like, how they will be achieved and how people will be affected by them. The aim is to ensure that unnecessary fears are allayed by keeping people informed using a variety of methods – written communications, the intranet, videos and, best of all, face-to-face briefings and discussions.

Developing and embracing a change culture

A positive change culture is one in which the values of the organization emphasize the importance of innovation and change and the norms of behaviour support the implementation of change. The existence of such a culture will assist in overcoming the problems associated with change, but the culture cannot be taken for granted. It will have been developed over time but can easily be damaged by an inept change management programme.

Change cultures result from the experiences of people who have undergone change. If they felt good about what happened they are more likely to embrace change in the future. And the opposite applies if change has consistently been mishandled. People embrace change when they are prepared to welcome it or at least judge it on its merits rather than resisting it automatically. Some people are more likely to embrace change than others because of their dispositions or their experiences. Others may be inherently suspicious of change but can be persuaded to accept it if the culture is right and they are dealt with properly.

For anyone to feel good about change, they must feel that they own the change – it hasn't been imposed upon them – and that they have benefited or at least not been harmed by it. They must be able to trust the organization because management have 'delivered the deal' – their promises of what change would involve and how people would benefit have been kept. They must understand that organizations cannot stay still – change is inevitable – but at the same time appreciate that management is aware of the needs of the members of the organization as well as those of the organization itself.

Identifying the need for change

A positive change culture provides the environment in which change can take place. But there is much to be done to manage change successfully. The first step in a change programme is to identify the need for change and to define why it is necessary. Effective reasons for change are those that are likely to be accepted by stakeholders – top management, middle management, employees generally and their trade union representatives. They must be persuaded that the change is necessary.

Strategic planning activities provide the most comprehensive basis for identifying the need for change. They can develop an integrated, coordinated and consistent view of the route the organization wishes to take and the changes needed to follow that route. Strategic planning also facilitates the adaptation of the organization to environmental change, which can be manifested in such aspects as the company's position in the market (leading the market, maintaining or losing market share), competitors' tactics, customer behaviour and government policies. Identifying this need means environmental tracking – noting what is happening and what is likely to happen, exploring the implications and deciding how the issues should be addressed. Proposals for changes because of environmental factors are more likely to be accepted if it can be demonstrated that the changes must take place and are appropriate and relevant.

The need for change may also emerge because of internal imperatives. This may be a proactive step arising from a review of areas for improvement. Or it may be a result of a systematic process of 'benchmarking' – finding out how other organizations are performing in certain areas – when it becomes evident that the organization is falling behind in such areas as profitability, productivity, cost management, quality or levels of customer service.

Reactive or remedial change may be required to respond to internal problems, even crises. In this case the need for change is determined by events. A proactive approach to anticipating the need for change has not happened and something has to be done in a hurry (often a recipe for disaster).

The identification process should generate hard evidence and data on the need for change. These are the most powerful tools for its achievement, although establishing the need for change is easier than deciding how to satisfy it.

The drivers of change

Change, as mentioned previously, can be driven by events – the need to change is forced upon the organization. More proactively, the driver for change may be an innovatory strategic plan or a positive response to environmental trends. Change may be inspired by an energetic and determined individual who wants to get things done. Continuous improvement programmes, as described in Chapter 19, may drive incremental change.

The benefits of change

Clearly, the main benefit of effective change is an improvement in organizational performance. Organizations can stagnate or decay. They may only revive or survive if radical changes take place to their ways of doing things. Change can be stimulating. Resistance to change may be a matter of a reaction to the 'shock of the new', but there is also such a thing as 'the challenge of the new'. Fortunately, most organizations will have people who, if they wanted a motto, would quote Horace – *carpe diem* (seize the day). They will be stimulated by the opportunity presented by change to the benefit of the organization and their own career. As Peter Drucker (1985) wrote: 'Opportunity is the source of innovation'.

Risks of change

There is a downside to change. It can go wrong because it is inappropriate or badly managed. Change can upset well-established and effective practices. The premise for change may be that if something is new it must be better, and this is by no means inevitable. There is such a thing as change for change's sake. Organizations can adopt the latest fashions or fads without thinking through their value or relevance. Failed changes can create a climate in which people become suspicious of any new ideas and unwilling to adopt them.

Planning the change programme

The basis for a change programme will be the business case. This defines the broad aims of the change, the benefits of the change and how it is to be achieved. In more detail, the programme needs to cover the following points.

Objectives

The goals to be achieved by the change should be discussed and agreed, wherever possible in quantified terms in the form of targets. If precise targets cannot be defined, then more generalized statements of the expected outcomes may have to be made, but these should be as specific as possible. It is often helpful to draw up success criteria so that everyone knows what they are striving to achieve and the extent to which the results have been achieved can be monitored and evaluated. A success criterion can be expressed in the form: 'This project (or aspect of the project) will be deemed to be successful if it delivers the following outcome…' It is important to involve as many people as possible in setting the objectives. This will increase their identification with the project and enhance their commitment.

Assessment of barriers to change and the development of solutions

The main barrier to change may be the sheer difficulty of planning and implementing a radical departure from the present way of doing things. The difficulties have to be anticipated – no surprises later on – and approaches to dealing with them decided in advance. A major barrier to change may well be the objections of those exposed to it.

Kurt Lewin (1951) produced a methodology for analysing change, which he called 'field force analysis'. This involves:

- Analysing the restraining and driving forces that will affect the transition to the future state – the restraining forces will include the reactions of those who see change as unnecessary or as constituting a threat.

- Assessing which of the driving or restraining forces are critical.

- Taking steps both to increase the critical driving forces and to decrease the critical restraining forces.

Defining responsibilities for managing change

The responsibility for managing change may be given to individual managers. This could be regarded as an important part of any manager's job and there is much to be said for making individuals accountable for results. In this role, as defined by Pugh (1993):

An effective manager anticipates the need for change as opposed to reacting after the event to the emergency; diagnoses the nature of the change required and carefully considers a number of changes that might improve organizational functioning; and manages the change process over time so that it is effective and accepted as opposed to lurching from crisis to crisis.

Project teams or task forces can be set up to plan and implement change, the members of which would probably include managers and other people affected by the proposed change as well as specialists. Ultimately, however, someone has to be made accountable for the whole project. The task force can contribute to planning and decision-making but cannot assume the final responsibility for making change happen.

It is often useful to identify people in the organization who welcome the challenges and opportunities that change can provide and can become 'champions for change'. They can act as 'change agents' with the role of facilitating change by providing advice on its introduction and management to project teams or individuals. This role can also be fulfilled by management consultants, who have the advantage of being independent and should therefore be able to take a fresher and more objective point of view. Their ideas may be more acceptable because they should have expertise in the area in which change is to take place and, as consultants, are in the business of introducing change. But their position as outsiders may be a drawback. They may not appreciate the subtleties of the organization's culture and needs, they may try to impose their own preconceived ideas and nostrums, and their ideas may be rejected simply because they are perceived to be 'not one of us'.

Organizations sometimes use process consultants as change agents. The role of the process consultant as defined by Schein (1969) is to 'help the organization to solve its own problems by making it aware of organizational processes, or the consequences of those processes and of the mechanisms by which they can be changed'. Processes such as inter-group or interpersonal relations and communications might be covered. Process consulting is one of the approaches that may be used in organization development (OD) programmes in which 'interventions' are made to increase the effectiveness of organizational processes. However, the massive and all-embracing OD programmes of the 1970s and 1980s have now largely been replaced by interventions that focus on more specific processes such as strategic management, total quality management, performance management or customer relations management.

Project planning

Project planning:

- identifies all the activities in the project and the order in which they have to be done – the aim is to break the change programme down into actionable segments for which people can be held accountable;

- estimates the time for each activity, the total length of the project and the time when each activity must be finished;

- finds out how much flexibility there is in the timing of activities and which activities are critical to the completion time;

- estimates costs and schedules activities so that overall cost is minimized;

- allocates and schedules resources;

- anticipates problems and takes the actions required to avoid them.

Monitoring and evaluating progress

Reporting systems should be set up so that progress can be measured against the plan. Milestones that can be used to monitor the project should be identified. Progress should be evaluated against the agreed objectives. Checks should be made after the change has been implemented to ensure that it is providing the expected benefits. These may indicate the need to reinforce the change or to make minor modifications.

Requirements for success in managing change

Success in managing change depends largely on thinking through the reasons for change, project planning, allocating the right resources, finding the right people to act as change agents and anticipating and dealing with problems, especially resistance to change. It is a good idea to positively encourage those concerned to articulate their reservations. It is better for these to come out into the open so that they can be dealt with than to allow them to fester. It is advisable to bear in mind the comments of Pettigrew and Whipp (1991) that change implies streams of activity across time and 'may require the enduring of abortive efforts or the build-up of slow incremental phases of adjustment'.

It is necessary to focus on short-term goals as well as longer-term deliverables. An incremental approach may well get better results in the long run than a 'big bang' approach. However, although flexible responses to new situations are important, it is necessary not to lose sight of long term goals.

Success in change management often depends on a climate in which innovation is fostered. As Drucker (1985) pointed out: 'change always provides the opportunity for the new and the different'. He went on to comment that: 'Systematic innovation therefore consists in the purposeful and organized search for changes, and in the systematic analysis of the opportunities such changes make for economic or social innovation' and that 'successful innovations exploit change'. But innovation involves risk and successful innovators define risks and confine them.

Ultimately successful change depends upon successful people management. It is necessary to understand and show empathy with people's needs, feelings and motivation.

Guidelines for change management

The following guidelines indicate how the effective management of change can best be accomplished:

- The achievement of sustainable change requires strong commitment and visionary leadership from the top.

- It is necessary to understand the culture of the organization and the levers for change that are most likely to be effective in that culture.

- Hard evidence and data on the need for change are the most powerful tools for its achievement, but establishing the need for change is easier than deciding how to satisfy it.

- Change is more likely to be successful if there is a 'burning platform' to justify it, ie a powerful and convincing reason to change.

- Those concerned with managing change at all levels should have the temperament and leadership skills appropriate to the circumstances of the organization and its change strategies.

- It is important to build a working environment that is conducive to change.

- Although there may be an overall strategy for change, it is best tackled incrementally (except in crisis conditions). The change programme should be broken down into actionable segments for which people can be held accountable.

- People support what they help to create. Commitment to change is improved if those affected by the change are allowed to participate as fully as possible in planning and implementing it. The aim should be to get them to 'own' the change as something they want and will be glad to live with.

- Change will always involve failure as well as success. The failures must be expected and learnt from.

- It is easier to change behaviour by changing processes, structure and systems than to change attitudes or the corporate culture.

- A coalition of support is needed to achieve change.

- There are always people in organizations who can act as champions of change. They will welcome the challenges and opportunities that change can provide. They are the ones to be chosen as change agents.

- The inept management of change will guarantee that it will be resisted.

- Every effort must be made to protect the interests of those affected by change.

Organizational transformation

Organizational transformation is defined by Cummins and Worley (2005) as 'A process of radically altering the organization's strategic direction, including fundamental changes in structures, processes and behaviours'. Transformation involves what is called 'second-order' or 'gamma' change, involving discontinuous shifts in strategy, structure, processes or culture.

Transformation is required when:

- significant changes occur in the competitive, technological, social or legal environment;

- major changes take place to the product life cycle, requiring different product development and marketing strategies;

- major changes take place in top management;

- a financial crisis or large downturn occurs;

- an acquisition or merger takes place.

Transformation strategies

Transformation strategies are usually driven by senior management and line managers with the support of HR rather than OD specialists. The key roles of management as defined by Tushman *et al* (1988) are envisioning, energizing and enabling.

Organizational transformation strategic plans may involve radical changes to the structure, culture and processes of the organization – the way it looks at the world. They may involve planning and implementing significant and far-reaching developments in corporate structures and organization-wide processes. The change is neither incremental (bit by bit) nor transactional (concerned solely with systems and procedures). Transactional change, according to

Pascale (1990) is merely concerned with the alteration of ways in which the organization does business and people interact with one another on a day-to-day basis and 'is effective when what you want is more of what you've already got'. He advocates a 'discontinuous improvement in capability' and this he describes as transformation.

Types of transformational strategy

Four strategies for transformational change have been identified by Beckhard (1989):

1. A change in what drives the organization – for example a change from being production-driven to being market-driven would be transformational.

2. A fundamental change in the relationships between or among organizational parts – for example decentralization.

3. A major change in the ways of doing work – for example the introduction of new technology such as computer-integrated manufacturing.

4. A basic, cultural change in norms or values – for example developing a customer-focused culture.

Transformation through leadership

Transformation programmes are led from the top within the organization. They do not rely on an external 'change agent' as did traditional OD interventions, although specialist external advice might be obtained on aspects of the transformation such as strategic planning, reorganization or developing new reward processes. The prerequisite for a successful programme is the presence of a transformational leader who, as defined by Burns (1978), motivates others to strive for higher-order goals rather than merely short-term interest.

Managing the transition

Strategies need to be developed for managing the transition from where the organization is to where the organization wants to be. This is the critical part of a transformation programme. It is during the transition period of getting from here to there that change takes place. Transition management starts from a definition of the future state and a diagnosis of the present state. It is then necessary to define what has to be done to achieve the transformation. This means deciding on the new processes, systems, procedures, structures, products and markets to be developed. Having defined these, the work can be programmed and the resources required (people, money, equipment and time) can be defined. The strategic plan for managing the transition should include provisions for involving people in the process and for communicating to them about what is happening, why it is happening and how it will affect them. Clearly the aim is to get as many people as possible committed to the change.

The transformation programme

The eight steps required to transform an organization have been summed up by Kotter (1995) as follows:

1. Establishing a sense of urgency – examining market and competitive realities; identifying and discussing crises, potential crises, or major opportunities.

2. Forming a powerful guiding coalition – assembling a group with enough influence and power to lead change.

3. Creating a vision – to help direct the change effort, and developing strategies for achieving that vision.

4. Communicating the vision – using every vehicle possible to communicate the new vision and strategies, and teaching new behaviours by the example of the guiding coalition.

5. Empowering others to act on the vision – getting rid of obstacles to change; changing systems or structures that seriously undermine the vision and encouraging risk-taking and non-traditional ideas, activities and actions.

6. Planning for and creating short-term wins – planning for visible performance improvement; creating those improvements and recognizing and rewarding employees involved in the improvements.

7. Consolidating improvements and producing still more change – using increased credibility to change systems, structures and policies that don't fit the vision; hiring, promoting and developing employees who can implement the vision and reinvigorating the process with new projects, themes and change agents.

8. Institutionalizing new approaches – articulating the connections between the new behaviours and corporate success and developing the means to ensure leadership development and succession.

Transformation capability

The development and implementation of transformation strategies requires special capabilities. As Gratton (2000) points out:

> *Transformation capability depends in part on the ability to create and embed processes which link business strategy to the behaviours and performance of individuals and teams. These clusters of processes link vertically (to create alignment with short-term business needs), horizontally (to create cohesion), and temporally (to transform to meet future business needs).*

Holding the gains

Perhaps the biggest challenge in change management is not deciding what changes should take place and introducing the changes, or even overcoming initial resistance to change. The ultimate and most difficult task is to ensure that the impetus provided by the change programme is maintained. There may be immediate gains but is it possible to hold on to them? Ensuring that this happens is one argument for incremental change, which provides time for reinforcement at each step without leaping too far ahead. But incremental change is not always possible. In these circumstances, holding the gains is a matter of first planning the change with implementation in mind – that is, with a clear idea of how it is going to be introduced and, importantly, how it is going to be consolidated. Careful monitoring of the process of bedding down the change is also required so that action can be taken in good time to deal with any deviations.

References

Bandura, A (1977) *Social Learning Theory*, Prentice-Hall, Englewood Cliffs, NJ

Beckhard, R (1969) *Organization Development: Strategy and models*, Addison-Wesley, Reading, MA

Beckhard, R (1989) A model for the executive management of transformational change, in *Human Resource Strategies*, ed G Salaman, pp 83–96, Sage, London

Beer, M, Eisenstat, R and Spector, B (1990) Why change programs don't produce change, *Harvard Business Review*, November–December, pp 158–66

Burns, J M (1978) *Leadership*, Harper & Row, New York

Cummins, T G and Worley, C G (2005) *Organization Development and Change*, South Western, Mason, OH

Drucker, P (1985) *Innovation and Entrepreneurship*, Heinemann, London

Gratton, L A (2000) Real step change, *People Management*, 16 March, pp 27–30

Kotter, J J (1995) *A 20% solution: Using rapid re-design to build tomorrow's organization today*, Wiley, New York

Lewin, K (1951) *Field Theory in Social Science*, Harper & Row, New York

Nadler, D A (1993) Concepts for the management of organizational change, in *Managing Change*, 2nd edn, ed C Mabey and W Mayon-White, pp 85–98, Chapman/Open University, London

Pascale, R (1990) *Managing on the Edge*, Viking, London

Pettigrew, A and Whipp, R (1991) *Managing Change for Competitive Success*, Blackwell, Oxford

Pugh, D (1993) Understanding and managing organizational change, in *Managing Change*, 2nd edn, ed C Mabey and W Mayon-White, pp 208–14, Chapman/Open University, London

Schein, E H (1969) *Process Consultation: Its role in organization development*, Addison-Wesley, Reading, MA

Thurley, K (1979) *Supervision: A Reappraisal*, Heinemann, London

Tushman, M, Newman, W and Nadler, D (1988) Executive leadership and organizational evolution: managing incremental and discontinuous change, in *Corporate Transformation: Revitalizing organizations for a competitive world*, ed R Kilmann and T Covin, pp 102–30, Jossey-Bass, San Francisco, CA

Woodward, J (1968) Resistance to change, *Management International Review*, **8**, pp 78–93

Part V
Enhancing Customer Relations

17

The Essence of Customer Relations

'The elite customer service companies:
- *design the right offers and experiences for the right customers;*
- *deliver these propositions by focusing the whole company on them;*
- *develop their capabilities – creating new capabilities, establishing direct accountabilities and constant renewal.'*

Allen, J, Reichheld, F F and Hamilton, B (2005) Tuning in to the voice of your customer, *Harvard Management Update*, October

Customer relations is concerned with all aspects of the ways in which an organization provides goods and services to its external customers and looks after its internal customers. Its essence is the development of a customer-centric culture as explained in the first section of this chapter. Within that culture the aim is to develop good relationships with customers and provide for high levels of customer service and satisfaction, as described in the next two sections of the chapter. More detailed consideration is given to practical approaches to customer service in Chapter 18.

Developing a customer-centric culture

A customer-centric culture is one in which everyone in the organization is aware of the importance of delighting customers by providing high levels of service to them, and works cooperatively with colleagues to achieve and exceed customer service standards. Everything done in the organization is focused on delivering service excellence for both external and internal customers. Singapore Airlines, as reported by Johns *et al* (2003), has 'created a culture which expects all staff to add value – to think about their processes, systems and routines all the time, to search for incremental improvements, even to think of radically different ways of delivering service enhancements to the customer'.

As reported by Sarah Cook and Colin Bates (2002), organizations such as Virgin and US retailer Nordstorm have created a customer-orientated culture by developing strong brands with powerful brand promises:

> *Through listening to customer needs and via consultation with employees, they have been able to identify brand values which form the backbone of how they do business with the customer and how employees are managed…The 'inside out' concept starts at the top of the organization. Employees look to the top team to model the desired behaviours… Organizations such as Barclays and AT&T have developed leadership behaviours and core competencies which directly reflect brand values. These in turn are linked to customer needs. How you lead is how you serve.*

The Lands' End approach

At Lands' End, the highly successful mail order clothing company, one of the key values is expressed as: 'Put the customer first. Achieve an even higher level of customer service through personal attention and new technology' (e-Reward, 2004). This is expanded by the following statement of 'what we believe in':

1. Satisfied customers and employees.

2. Integrity, honesty, friendliness, respect and trust.

3. The imperative to offer quality products and services at a fair price.

4. Lasting relationships with customers who appreciate our brand and its value.

5. Innovation in all we do.

The reason why the company wants to inspire staff is because it believes that the difference between doing something and doing it well comes down to the amount of effort people will put into their work. While an individual cannot be blamed for not taking an initiative or only working to their job description, their willingness to do that little bit extra is the difference between a good experience for customers and a poor one.

Lands' End staff are willing to make that extra effort because of their sense of pride in what the organization stands for: quality, service and value. Management believes that every employee wants to do a good job, and is motivated by doing so, but that their ability to do this depends on their 'amount of space', in the sense of not being frantically busy the whole time, and the degree of responsibility that you give them. So, Lands' End ensures that staffing levels are such that employees have the time to offer a good level of service, which in turn creates greater pride and so on in a self-fulfilling cycle. The company takes pride in its history of good service and publishes a book of 'great service stories' to help people understand how far they can go to help a customer.

Lands' End says that what front-line staff do has a far greater impact on customers than what the executive team does, which is why every staff member, including the managing director, works in a front-line job for four hours a week for the busy six weeks before Christmas. This reminds everyone of the importance of the front-line jobs and demonstrates to front-line staff that everyone else understands and values what they do.

Lands' End believes that where jobs are repetitive or less challenging, it is particularly important to provide some challenge and fun. And if it isn't possible to give people a choice as to the type of work they do, they can be given a choice as to how they do it. So, for example, in the Lands' End call centre, unlike many others, good performance is not primarily measured by the number of calls, call duration or the amount of time a person is available to take a call. If a customer wants a service assistant to go to the distribution centre, pick the item they want to buy, call them back and describe the feel of the garment, then that is what the assistant does. The company invests more heavily in staff training and giving people more responsibility than in putting in controls.

Steps to creating a customer-centric culture

1. Articulate the core values for service excellence that will be adopted by the organization.

2. Communicate those values to all staff.

3. Live the values at top management level – how they lead is how others serve.

4. Implement programmes of continuous improvement that provide for incremental but significant enhancements to service levels.

5. Implement total quality management or Six Sigma programmes (see Chapter 20), which provide for the achievement of high levels of product and service quality.

6. Focus on internal as well as external customers.

7. Define the attitudes and behaviours expected of all those dealing with external and internal customers.

8. Select people with the right attitudes, train them in the customer service skills they need and empower them to provide them with greater autonomy in relating to customers.

9. Monitor performance by reference to core customer service values and expected attitudes and behaviour.

10. Recognize and reward high levels of customer service achieved by individuals and teams.

Customer relationship management

Organizations must establish and maintain good relationships with customers – instilling confidence that their requirements will be met, on time, with cost-effective solutions and adequate support. To do this, it is necessary to understand what their needs are and to take steps to satisfy them through the development of the products and services required, targeting individual customers as much as possible, and providing the infrastructure in the shape of the required delivery (order processing and fulfilment) and customer support systems.

Customer relationship marketing is an approach to marketing that emphasizes the continuing relationships that should exist between the organization and its customers, with the emphasis on customer service and quality. It adds customer service and quality to the traditional marketing mix of product, price, promotion and place. Relationships with customers can be enhanced by relationship management supported by CRM (customer relationship management) systems as described at the end of this section.

The term 'relationship management' was first formulated by Theodore Levitt in *The Marketing Imagination* (1983). He suggested that the relationship between a seller and a buyer seldom ends when the sale is made. He wrote: 'In a great and increasing proportion of transactions, the relationship actually intensifies after the sale. This becomes the central factor in the buyer's choice of the seller the next time round'. According to Levitt, the relationship between the buyer and the seller is 'inextricable, inescapable and profound'.

The three objectives of customer relationship marketing are:

1. To achieve competitive advantage by creating value for the organization's customers.

2. To ensure that enough value is created in the sale to bring customers back for more.

3. To build and maintain mutually satisfying relationships with customers.

The essence of relationship marketing is the concept of the value chain, developed by Michael Porter (1980) as a tool to identify which of an organization's activities are strategically relevant. The value chain consists of five activities:

1. Inbound logistics – the reception, storage and internal transport of inputs to the product.

2. Operations – the transformation of those inputs into the final product.

3. Outbound logistics – the collection, storage and distribution of the product to buyers.

4. Marketing and sales – persuading buyers to purchase the product and making it possible for them to do so.

5. Service – the provision of service to enhance or maintain the value of the product.

Michael Porter believes that service and the value provided to the customer are integral and key parts of the chain, leading to competitive advantage.

Customer relationship marketing involves the provision of service support activities that will be perceived by the customer as being of unique value, thus extending the offer beyond the customer's expectations and contributing to a shift in the customer's perception of the organization. Service support includes such activities as pre-sale information, objective advice, care and attention during the sales negotiation, financing options, and after sales support in the form of warranties, accessories, repair centres and help lines.

The development of customer relationship management requires the alignment of the three activities of marketing, customer service and quality. The starting point is to chart the service delivery system and to identify critical service issues by research and analysis of customer wants, needs and reactions, as described in the next section. Service standards are then set for each part of the system, especially the 'encounter points' – the critical events in the system when the customer comes face to face with the service process. Monitoring systems are developed, which check how well the service standards are being achieved and programmes are established for maintaining continuing good relationships with customers on the basis of this control information.

Above all, customer relationship marketing has to focus on the organization's staff in all functions – product development, operations, distribution and support services, as well as sales and marketing. Their responsibility for building and maintaining good relationships with customers should be constantly emphasized and supported by training and the performance management and reward systems.

CRM systems

CRM (customer relationship management) systems are used by businesses to manage the information they gather on their customers and so enhance the quality of their customer relationships. Their main purposes are first to improve the speed and efficiency with which customer queries are addressed and resolved, and secondly to analyse customer data to predict their behaviour, find ways to make them more profitable and ensure that customer loyalty is enhanced. CRM is sometimes described as 'one-to-one marketing' because it enables businesses to focus on meeting the needs of individual customers who can be differentiated according to their buying habits and offered a personalized service. Customers are always a moving target and CRM systems can keep track of them. Much of the thinking behind CRM is based on the 20/80 rule that the top 20 per cent of an organization's customers account for 80 per cent of its revenues.

A CRM system contains a database that provides the company with the means to target advertising and mailshots because a better understanding has been achieved of the buying habits and wants of individual customers. Telesales can be facilitated by providing the telesales team with immediate access to customer information. Queries and complaints can be handled more easily from the online customer database.

A CRM system is based on a number of software applications. It starts with an integrated 'front-office' system. This is used by the people in immediate contact with customers, ie those in sales, marketing and customer service (helpline) teams. Customer information can be viewed on screen and relevant data can be captured for future reference. In addition, the system can provide a 'data warehouse' and 'data mining tools'. Customer information obtained at the front-line level is fed into the data warehouse. There, the information is used to identify customer behaviour, and from that behaviour, product and service configuration, sales and marketing strategies and loyalty schemes can be devised and directed to specific customers.

A complete CRM system contains four distinct sub-processes that feed into each other in a loop:

1. Data gathering – customer data is gathered and organized by segment. Data on customer purchasing patterns and complaints is particularly important.

2. Data analysis and value identification – the segmented data are analysed to provide information on customer motivations and behaviour.

3. Value delivery – the new insights obtained by the analysis are used to indicate where changes to the marketing mix (product, price, promotion and place) are required.

4. Monitoring, feedback and control – ensuring that the changes are viable and make overall strategic sense.

Customer service

Good customer relations largely depend on good customer service – all the activities carried out by organizations that meet customer needs and expectations. It is concerned with both external customers who purchase goods or services and internal customers within an organization who rely on the services provided by others to carry out their work.

Customer needs will be expressed in terms of the types of products or services they want. Expectations will consist of what customers believe to be a satisfactory level of quality and reliable service in terms of providing what they want (service delivery), attention to their needs, value for money, speed in dealing satisfactorily with orders, enquiries and requests, level of support and after-sales service, and willingness to listen to complaints and respond to them.

An external customer who makes a purchase enters into a relationship with the supplier or provider, who is obliged to meet the customer's expectations if they want to create a satisfied customer. External customers can be distinguished from: (1) users, who simply take advantage of a service that is available to them, eg the National Health Service; (2) clients with whom suppliers, eg management consultants, enter into a fiduciary relationship for the provision of paid advice or other services; and (3) payers who, for example, are members of an accounts payable department and arrange the payment, eventually, for something another person has purchased. Users and clients expect good service and should be provided with the same level of service as other customers. Payers need to be treated with courtesy even if an invoice from a supplier has not been paid for three months or more (it may not be their fault).

Internal customers also have relationships with their colleagues that involve expectations about levels of service.

Customer service is concerned with both product (what the customer actually gets) and process (the way in which the service is delivered). These two facets of customer service are closely interlinked. Customer satisfaction is only attained if they are both attended to.

It is not enough simply to offer what the organization believes to be good products or services to external customers. An organization will only succeed if its products or services meet consumer or user requirements. These may be expressed as service standards or targets in public sector or not-for-profit organizations, or quality, value for money and service level expectations in private sector companies. If these are not met, a public or not-for-profit sector organization will be deemed to have failed in achieving its purposes, with adverse consequences for its future. In the private sector, poor levels of customer service will result in inability to attract and, importantly, retain customers, and thus falling sales and therefore profitability, again with undesirable consequences for the management and staff of such organizations.

Aims of customer service

The overall aim of customer service for external customers is to meet and exceed customer expectations in order to increase the profitability of a business or the effectiveness of a service provider organization. Specifically, the aim is to provide a reliable product to fit customer needs, complemented by helpful and efficient service and support. This involves improving customer service by managing all customer contacts to mutual benefit and persuading customers to purchase again – not to switch brands or change to another supplier.

The aim for internal customers is to ensure that efficient services are provided for colleagues, bearing in mind that it is the customer who buys the products or services who matters and that everyone's efforts within the organization should be channelled towards helping those at the 'sharp end' deliver the best possible service to the customer.

The following ways in which customer care can increase profitability have been listed by Stone (1997):

- less lost business;
- fewer lost customers;

- repeat sales through increased customer loyalty;

- better opportunities for communicating effectively with customers to increase sales;

- more scope to identify the potential for increasing revenue from existing customers;

- increased revenue and profit through targeting sales to customer needs;

- more revenue due to the ability of sales staff to concentrate on calling on higher-revenue prospects;

- better and more efficient arrangements for service delivery and therefore lower staff and administration costs.

Customer service priorities

The customer service ethos in an organization should be founded on the principle that everything that anyone does will ultimately impact on customers and that meeting their needs should be given priority. As the slogan in one retail organization put it: 'If you're not serving a customer, you should be serving someone who is'. This is a good reason for developing improved standards of service for internal customers, as well as focusing on the needs and expectations of external customers. Customer service priorities should be reflected in statements of core values, training, performance management and reward policies and practices, which influence the behaviour of employees to customers, as well as developing better customer service processes.

Customer service activities

The following are the main customer service activities:

- ascertaining customer needs and expectations;

- using CRM processes to identify those needs and target sales;

- developing products and services that meet those needs and expectations;

- seeking and taking orders for products or services by advertising, promotions, direct selling, and the use of call centres or telesales;

- delivering the product or service effectively and efficiently;

- conducting effective interpersonal working relationships between employees and external customers and between individuals within the organization and their internal customers;

- setting standards and targets for customer service;

- developing customer service skills and influencing the behaviour of staff to customers;

- setting up customer service centres and websites;

- providing after-sales service – help, advice, repair and maintenance;

- dealing with customer queries and complaints;

- measuring the effectiveness of customer service and taking remedial action when necessary.

Elements of customer satisfaction

The fundamental aim of an organization's customer service policies and practices is to create and maintain customer satisfaction and retention. Loyal customers are worth nurturing. They buy more and buy more regularly. And the cost of selling to them is low, whereas finding new customers can be expensive. Satisfied customers will recommend products and services to others. Dissatisfied customers will complain to as many as 10 other customers and potential customers.

To achieve and sustain customer satisfaction the following requirements must be met:

- Quality – the product or service meets customer expectations on the degree of quality they require by delivering what was promised. For products this will refer to such criteria as fitness for purpose, reliability, durability and low maintenance. For services it will be concerned with the achievement of an acceptable level of provision, reliability and accessibility.

- Value for money – the product or service meets customer requirements on value for money in the sense of giving them at least what they paid for and preferably more. Belief on whether value for money is provided will often be on a comparative basis, setting off one manufacturer or supplier against others.

- Reliability – customers are most likely to be satisfied when the manufacturer or supplier 'delivers the deal' by achieving a consistent level of performance and dependability.

- Responsiveness – increasingly, customers expect their supplier to be willing and ready to provide prompt service and help at the point of sale and afterwards. Individual attention, speed and flexibility are required.

- Competence – the supplier must have the required skills and knowledge to produce value for money and to provide a satisfactory level of service.

- Access – customers must be able to gain access to the supplier or provider with the minimum of trouble. They have learnt to put up with mechanized answering services but hate endless delays in getting through listening to *The Four Seasons* and to seemingly insincere assurances that their custom is valued. They like to talk to human beings who will respond to their query or complaint.

- Courtesy – customers require politeness, respect, consideration and friendliness from the people they contact over the counter, in a call centre or when faced with a service problem.

- Communication – it is essential to keep customers informed in language they can understand about the product or service and how they can make quick and easy contact if they have a problem. It should be obvious that when they make contact they are listened to so that their specific query is dealt with quickly.

- Credibility – customers are more likely to be satisfied if they find as a result of their experiences that the supplier or provider is trustworthy, believable and honest. This is based on the knowledge and courtesy displayed by staff and their ability to inspire trust and confidence.

- Security – customers want to be confident that the product or service will be safe.

- Tangibles – physical facilities, equipment and staff appearance.

Changing customer dynamics and satisfaction

When considering how to satisfy customers it should be remembered that customer expectations tend to rise. They expect continually rising levels of service and more choice and will be dissatisfied if standards are only maintained at a level that they once found acceptable. Customers are changing the way in which they purchase, especially through the internet, which gives them more choice and enables them to compare product prices and attributes. It should also be noted that other organizations will improve the services they offer and competitive edge will be lost if these improvements are not matched or preferably exceeded.

Simply to seek satisfaction is not enough. It is necessary to go beyond satisfaction by exceeding expectations in anticipation of what customers will want in the future and what competitors will be doing. It is for this reason that careful attention has to be given to assessing and meeting customer needs, as discussed in the next chapter.

References

Cook, S and Bates, C (2002) How to create a customer orientated culture, *Customer Management*, **10** (2), pp 30–32

e-Reward (2004) *Research Report on Lands' End*, e-Reward, Stockport

Johns, E, Wirtz, J and Johnston, R (2003) Singapore Airlines and the service template, *Customer Management*, May/June, pp 38–41, and September/October, pp 38–41

Levitt, T (1983) *The Marketing Imagination*, The Free Press, New York

Porter, M (1980) *Competitive Strategy*, The Free Press, New York

Stone, M (1997) Evaluating the profitability of customer service, in *The Gower Handbook of Customer Service*, ed P Marley, pp 3–16, Gower, Aldershot

18

Delivering High Levels of Customer Service

'*To achieve world-class customer service a business must:*
1. *Deliver what it promises.*
2. *Provide a personal touch.*
3. *Go the extra mile if it has to.*
4. *Resolve problems well.*'

Ted Johns, Chairman, Institute of Customer Service

High levels of customer service are achieved and maintained by developing and implementing a customer service strategy, building a customer-centric culture, defining the attitudes, skills and behaviours in relation to customers required by staff, and ensuring that employees adopt those attitudes, possess the necessary skills and behave appropriately when in contact with customers.

The Institute of Customer Service (ICS) model for world class service (Figure 18.1) provides a comprehensive basis for the development and implementation of customer service strategies and processes.

A systematic approach is required to ensure the delivery of high standards of customer service for external customers. Fundamentally, as described in the last chapter, this means that the organization has to pay close attention to customer relationship management – creating and maintaining good relationships with customers in order to ensure that they will continue to want the goods or services provided by the organization because their expectations have been met. It is not enough for a commercial company to obtain customers, they must be retained as well by establishing a continuing relationship that satisfies their needs and thus contributes to business success. This attitude to customer service is just as important in organizations in the public sector

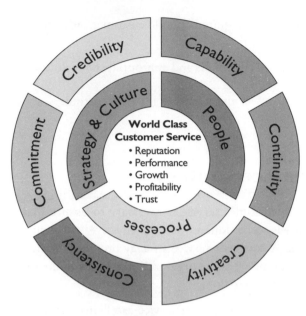

Figure 18.1   The ICS model for world class service

such as local authorities and NHS Trusts, where they are expected to achieve defined customer service standards. Not-for-profit organizations such as housing associations and charities are equally concerned with meeting the needs of their customers or clients, for example when they contract with an international or public sector organization to provide certain services.

The approach outlined above is the basis for the other customer service activities discussed in this chapter, namely:

- developing a customer service strategy;

- assessing customer needs and expectations;

- identifying target customers;

- communicating the availability and benefits of goods and services;

- measuring customer satisfaction and entering into dialogues with customers;

- developing products and services that will meet customer needs and increase or at least maintain customer satisfaction;

- providing the required infrastructure for customer service;

- evaluating models of customer service;

- setting standards for customer service;

- monitoring the delivery of those standards;

- taking whatever steps are required to build customer satisfaction and therefore to keep customers;

- developing customer service skills and appropriate behaviours.

The actions necessary to meet the needs of internal customers are also examined in this chapter.

Customer service strategy

A strategic approach to customer service is necessary to ensure that a longer-term view is developed on what needs to be done to develop effective, coherent and integrated policies, processes and practices. A customer service strategy provides the framework for continuous improvement. It will indicate what the organization intends to do about customer service in the future and how it proposes to do it.

The aim of the strategy will be to achieve service excellence. As defined by Robert Johnston (2002): 'Service excellence is simply about being easy to do business with'. He suggests that a reputation for service excellence can be developed and sustained by having a strong service culture, a distinct service personality, committed staff and customer-focused systems.

The strategy will cover what action will be taken to create a customer-centric culture, how the customer service infrastructure will be developed, the processes required to identify and meet customer needs and expectations and measure satisfaction, how the right attitudes, skills and behaviours will be fostered, and how the various internal systems and processes – the infrastructure that supports customer service – can be improved. The strategy will deal with both external and internal customers. It will be concerned with integrating the programmes for continuous improvement and quality management that ensure that a quality product or service is delivered to customers. It will also address issues relating to the recruitment, training and reward of customer-focused staff.

Assessing customer needs

Customer service policies should be based on assessments of what customers want and need. Expectations can be defined as 'deliverables' – what the organization intends to provide for customers and what customers expect organizations to provide for them. Deliverables can be expressed in terms of the type of product or service to be provided, quality, conformity to specifications, price, reliability, delivery and after-sales service. Needs can be established in four ways: (1) using CRM (customer relationship management) techniques as described in Chapter 17; (2) buying behaviour analysis; (3) marketing research; and (4) competitor analysis.

Buying behaviour analysis

Buying behaviour analysis determines the factors affecting the behaviour of customers with regard to the purchase of existing or proposed products or services. The analysis has to be based on an understanding of what influences buyer behaviour, and uses various models.

Influences on individual buying behaviour

The psychological concepts explaining individual buying behaviour are:

- Motivation, ie goal-directed behaviour – the emotional and rational motives that offer buying decisions and involve a reaction to a stimulus.

- Self-concept – consumers tend to make purchases that confirm their self-image so that they can safeguard and boost it.

- Personality – this strongly influences buying behaviour and an aim of buyer behaviour analysis will be to identify what sort of products or services might appeal to different personality types.

- Perception – the analysis identifies the meaning buyers attach to stimuli and how they discern between products and services and how these fulfil their need satisfaction.

- Attitudes – the set of perceptions an individual has leading to beliefs a buyer might have regarding a possible purchase. Potential positive or negative attitudes need to be identified so that marketing action such as repositioning can be taken.

Models of consumer buying behaviour

The simplest model simply means responding to immediate needs in the following 'AIDA' sequence: awareness > interest > desire > action.

An alternative model is the buyer/decision sequence:

- problem recognition – establishing a need;

- information search – seeking ways of satisfying the need, which can be influenced by marketing;

- evaluation of alternatives – this can be influenced by promoting the product or service;

- purchase decision – to purchase or not to purchase based upon the evaluation;

- post-purchase behaviour – the degree of satisfaction or dissatisfaction will affect future purchasing decisions and customer service tactics will aim to produce a positive reaction.

Marketing research

Marketing research provides information on consumer tastes, preferences and buying habits. Importantly, it can identify consumer beliefs, opinions and attitudes not only about products and services but also about the level and type of customer service provided.

Research into competitors

A comparative analysis can be made of competitors' products or services and customer service arrangements from the viewpoint of how and why they attract customers. This leads to decisions on what changes need to be made to maintain competitive edge. The analysis can be conducted by individual interviews or through focus groups or by using the Kelly repertory grid. The latter technique involves obtaining the opinions of respondents on competing products and their brand images. The interviewer presents informants with the names of products in groups of three for them to select the product that is different from the other two and how it is different. A final sifting then takes place through all the products to check out the characteristics attributed to them.

Identifying target customers

Target customers need to be identified to ensure that products or services are developed specifically to meet their needs, and promotion, sales and customer care practices are aligned to their preferences. Field research is used to establish user and non-user profiles, the factors affecting choice and preference, and reactions to new product concepts. The techniques used are described in the following section.

Sampling

Sampling involves the analysis of attitudes, opinions and facts about products or services – planned or on offer – from a representative sample of people in the total population. The typical technique is random sampling, which means picking the people from whom information is to be obtained on the basis that every individual has an equal chance of being selected.

Interviewing

Face-to-face interviews enable direct contact to be made with potential users to find out who is most likely to want to buy the product. Interviews can be structured (ie the interviewer has to cover predetermined areas) or unstructured (ie in-depth interviews that aim to obtain information on feelings and attitudes).

Panels

Panels measure the consumer behaviour of a representative sample of individuals or households over extended periods. The two basic methods are home audits, in which levels of household stocks of specified products are checked, and diaries, in which panel members record all purchases made.

Communicating to customers

It is necessary to inform customers of what is on offer and how it will satisfy their needs.

Availability of goods or services

The availability of goods or services is communicated by means of promotion activities. These consist of:

- Selling, which involves direct contact with customers to explain the product and persuade them to purchase it. This is carried out by sales representatives and assistants in retail outlets, by telephone (telesales), via websites and through call or contact centres.

- Merchandizing, which ensures that retailers display products prominently.

- Display, which displays the products in retail outlets or in exhibitions.

- Advertising, which aims to present the product to customers in a way that will persuade them to purchase it. Advertising is sometimes referred to as 'above the line' when agencies receive a commission for placing the sponsor's advertisements.

- Sales promotions, which refer to short-term activities like competitions and free samples that encourage quick action by buyers. This is referred to as 'below the line' because a direct charge is made to the sponsor for the work performed and the advertising agency does not receive a commission.

- Public relations, which publicizes information about the company's products or services through the media.

- Exhibitions, in which the company's products are displayed and promoted.

Helping customers to select the products and services they need

The communications to customers should indicate how the products or services will meet their needs. This message is referenced to the research that has established what those needs are, and the characteristics of the product or service and the benefits it provides.

Measuring customer satisfaction

It is essential to measure the extent to which customers are satisfied with the products or services provided by the organization. This means entering into dialogues with customers through responses to enquiries and complaints, questionnaires, surveys, focus groups (group discussions) and employee feedback.

Responses to enquiries and complaints

Every time a customer contacts an organization an opportunity is created to assess the level of satisfaction. Formal procedures can be set up to log enquiries and complaints under appropriate headings. These can be analysed and the outcome distributed to staff with an indication as to what action is required or, better still, a request that they should get together with colleagues and discuss what needs to be done.

Customer questionnaires

Customer questionnaires are a commonly used method of measuring satisfaction. Answers are often obtained just after the service has taken place, for example staying in a hotel or purchasing a car. Customers are asked to assess the service provided on a rating scale covering such aspects as helpfulness, courtesy, meeting needs, delivering as promised and the overall quality of the services provided. The questionnaires are analysed, the analysis is fed back to staff, and steps are taken to deal with any problems. Customer questionnaires provide immediate reactions but they may only be completed by an unrepresentative sample of customers, for example those who were highly satisfied or dissatisfied.

Customer surveys

Customer surveys, often conducted by specialized consumer research firms, cover a much wider and more balanced sample of customers. They can be carried out by means of face-to-face interviews, postal questionnaires or through the internet. Surveys will ask questions or get customers to respond on a scale (eg fully agree, generally agree, disagree) to statements such as:

- Staff are polite.
- Staff are helpful.
- Customer requests are dealt with politely and promptly.
- Staff do not provide individual attention.
- You have to wait ages to get through to someone in the company by telephone.
- Staff return your calls quickly.

Customer surveys are best conducted regularly in order to analyse trends. Results should be fed back to staff so that action can be taken. But surveys, like questionnaires, cover only shoppers who buy, and therefore they do not identify any aspects of customer service that put customers off.

Focus group discussions

Group discussions, commonly called focus group discussions, are frequently used as a means of conducting dialogues with customers. A small group of typical customers is assembled and pre-prepared questions are put to them on products or services and how they have been treated as customers. The person conducting the focus group acts as a facilitator, encouraging but not dominating the discussion. The aim is not only to obtain direct responses from individuals but also to get group members to discuss the questions amongst themselves so that an in-depth response can be achieved. Facilitators have to be careful to pose open questions, which prompt discussion but do not reveal what answer is expected.

The effectiveness of a focus group depends on the quality of the facilitation process. Because only small numbers of people are usually involved it is risky to infer too much from them. They indicate what some customers feel about what the organization provides, but they are only a sample.

Employee feedback

Employees can be encouraged to feed back to management and each other anything they have learnt about customer concerns and attitudes.

Popularity of measures

A survey conducted by CRL Solutions (*Measuring Customer Satisfaction: The Views of Customer Service Professionals*, 2002) established that enquiries and complaints data were the most popular method of measuring customer satisfaction, followed by telephone surveys, employee feedback and mail surveys.

Use of measures

Measures are only useful if they lead to action. That is why any data collected must be distributed to management and all staff concerned with customer service, which might mean every employee. Processes need to be established to allow people to learn from the data and do something about it. These might consist of regular meetings to review customer service issues or improvement groups (groups set up to deliver continuous improvement programmes, see Chapter 19).

214 Enhancing Customer Relations

Measures should be used to identify customers at risk. It is also desirable to segment customers according to their value to the organization. An important aim of customer satisfaction surveys should be to maximize the satisfaction and loyalty of those customers making the most significant contribution to profitability. It is advisable to record trends so that improvements or declines in satisfaction can be noted, allowing improvements to be maintained and declines arrested.

Developing products and services to meet customer needs

The process of developing products and services is usually referred to as product planning. This is defined as the activities required to inform decisions on the introduction of new products or services, changes to existing products or services, and the withdrawal and replacement of unwanted products or services. The aim of product planning is to keep customers by ensuring that the organization continues to supply products that they need and want over the long term.

Providing the infrastructure for customer service

The infrastructure for customer service consists of:

- the counters, showrooms and display units that offer and show goods for purchase;
- the arrangements for order processing or fulfilment;
- the distribution system;
- customer service or contact centres and helplines to answer enquiries and deal with problems;
- call centres to receive and process orders.

In each case, it is necessary to ensure that the arrangements are customer friendly and provide the basis for achieving high standards of customer service.

Models of customer service

The following models of customer service are available. Each needs to be evaluated in terms of fitness for purpose, operational efficiency and effectiveness, and the extent to which defined customer service standards are being met.

Customer service centre

A customer service or contact centre is a facility that provides help and advice to customers and deals with their enquiries, problems and complaints. There are three evolutionary stages to most service centres, ranging from a reactive cost centre to the proactive high-value service centre:

- Stage 1: The message centre – this is someone who simply routes enquiries and complaints to someone who can respond to them. Problem resolution is not attempted and the service is entirely reactive. Automated telephone queuing systems may be used and they do help to channel enquiries. However, they can create dissatisfaction on the grounds that it seems to be more difficult to make contact with a human being. This may lead customers to conclude that the company is using the system solely as a means of economizing on staff rather than making life easier for customers.

- Stage 2: The reactive/problem service centre – this may be a 'helpline' or 'help desk' that is staffed by one or two people and acts as a single point of reference for customers, attempting to resolve problems such as defective products, delivery delays and difficulties in setting up or operating equipment. It is better than a message centre but it is still reactive with typically low levels of problems resolved following the first call.

- Stage 3: The full customer service centre – this is staffed by trained people fully supported by software and, where appropriate, including technicians who can resolve technical problems. The aim is to achieve a quick and accurate resolution of customer issues with the help of automated processes.

Call centres

Call centres use specially trained staff to handle sales, enquiries and orders by telephone. They usually focus more on gaining new customers than on services for existing customers.

Websites

Websites are used by many companies (eg Amazon) to enhance customer service. They are also useful sources of data on customers as part of a CRM system.

Service level agreements

A service level agreement is an agreement between the provider of a service and the customers who use that service. The starting point of a service level agreement is a clarification of what the needs of customers are and which of these are the more important. The aim in setting service targets is that they should be stretching but achievable, although some providers under-promise so that they can appear to over-achieve. A service level agreement defines the nature of the service(s) provided, the volumes and quality to be achieved by each of the services, and the response times to be achieved by the providers when their services are requested. Service level agreements are most commonly found in the public sector but they are equally applicable elsewhere. They can operate between providers and either external or internal customers.

Preferred supplier status

Organizations can designate firms as preferred suppliers, which means that the supplier will be given the first opportunity to provide the goods or services and can safely assume that any preferred supplier contract will run over a period of time and will be renewable.

Telesales

Businesses selling products such as double glazing often rely to a large extent on doing so by means of unsolicited telephone calls. The proportion of sales in relation to calls made by this direct approach may appear to be small, but as long as well-trained, highly motivated and persistent staff are used, this method pays off.

Accounts management

Businesses with customers who buy heavily and continuously from them may appoint accounts managers whose job is to 'nurse' customers and ensure that their needs are met and any problems are resolved swiftly. Accounts managers monitor sales and levels of service and take action if sales decline or levels of service show signs of slipping.

Setting standards for customer service

Customer service standards define the levels of service to be achieved for each of the main aspects of customer service. Levels of service standards can be classified under these three headings:

1. Desired level of service – what customers would really like to experience by reference to the best level of relevant experience the customer has received.

2. Expected level of service – what customers expect, given their knowledge of circumstances and their experience.

3. Minimum acceptable level of service – the minimum level of service customers will expect, which will lead to loss of business if it is not achieved.

The standards form the basis for guidelines to staff on what they should achieve and for monitoring service levels. The areas covered can include:

- Order processing – speed of response and delivery of products ordered by customers, including replacement parts and requests for service. Response rates can be measured by recording the proportion of letters or calls answered in a defined number of hours or days, and delivery standards can be expressed as the time taken between taking the order and delivery. Standards can also be set for the backlog of unprocessed orders at the end of a day or week (ideally none, but a small incidence of backlog orders may be allowed in peak periods, eg before Christmas) or when order fulfilment is highly complex.

- Quality of relationships with customers – how customers should be approached and responded to; how complaints should be dealt with; the information that should be provided in response to enquiries; and the levels of service to be achieved in terms of reliability, responsiveness, competence, access, courtesy, communication, understanding customers and dealing with difficult customers.

- Complaints – assessed by reference to the number of complaints as a proportion of total orders, the backlog of complaints, the proportion of complaints dealt with satisfactorily when first raised and the quality of response to complaints.

- Service and call centres – assessed through call pick-up rates (proportion of calls answered in so many seconds or within a certain number of rings), lost call rates (proportion of in-bound calls lost), proportion of problems resolved at first contact, backlogs (number of orders, enquiries or complaints outstanding at the end of a day or week), and quality of response to enquiries or complaints.

Monitoring the delivery of service standards

To monitor the achievement of service standards it is necessary to set up systems for recording the number of enquiries and complaints, analysing the reasons for complaints, and monitoring response rates (time taken to deal with complaints and enquiries), lost calls, backlogs and delivery times. The quality of relationships with customers can be assessed by observation, by recording telephone conversations and by collecting and reviewing documented evidence of how complaints were dealt with and how customers reacted. The outcomes of customer satisfaction surveys should also be analysed to determine areas for improvement against the standards set.

Mystery shopping

Mystery shopping enables the quality of customer service to be assessed at the critical point at which customers come into contact with sales staff – in a retail or service outlet or over the telephone. People (usually from market research firms) are sent into a retail outlet to observe how they were treated. Or they may make a telephone enquiry. They then record their observations of how well or badly they were handled against a set of basic standards covering such aspects of service as friendly reception, paying attention to the shopper's wants, helpfulness, knowledge of the product, willingness to listen and respond to the customer's requests and queries, and avoiding pressurized sales techniques.

Building satisfaction and keeping customers

Loyalty cards are used by stores, and airlines have air miles to keep customers, but customer loyalty is best achieved by building and maintaining high levels of satisfaction and developing a customer-centric culture as discussed in Chapter 17. This culture should be based on a well-defined customer relations strategy supported by the processes of managing customer relationships, assessing needs and expectations, measuring customer satisfaction, developing products and services that meet customer needs, providing the infrastructure for customer service, setting and monitoring service delivery standards, and taking action to overcome shortfalls in the achievement of those standards.

Internal customers

An internal customer is anyone who makes use of the outputs or services provided by other departments or individuals in the organization. This means everyone – all employees are customers of other employees and they all provide services to other employees. Some departments such as IT, HR and facilities management exist primarily to provide professional or technical services directly to other departments. Some departments exist to produce outputs upon which other departments rely to achieve their objectives. Research and development has to deliver products that can be promoted and sold by marketing and sales departments. Production or operating departments exist to deliver the products or services that are required by sales to meet customer demands. Marketing and sales departments produce the information on forecast demand that enables production and operating departments to plan their activities.

J M Juran (1989), the quality guru, has stated that: 'meeting the needs of internal customers is a prerequisite for meeting the needs of external customers'. If, for example, marketing gets its sales forecasts wrong or manufacturing fails to meet the requirements specified by sales, then it is the level of service to external customers that suffers and this has a negative impact on satisfaction and loyalty.

The basic approach to creating high standards of service for internal customers is to define how the different parts of the organization interrelate and spell out who serves whom and who receives service from whom. It is then necessary to ensure that all the parties concerned know how important service to internal customers is and what is expected of them from their internal customers. This can be defined formally as a service level agreement. For example, an agreement for an HR department could set out standards under the following headings:

- level of response to requests for help or guidance in areas such as recruitment, training, handling disciplinary cases and grievances, and health and safety;
- the time taken to prepare and agree role profiles, fill vacancies or conduct a job evaluation exercise;
- the quality of candidates submitted for appointments;
- the proportion of discipline or grievance issues settled at the first time HR is involved;
- the number of appeals (successful and unsuccessful) against job grading decisions;
- the results of evaluations of training carried out by participants in training programmes;
- the outcomes of employee attitude surveys.

Defining required attitudes, skills, knowledge, behaviours and competencies

It is necessary to define the attitudes, skills and behaviours required of all those involved in customer service in order to provide a basis for managing customer service, recruitment, training, performance management and reward.

Attitudes

Customer service excellence is achieved by people whose attitudes can be summed up in the phrase 'put the customer first'. They must believe that they exist because customers exist and that being responsive to customer needs and expectations is a vital part of their role.

Skills

The main skills required are:

- interpersonal skills – ability to relate well to people during person-to-person contacts;
- listening skills – ability to pay attention to people, absorb what they are saying and react appropriately;
- communication skills – ability to explain matters to customers clearly and with conviction and to handle telephone conversations;
- complaints handling skills – ability to deal with complaints and handle angry customers.

Knowledge

Knowledge will be required of the product or service offered by the organization. This could be quite advanced knowledge enabling individuals to identify and deal with faulty equipment or provide technical advice. It will also be necessary to understand the customer service systems and procedures used in the organization.

Behaviours

The following are examples of the sort of behaviours typically required of anyone involved in customer service:

- Be helpful, polite, friendly and positive with customers.
- When dealing with customers, smile, make eye contact and look and sound enthusiastic.
- Speak clearly.
- Show personal interest.
- Show sympathy with customers making complaints – listen to what the customer has to say, establish the facts, agree what needs to be done, and keep the customer informed.
- Provide information immediately or let customers know when they can expect it.
- Keep promises.
- Answer telephones promptly.
- Reply to e-mails, voicemail messages and letters quickly.
- Concentrate on the needs of customers, not on what is easiest to sell.

According to O'Connor (2003) the top 10 behaviours are:

1. Takes time to understand the specific needs, requirements and any current pressures the customer may be under.

2. Shows an immediate understanding of the problem and the possible consequences.

3. Demonstrates empathy.

4. Generates a range of solutions to address a difficulty.

5. Uses organizational policy to guide the solutions rather than to act as blocks, or worse, reasons not to assist the customer.

6. Takes decisions quickly.

7. Is honest about the situation and what the organization can do to help.

8. Looks for ways to delight the customer.

9. Demonstrates an understanding of the commercial implications of decisions taken.

10. Seeks the appropriate guidance where required and does this efficiently, retaining ownership of the customer.

Competencies

Organizations with competency frameworks frequently use customer service as one of the headings. An analysis carried out by Rankin (2002) of the core competency frameworks of 40 employers showed that the second equal most common heading was Customer Focus, used in 65 per cent of the organizations surveyed.

Defining competency levels for customer service is a good way of expressing the values and requirements of the organization for customer care. It provides the basis for recruitment, training and development programmes, and performance management and recognition and reward schemes. Two examples are given below.

Britannic Assurance

Levels of performance in the customer service competency

Level 1

- Take ownership of customer problems.

- Treat each and every customer contact as an opportunity to impress them with your professional service.

- Take care of your customers.

Level 2

- Offer flexible service, taking time to build a rapport and assess customer needs.

- Present a range of alternative options to your customers.

- Put yourself in the customers' shoes.

Level 3

- Are always prepared to go 'the extra mile' to deliver the highest quality service, on time, every time.

- Identify customer needs – beyond those expressly stated.

- Establish a personal relationship based on understanding their personality and individual traits.

- Offer a commitment to customer service excellence and can spot when things are going off track.

Level 4

- Identify new and emerging areas of service and seize on these as opportunities.

- Conceive schemes which are mutually beneficial to the customer and other stakeholders.

- Act as the customers' champion, constantly driving the business forward in delivering service.

- Persuade others to see things from a customer's point of view.

Source: Customer Management, **12** (2), pp 18–21

Peabody Trust

Manage Customer Service			
Provide high levels of service to internal and external customers in accordance with exacting standards			
Level	Standard	Positive behavioural indicators	Negative behavioural indicators
1	Provide good services to internal and external customers.	Meets expressed needs of customers.	Has no appreciation of customer needs or pressures. Doesn't listen to customers.
2	Build and maintain good relationships with customers.	Handles customer queries effectively and knows where to channel queries in the organization. Understands customer problems.	Unaware of customer needs. Passes enquiries when they should have taken action themselves.
3	Contribute to the development and maintenance of high standards of customer service.	Identifies potential opportunities to help customers. Asks customers how services could be improved.	Fails to respond to customer requests or queries. Does not deliver the standards of service customers have the right to expect.
4	Contribute to the development of customer service standards in the department and play an active part in achieving them.	Builds collaborative relationships with customers. Establishes high levels of trust amongst customers as witnessed by customer feedback.	Customer enquiries and complaints are not attended to swiftly. Gets negative feedback from customers.
5	Contribute to the development of customer services in the function and play an active part in achieving them.	Develops extensive customer networks. Sets standards of customer service and ensures they are met.	Too little concerned with setting and monitoring customer service.

Manage Customer Service			
Provide high levels of service to internal and external customers in accordance with exacting standards			
Level	Standard	Positive behavioural indicators	Negative behavioural indicators
6	Lead and promote a culture which recognizes the importance of meeting the needs of both internal and external customers in key aspects of the Trust's operations.	Actively involved in promoting high levels of customer service across the organization. Continuously monitors customer service levels and takes swift corrective action when necessary.	Takes a narrow view of customer service. Not concerned with wider issues.

Developing attitudes, skills and behaviours

The development of appropriate attitudes, skills and behaviours is achieved through recruitment, training, performance management and reward processes. But it is also generally accepted that if employees are satisfied then customers are more likely to be satisfied, which means paying close attention to employee needs and measuring their attitudes through regular surveys.

Recruitment

At the recruitment stage the aim should be to obtain people with the right attitudes to customer service who are potentially likely to behave effectively in delivering customer services. The role specification should indicate what attitudes and competencies are required and the interview plan should set out what evidence will be sought on behavioural patterns. This can form the basis for a behavioural-based, structured interview in which candidates are asked to tell the interviewer how they would behave in situations that have been identified as critical to successful performance with regard to customer contacts, for example how they would deal with an angry customer, internal or external. Businesses such as Selfridges use psychological tests to provide additional information.

Training and development

At one time the 'big bang' approach to training in customer service was adopted, everyone in the organization from top to bottom being put through a one or two day course of 'smile training' as at British Airways. This method is now largely discredited because experience has shown that this 'one-off' method does not produce lasting changes in behaviour. The focus is now on formal induction training – getting the message across when people start, followed by continued learning on the job. Team leaders and supervisors are given the responsibility to ensure that learning does take place and that this results in the required behaviour. They require training and guidance on how to exercise this responsibility and in the skills they need to use. It should be emphasized that this is a key part of their role and that their performance in developing staff will be monitored and reviewed. This continuous development process can be supplemented by short training sessions to build knowledge, eg product knowledge, and skills, eg dealing with complaints.

NVQ/SVQ in customer service

Employees can be encouraged to take an NVQ/SVQ in customer service. The standards are set out in the following box.

Key purpose

- Deliver continuous improvement in service to achieve customer satisfaction.
- Maintain reliable customer service.
- Maintain records relating to customer service.
- Organize own work pattern in response to the needs of customers.
- Work with others to benefit the customer.
- Communicate with customers.
- Select information for communication to customers.
- Improve the flow of information between the organization and customers.
- Adapt methods of communication to the customer.
- Develop positive working relationships with customers.
- Respond to the needs and feelings expressed by the customer.
- Present positive personal image to the customer.

- Balance the needs of customers and the organization.

- Solve problems on behalf of customers.

- Identify and interpret problems affecting customers.

- Generate solutions on behalf of customers.

- Take action to deliver solutions.

- Initiate and evaluate change to improve service to customers.

- Obtain and use feedback from customers.

- Propose improvements in service delivery based on feedback from customers.

- Initiate change in response to customer requirements.

- Evaluate changes designed to improve service to customers.

Performance management

Competency frameworks such as those illustrated in the last section can be used as the basis for performance management processes. Dialogues between managers or team leaders and their staff can take place that achieve understanding of customer service performance expectations and how they can be met. Periodical reviews take place (not just once a year) that refer to agreed expectations and how individuals have actually performed. The dialogue in review meetings covers any changes in behaviour required and how those changes should be achieved by individuals with the support of their manager.

Reward

Rewards are used to recognize and motivate appropriate behaviour. They can be financial (some form of performance or contribution pay) or non-financial (some form of recognition). Formal recognition programmes can be more effective than awarding pay increases or bonuses. Programmes can provide for 'applause', which publicly recognizes exceptional performance in house journals, the intranet or notice boards. This can include naming people as 'employee of the month', or more comprehensibly, highlighting what they have actually done to achieve such recognition. Recognition programmes can include various forms of gifts, certificates, badges and appearance at presentations.

World-class customer service examples

A world-class organization will generally exhibit any or all of the following characteristics:

- market leader;
- high-quality leadership;
- exceptional results;
- a leading employer of choice;
- meet highest standards of corporate responsibility – for stakeholders and the environment;
- meet demanding standards of customer service as indicated not by the rhetoric – what they say they do – but by the reality – what they actually achieve as measured against the highest standards elsewhere.

References

Johnston, R (2002) Why service excellence = reputation = increased profits, *Customer Management*, **10** (2), pp 8–11

Juran, J M (1989) *Juran on Leadership for Quality*, The Free Press, New York

O'Connor, Z (2003) The human touch, Topics, *ER Consultants*, pp 8–10

Rankin, N (2002) Raising performance through people: the ninth competency survey, *Competency & Emotional Intelligence*, January, pp 2–21

Part VI

Enabling Continuous Improvement

Continuous Improvement

'Develop programmes for continuous improvement of costs, quality, productivity and service.'
William Deming (1986) *Out of the Crisis*, MIT Center for Advanced
Engineering Study, Boston, MA

The notion of continuous improvement is based on the Japanese concept of *kaizen*, which is a composite of the word *kai* (meaning change) and *zen* (meaning good or for the better). The kaizen management style relies on a foundation of gradual change, building up a culture of quality awareness and constant learning. This chapter starts by examining the nature of continuous improvement and continues by dealing in turn with its requirements, framework and programmes. The chapter ends with examples of approaches to continuous improvement.

The nature of continuous improvement

Continuous improvement is a management philosophy that contends that things can be done better. It is a set of concepts, principles and methods developed from the quality principles proposed by the quality gurus W Edwards Deming, Joseph Juran and Philip Crosby. Continuous improvement is defined by Bessant *et al* (1994) as 'a company-wide process of focused and continuous incremental innovation sustained over a period of time'.

The key words in this definition are:

- Focused – continuous improvement addresses specific issues where the effectiveness of operations and processes needs to be improved, where higher-quality products or services should be provided and, importantly, where the levels of customer service and satisfaction need to be enhanced.

- Continuous – the search for improvement is never-ending; it is not a one-off campaign to deal with isolated problems.

- Incremental – continuous improvement is not about making sudden quantum leaps in response to crisis situations; it is about adopting a steady, step-by-step approach to improving the ways in which the organization goes about doing things.

- Innovation – continuous improvement is concerned with developing new ideas and approaches to deal with new and sometimes old problems and requirements.

Continuous improvement is closely associated with quality control and assurance, as described in the next chapter, but these are concerned more with prevention and cure than positive incremental improvements. However, the concept of continuous improvement is fundamental to the philosophy of total quality management, as also described in the next chapter.

Although continuous improvement is essentially incremental it can result in organizational transformation. This is the process of ensuring that the organization can develop and implement major change programmes that will ensure that it responds strategically to new demands and continues to function in the dynamic atmosphere in which it operates.

Aims of continuous improvement

Deming (1986) considers that customers are the most important part of the production line. The ultimate aim of continuous improvement is to recognize this fact by developing operational and business processes that ensure that customer expectations are fully met, indeed exceeded. In achieving this ultimate aim it is also necessary to ensure that the organization is profitable (private sector) or is fulfilling its purpose effectively (public and not-for-profit sectors). The more detailed aims are to improve the quality and reliability of products or services and their customer appeal, enhance operational systems, improve service levels and delivery reliability, and reduce costs and lead times.

The importance of continuous improvement

Organizations that fail to pursue actively policies of continuous improvement will stagnate, decline and eventually die. All organizations have to exist in a constantly changing environment with new challenges and demands to meet from competitors, customers, clients, central or local government and regulatory bodies. They cannot afford to stand still. The importance of continuous improvement has been emphasized by Oakland (1998) as follows:

Never-ending or continuous improvement is probably the most powerful concept to guide management. It is a term not well understood in many organisations, although that must begin to change if those organisations are to survive. To maintain a wave of interest in quality, it is necessary to develop generations of managers who not only understand but are dedicated to the pursuit of never-ending improvement in meeting external and internal customer needs.

The rationale for continuous improvement

The rationale for continuous improvement is the need to pay constant attention to what needs to be done to delight customers. As IRS (1997) points out, the focus of continuous improvement 'is customer satisfaction, although resource utilisation is just as important, since it enables an organisation to bring a product or service to a customer at the lowest possible cost'.

A critical assessment of this proposition suggests that it is based on the notion that the only purpose of an organization is to serve its customers. But it could be argued that organizations exist to achieve other purposes, for example to be profitable, to increase shareholder value, to fulfil their obligations to their employees, their clients and the public at large, and to meet the requirements of government departments and statutory authorities. However, these purposes all embrace the notion of customer service. Profitability and increased shareholder value can only be achieved through customers and clients. All stakeholders – employees, boards, trustees, governors, public sector organizations and the recipients of aid and support – are customers of the organization. Their needs and expectations must be met and continuous improvement processes provide important means of doing so.

The rationale for transformation through continuous improvement

Organizational transformation programmes, as described in Chapter 16, are business-led. They focus on what needs to be done to ensure that the organization performs more effectively in adding value for its customers and owners and achieving competitive advantage. The rationale for transformation is that unless something is done about it, organizations typically follow a life cycle pattern of growth, maturity and decline. It is all too easy for what was once a successful business to stagnate and then fail to arrest the decline because of consumer shifts in taste, increased competition, the availability of substitute products, reluctance to take advantage of technological advances, complacency, and inability to spot and deal with process inadequacies. Faced with this situation, organizations often take drastic transformational steps. But it is much better to adopt the incremental approach of continuous improvement, which can progressively lead to organizational transformation and continued success, than to be forced to take precipitant action in a crisis.

The implications of continuous improvement

The pursuit of continuous improvement implies that the organization is fundamentally concerned with the achievement of excellence and therefore success. It specifically means that the organization intends to develop world-class levels of customer service – delivering quality products or services to customers. It should be remembered that although continuous improvement is carried out by people working together, most problems, as Deming (1986) noted, are found in systems, not people. Continuous improvement seeks to find better ways of doing things, not to attach blame.

The requirements for continuous improvement

Continuous improvement requires concerted effort to enlist the ideas and enthusiasm of everyone in the organization to ensure that a steady stream of decisions are made that will generate incremental improvements to operational and quality performance and deliver increased value to customers. It is most effective when it becomes a natural part of the way everyday work is done. A culture of continuous improvement therefore needs to be fostered and this requires attention to many factors including leadership, shared organizational values, the development of structures, processes and people, and, overriding all these, the establishment of a high-performance culture incorporating challenging goals. Continuous improvement programmes must have a consistent focus that addresses these broad issues holistically, as well as concentrating on particular requirements or problems.

Leadership

Top management provides the leadership and direction and ensures that their vision for continuous improvement is conveyed to everyone in the organization. They communicate the values underpinning continuous improvement as set out in the next section and see that people live those values. Middle management and supervision support the concept of continuous improvement and are actively engaged in the programmes and processes involved.

Shared organizational values

Continuous improvement values are based on the belief that the achievement of customer satisfaction is crucial and that continuous improvement programmes are the best way to achieve this aim. The values that drive continuous improvement are essentially the values that impel the satisfaction of customers. This overarching value is supported by the following specific values:

- Respect for people – listening to their ideas and concerns, communicating with them openly and believing that they have the intelligence and expertise to contribute positively.

- Trusting people – management must trust employees to act independently and employees must trust management not to exploit their ideas to their detriment. This trust must be earned. Management must deliver their promises and employees, with guidance, encouragement and help, must show that they can be trusted to get on with it.

- Cooperation – Oakland (1998) has stated that in an environment of cooperation a greater variety of complex problems can be tackled, which are beyond the capability of any one individual or department. Processes and problems are exposed to a greater diversity of knowledge, skill and experience and are addressed more efficiently; this is particularly important when the problem extends across departmental boundaries.

- Openness – progress is more likely to be made if information is shared, opinions are voiced without fear or favour and people are honest with one another.

Structure

The organizational structure should support continuous improvement values. A rigid functional organization is likely to prevent this happening. A more flexible, team-based structure is likely to foster cooperation and ensure that the collective wisdom of a number of people is brought to bear on problems. These can be permanent teams within departments or, usefully, cross-functional teams. Groups can be assembled that are dedicated to reviewing the scope for improvements and making specific recommendations on what needs to be done. Extended teams can be set up that include customers and suppliers. Diverse contacts outside a person's own group can enhance innovation and the generation of ideas.

Process

Process is concerned with 'the way things get done around here'. It refers to how effort is directed and coordinated, how planning and control take place, how decisions are made and how influence is exercised. If they function effectively, all these processes can contribute to the achievement of continuous improvement.

Comprehensive people development

Continuous improvement programmes require people with the knowledge and skills needed to analyse opportunities and problems, innovate and reach practical solutions. They should be prepared to behave in a cooperative way, sharing knowledge and information and working effectively with others. Training programmes can help people to acquire the necessary knowledge and skills, and performance management and personal development processes based on a competency framework can encourage and help people to behave appropriately as contributors to continuous improvement.

High-performance culture

A high-performance culture is conducive to continuous improvement. The characteristics of such a culture were described in Chapter 6.

The conditions and behaviour that promote continuous improvement

Continuous improvement is promoted if people live the values and attention is paid to structural, process, people and cultural issues, as mentioned previously. The behaviours required for continuous improvement have been defined by the Peabody Trust in their competency framework as set out in Table 19.1.

Table 19.1   Competency framework for continuous improvement (Peabody Trust)

Manage Continuous Improvement			
Constantly seeks ways of improving the quality of services, the relevance and appeal of these services to the needs of customers/clients, and the effectiveness of support and operational systems			
Level	Standard	Positive behavioural indicators	Negative behavioural indicators
1	Take steps to improve task performance. Improve work methods to achieve higher levels of efficiency. Ensure that quality considerations are given proper attention.	Continually strives to improve task performance. Makes suggestions to manager on better ways of carrying out the work.	Not interested in doing anything different.
2	Develop new procedures and systems for carrying out work. Identify areas for improvement and take action to achieve improvement plans. Give close and continuous attention to the delivery of high-quality services.	Prepared to try doing things differently. Aware of quality standards and takes steps to ensure service delivery.	Complacent, believes that there is no room for improvement.

Table 19.1 *continued*

Manage Continuous Improvement			
Constantly seeks ways of improving the quality of services, the relevance and appeal of these services to the needs of customers/clients, and the effectiveness of support and operational systems			
Level	Standard	Positive behavioural indicators	Negative behavioural indicators
3	Set targets for improvement. Deliver and implement programmes for introducing change. Contribute to the development of quality assurance and control processes and ensure they are implemented.	Encourages the development of new ideas and methods, especially those to do with the provision of quality services. Conscious of the factors that enable change to take place smoothly.	Doesn't try anything that hasn't been done before.
4	Develop and oversee the implementation of quality assurance and control processes. Develop and monitor continuous improvement programmes and stimulate action as required. Contribute to the successful outcomes of the management of change.	Discusses ideas with colleagues and customers and formulates view on how to improve services and processes. Understands the need to seek ideas from outside own experience. Takes action to ensure that change is accepted and implemented.	Follows previous practices without considering whether there is any need for change.
5	Contribute to the development of a culture which encourages innovation and continuous improvement. Manage major change programmes in areas of responsibility.	Continually seeks to improve. Generates different options and assesses the risks and implications of pursuing them.	Reluctant to admit that there is any need for change.

Table 19.1 *continued*

Manage Continuous Improvement			
Constantly seeks ways of improving the quality of services, the relevance and appeal of these services to the needs of customers/clients, and the effectiveness of support and operational systems			
Level	Standard	Positive behavioural indicators	Negative behavioural indicators
6	Lead the development of a culture which encourages innovation and continuous improvement. Manage major change pro-grammes affecting the Trust as a whole.	Challenges people and inbuilt prejudices. Is prepared to take risks and challenge assumptions.	Accepts the status quo. Risk averse.

The framework for continuous improvement

The framework for successful continuous improvement produced by The Continuous Improvement Research for Competitive Advantage (CIRCA) Unit at Brighton University (1998) consists of five elements:

1. Strategy: Clear strategic goals need to be set for continuous improvement, providing 'sign-posted destinations'. These goals should be communicated across the whole organization and translated into specific targets for teams and individual workers.

2. Culture: The culture of the organization should be developed to support continuous improvement and develop quality awareness. This means defining and communicating values about the need to persist in making incremental improvements to quality as per-ceived by customers, and about autonomy and empowerment for those involved in improvement on a continuous basis.

3. Infrastructure: As recommended by CIRCA, the type of organization-wide framework necessary for the successful development of continuous improvement includes open man-agement systems, cross-functional management and structures, teamworking, two-way communication processes, joint decision-making and employee autonomy and participa-tion. This framework depends largely on trust: 'Managers have to trust their workers if

they are going to grant them greater responsibility and authority. Empowered employees, similarly, have to trust those in senior positions not to take advantage of employees' ideas to cut jobs. Information is a key component of the creation of greater trust' (CIRCA, 1998).

4. Process: The processes used in continuous improvement include individual problem-seeking activities, problem-solving groups, suggestion schemes and company-wide campaigns to promote continuous improvement. Continuous improvement does not simply happen by itself. It has to be encouraged and facilitated by management action.

5. Tools: Continuous improvement is enhanced by the use of the various problem-solving tools available for individuals and groups. These include Pareto diagrams and cause and effect diagrams, as described later in this chapter, and various statistical tools such as control charts and scatter diagrams. Benchmarking is another important tool used to establish standards for continuous improvement. Groups can use brainstorming techniques to develop ideas.

Approaches to continuous improvement

Continuous improvement involves constantly adapting by getting and using information and by evaluating changes to make sure they are effective. It requires good information from a variety of sources to evaluate outcomes (what is achieved) and processes (how it is achieved). It is necessary to pull people together from different functions or disciplines and levels to freely discuss the information and issues involved, come up with ideas, critically evaluate them, ensure they are put into practice, and measure progress and outcomes. The guidelines on improvement efforts are:

- before you try to solve a problem, define it;

- before you try to control a process, understand it;

- before trying to control everything, find out what is important and work on the most important process or the one that makes the biggest impact.

The approach to continuous improvement programmes starts with a strategy that forms the basis for the development of an infrastructure of teams, processes and systems and for the conduct of the work of continuously reviewing and improving processes and systems and the ways in which they are managed.

The strategy for continuous improvement

A continuous improvement strategy needs to be formulated to provide a sense of purpose and direction. It will be concerned with how the organization intends to improve quality, processes and customer service. The strategy is produced in six steps: (1) establish corporate objectives;

(2) determine the effects of current practices; (3) identify problems and their causes; (4) decide on actions; (5) prepare a programme for implementation; and (6) define resources required, including the infrastructure.

The infrastructure for continuous improvement

The arrangements for implementing the continuous improvement strategy consist of the creation of an infrastructure of involvement processes including suggestion schemes and improvement groups and the development of tools and assessment procedures. The infrastructure will be composed of people who have been given responsibility for promoting and coordinating continuous improvement programmes, and systems for analysing problems and recording outcomes and proposed actions, assessing results and ensuring that innovations are embedded.

Quality circles as a formal part of the infrastructure of continuous improvement achieved some popularity in the 1980s. They consisted of small groups of volunteers who carried out related work and who met regularly to discuss and propose ways of improving working methods or arrangements under a trained leader. Unfortunately it was not appreciated that the approach to using such groups in Japan was only part of a much more comprehensive kaizen programme in which everyone was involved and they therefore often failed.

To get over the somewhat discredited image of quality circles, they were sometimes renamed 'improvement groups'. But as formal entities these often failed too, for the same reasons. The tendency now is to set up ad hoc improvement groups to deal with specific problems, although these might and indeed should be treated as part of the infrastructure of a total continuous improvement programme. However, there is one important legacy of the quality circle movement. That is the emphasis on formal training for group leaders and members in analytical and problem-solving techniques, as described later in this chapter.

Applications for continuous improvement

Continuous improvement is proactive – it explores new ways of doing things; it does not wait for a problem to emerge. It is about seeking opportunities, not fire-fighting. It can be intuitive, based on immediate apprehension or insight without empirically based reasoning. But intuitions have to be evaluated and for this purpose experimentation takes place to test the hypothesis that action will lead to improvement. Overall, the process of continuous improvement involves empowerment. Individuals and teams are empowered to investigate opportunities, solve problems, produce ideas and solutions, and take action.

These applications need to be differentiated and evaluated in continuous improvement programmes. They ought to be proactive but there will be occasions where it is necessary to react to a pressing problem. Intuition has its place but it should not be allowed to go too far without proper testing. Experimentation is desirable but there will be times when something has to be done now – it can't wait. Empowerment is highly desirable but there will be occasions when management has to take the lead and make the decisions.

Continuous improvement techniques

Improvement is based on building knowledge of what works and does not work and then applying it appropriately. The three basic questions are:

1. What are we trying to accomplish?

2. What changes can we make that will result in an improvement?

3. How will we know that a change is an improvement?

The Plan-Do-Check-Act cycle as set out by Deming (1986) is used as the basis for developing and testing changes: plan the change strategy, including who will be involved, what data will be collected and when the data will be considered adequate for study; do the intervention; check the results; act on the knowledge gained from the data – maintain the plan, modify the plan, add to the plan. If the change is successful, embed it by expanding it to the rest of the system, establishing processes to support it and identifying ways in which further improvements can be made.

A number of problem-solving and analytical techniques are available, as described in the following sections.

Problem-solving

Problem-solving is carried out in ten steps:

1. *Define the situation* – establish what has gone wrong or is about to go wrong.

2. *Specify objectives* – define what is to be achieved.

3. *Develop hypotheses* – develop ideas about what has caused the problem.

4. *Get the facts* – find out what has actually happened and contrast this with an assessment of what ought to have happened.

5. *Analyse the facts* – determine what is relevant and what is irrelevant and diagnose the likely causes of the problem.

6. *Identify possible courses of action* – spell out what each involves.

7. *Evaluate alternative courses of action* – assess the extent to which they are likely to achieve the objectives, the cost of implementation, any practical difficulties that might emerge and the possible reactions of stakeholders.

8. *Weigh and decide* – determine which alternative is likely to result in the most practical and acceptable solution to the problem.

9. *Plan implementation* – timetable, project management resources required.

10. *Implement* – monitor progress and evaluate success.

Cause and effect diagrams

Cause and effect diagrams are used to clarify the causes of a problem. They are sometimes called 'fishbone diagrams' (because of their shape) or 'Ishikawa diagrams' (after Kaoru Ishikawa, the Japanese quality expert who championed their use).

Suppose a customer complains at a restaurant. The fault may be caused by the raw materials, the cooking, the staff or the facilities. Problems with the raw materials may in turn be caused by quality, storage or costs. A cause and effect diagram draws these relationships in the form of spines like a fish bone, as shown in Figure 19.1.

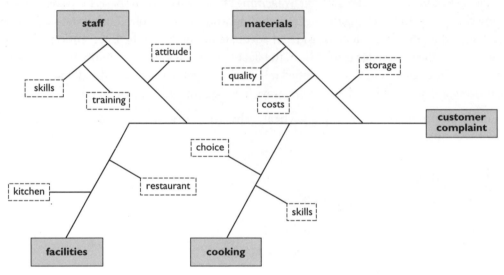

Figure 19.1 Cause and effect diagram
Source: Armstrong, M (2001) *A Handbook of Management Techniques*, 3rd edn, Kogan Page, London

Pareto charts

Pareto charts are used to focus on key problems. They are based on Pareto's Law. Pareto, an Italian economist, observed that 20 per cent of the population owned 80 per cent of the wealth. In the 1940s Dr Joseph Juran recognized a universal principle that he called 'the vital few and trivial many'. This principle – that 20 per cent of something produces 80 per cent of the results – became generally known as Pareto's Law. In his original work, Juran noted that 20 per cent of the defects caused 80 per cent of the problems. Many investigations have revealed that this law applies more generally; for example 80 per cent of stock comes from 20 per cent of suppliers, 80 per cent of sales come from 20 per cent of sales staff. It is also sometimes argued that 20 per cent of an organization's staff will produce 80 per cent of its problems, but it works the other way round too, ie another 20 per cent of staff will produce 80 per cent of added value. The principle has also been applied to the process of management, suggesting that people should identify the 20 per cent of the important things they do during a day and concentrate more on these than the remaining 80 per cent.

The problem is that of identifying the vital 20 per cent, and Pareto charts are used for this purpose. They illustrate the relative importance of problems by showing their frequency or size in a descending bar graph, as illustrated in Figure 19.2. They are constructed by listing the problems and then assessing how significant they are in relation to one another.

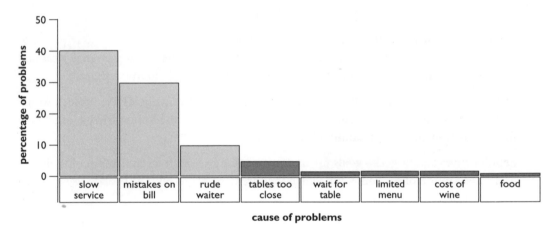

Figure 19.2   A Pareto chart
Source: Armstrong, M (2001) *A Handbook of Management Techniques*, 3rd edn, Kogan Page, London

Brainstorming

Brainstorming gets a group to generate as many ideas as possible without pausing to evaluate them. The rationale for the process is that people are more likely to come up with ideas if they are not subjected to criticism or even ridicule. Any idea goes and no one is allowed to comment on what others say. The aim is to produce as many ideas as possible. The majority (possibly 80 per cent) are likely to be useless, but some possible ideas (20 per cent perhaps) will emerge. Evaluation of the ideas only takes place after the session has finished and no one gets the credit for any accepted ideas or the blame for any of those rejected.

Nominal group technique

The nominal group technique gets a group to achieve consensus on the ranking of problems, issues or solutions in order of importance.

Benchmarking

Benchmarking involves identifying good practice in other organizations, comparing these practices with practices within the benchmarker's own organization, and drawing conclusions on the lessons learnt from good practice elsewhere that can be applied within the organization. The comparisons concentrate on the areas for improvement that have been identified and the aim is to learn as much as possible about how other organizations have tackled similar problems, bearing in mind that what works well in one organization does not necessarily work well in another.

Continuous improvement programmes

Continuous improvement programmes can take place in the following stages:

1. Set up project teams – they will consist of people who have the knowledge required to address continuous improvement issues. The members will be trained in analytical and problem-solving techniques and the leader will be trained in facilitation skills.

2. Define terms of reference – the terms of reference define the scope of the project, which includes a statement of the issue or problem, a definition of the boundaries, a target date for completion and an indication of the resources available.

3. Set objectives and targets – goals for improvement are set with an indication of their size and a description of the context in which they are to be achieved. The broad areas covered may include:

   – increasing customer satisfaction and therefore retention by means of specific improvements to quality and levels of service;

   – improvements to the efficiency and effectiveness of selling, production and distribution processes;

   – reduction in defects or errors and the achievement of 'right first time';

   – improvements in productivity;

   – the use of value analysis (a cost reduction technique that uses organized procedures for the identification of unnecessary cost elements in a component or product by the analysis of its function and design – function being defined as that aspect of the product that makes it work or sell).

   These broad areas may be defined more closely in terms of specific targets for such requirements as reducing errors, speeding up processes or responding to customer complaints.

4. Plan the project – this involves planning: fact collection and analysis; diagnosis of the causes of problems; development of solutions; implementation of the changes; and review of the results.

5. Fact collection and analysis – the aim is to understand the process or system, which means getting the facts about how it works (or does not work). The questions asked at this stage include: What does the process do?, What are the stages of the process?, What are the inputs and outputs of the process?, Who are the suppliers and customers (internal and external) of the process?, Are there any problems with the process? Use is made of flow charts, which provide a picture of the process by tracing each of its stages and their interconnections.

6. Define the problem – on the basis of the analysis, describe what the problem is and what impact it makes. Use Pareto charts to describe the relative significance of the problems so that attention can be focused on them during the diagnostic stage.

7. Diagnose causes – use problem-solving techniques and cause and effect diagrams to establish the cause or causes of the problems.

8. Develop solutions – ideas are generated for solutions by studying the facts and the diagnosis and by investigating alternative ways of doing things based on the group's experience supplemented by specific enquiries and reading the appropriate literature. Critical evaluation techniques are used to identify solutions. The group may decide at this stage to benchmark, ie find out how other organizations are tackling the problem (problems are seldom unique).

9. Implement the solution – the Plan-Do-Check-Act sequence described earlier in this chapter is adopted to implement the selected solution. Define exactly what changes need to be introduced, the sequence of activities required to make them, the responsibilities for implementation, the resources required and the timetable.

10. Monitor – review and evaluate the impact of the changes, answering the following questions: Were the expected benefits achieved? If not, what needs to be done about it? What lessons can be learnt? How can we ensure that the improvements are maintained (hold the gains)?

Barriers to continuous improvement

The main barrier to continuous improvement is complacency on the part of management. If they believe that everything is fine, it is unlikely that any serious attempt will be made to do things better. The other barrier is indifference or lack of cooperation from staff.

Complacency is difficult to deal with if it is engrained into the culture of the organization. It can be shaken if major problems of performance or profitability arise but it may then be too late. If it exists amongst top management it can only be hoped that there are some people in the organization who are armed with the facts and are determined enough to pressurize management into taking action. If not, management complacency may only be shattered when shareholders, government departments, governors or trustees make their concerns felt. And it may then be too late.

Indifference or hostility to continuous improvement changes from staff can be countered by recognizing that it is a situation that requires systematic change management approaches, including communication, involvement and training. These are considered in Chapter 16.

Holding the gains

It is necessary to ensure that the outcomes of a continuous improvement programme should be embedded to become a permanent and effective part of the organization's processes. Juran (1988) used the phrase 'holding the gains' to emphasize this requirement.

Holding the gains begins when a solution is created to develop better practices and processes, produce cost savings or deliver improved customer service. It must be a solution that is not only practical in terms of its immediate implementation but is also sustainable without undue effort. The momentum created by the change should continue. Quality assurance techniques can be introduced to keep the process under continuous review so that any failings can be identified quickly and dealt with. It must never be assumed that a changed process will go on operating as planned of its own volition. Continuous effort is required to ensure that incremental gains are consolidated and become part of normal working practices to the benefit of customers and, therefore, the organization.

Examples of approaches to continuous improvement

The following examples illustrate the imperatives for and application of continuous improvement in a sample of different organizations and sectors.

Higher education – The University of Sydney

The University of Sydney states that its approach to continuous improvement is to learn from best practice, locally and internationally, and benchmark against leading research universities. It claims that its quality assurance processes are evidence-based and intrinsic to the work of all staff. The features of their policy are critical self-evaluation, methodical collection of evidence about service satisfaction and student experience and a 'focus on efficient planning, management and resource processes to achieve excellence and ensure continuous improvement'. A process of cyclical reviews (five years) is followed to assist in safeguarding and enhancing the quality of its core activities, ie teaching, learning and research. These include reviews of administrative services to identify, evaluate and appraise the quality of deliverables and to implement improvements in a planned, timely and effective manner.

Finance – Mortgage Express

Mortgage Express is committed to the principles of the EFQM Excellence Model (see Chapter 20). Self-assessment against the model revealed a number of areas for improvement, including the need for a review of mission, vision and values, better training on customer service, development of staff communications, a new process to capture improvement ideas from staff, a system for getting regular feedback about staff satisfaction, and a requirement to train management in facilitating change skills. An 'Exceeding Expectations' programme was introduced to support the 'Customer Value Proposition' for the achievement of outstanding customer service. A database was launched to record staff improvement ideas. This comprised IF and DONE processes. IF is the name given to an ideas forum and DONE refers to the actions taken to evaluate and implement improvements.

Local authorities

Merthyr Tydfil County Borough Council has set up a continuous improvement programme to achieve excellence by encouraging staff to make improvement suggestions. There are about 50 teams working to suggest and create improvements.

One of the four key corporate priorities at North Somerset Council is 'to ensure that the customer is at the heart of the Council's approach to service delivery'. The aim is to improve the Audit Commission's Performance Assessment. Indicators have been developed such as the proportion of people who say that they received friendly and polite service when they approached the Council, the percentage of telephone calls answered within 15 seconds, the number of people who think the Council keeps them well informed, and the percentage of invoices that were paid promptly.

Manufacturing – The Boeing Company

The Boeing Company lays down that the organization 'Shall develop and document a continuous improvement system. This system is to include performance measures, such as measures of waste, quality, cycle time and customer satisfaction. The organization shall conduct periodic management reviews of the system, paying close attention to the performance measures and modifying improvement activities as necessary.' The requirement is that: 'Procedures are coordinated enterprise-wide for consistency and standardisation, so that all departments practice continuous improvement'.

Service – Serco

As one of the world's leading service companies, Serco has defined its approach to continuous improvement as follows:

Competitive pressure creates a continuous challenge to generate fresh ideas to win and retain contracts. The challenge is to create an environment and culture that recognise the need for continual improvement and innovation in the way we develop our service throughout the life cycle of each contract. The following elements drive continuous improvement:

- *Strategic planning – the contract development plan, cost reduction strategy and procurement strategy.*

- *Service management – manage customer expectations (demand) and the delivery process (service), improve user interface and communications, introduce better financial control.*

- *Operational delivery – introduce and monitor systems that define service requirements such as service level agreements, produce performance standards and measurements for incorporation into contracts and in service appraisals and continued development of procedural and operating manuals.*

External benchmarking is used to gain understanding of how Serco is performing in different areas in comparison to other operations. Internally, the Serco Best Practice Centre has been set up to evaluate the needs of the business, design tools and processes to improve effectiveness, and provide training. It is also responsible for identifying the intellectual property in the organization, capturing that knowledge and using it in the business.

References

Bessant, J et al (1994) Rediscovering continuous improvement, *Technovation*, **14** (3), pp 17–29

The Continuous Improvement Research for Competitive Advantage (CIRCA) Unit (1998) *The Framework for Continuous Improvement*, Brighton University, Brighton

Deming, W E (1986) *Out of the Crisis*, MIT Center for Advanced Engineering Study, Boston, MA

Industrial Relations Services (1997) Variety through continuous improvement, *IRS Employment Trends*, **624**, pp 8-16

Juran, J M (ed) (1988) *Quality Control Handbook*, McGraw-Hill, Maidenhead

Oakland, J S (1998) *Total Quality Management: The route to improving performance*, Butterworth-Heinemann, Oxford

Quality Management

'Build quality into the product.'
William Deming (1986) *Out of the Crisis*, MIT Center for Advanced
Engineering Study, Boston, MA

Continuous improvement as described in Chapter 19 is closely associated with quality management. They both aim to deliver excellence to the customer by attaining high-quality standards. The difference is that quality management as discussed in this chapter is concerned more with the assurance and control of quality rather than the achievement of incremental improvements by developing new approaches to managing processes and systems.

This chapter starts by defining the concepts of quality and quality management and describing the contribution of the quality 'gurus' to it. It continues with a description of the main approaches to quality management (quality assurance, quality control, total quality management and 'Six Sigma'), the use of quality standards, and quality management issues.

Quality defined

There are two views of quality: the traditional internal view, which indicates that a product that meets the standards of the organization should meet the needs of customers, and the more acceptable, current external view that it is customers who decide when a product meets their expectations. These broad descriptions of quality can be expanded as indicated below.

Quality can be defined and assessed in the following terms:

- innate excellence;

- convenience of use;

- performance;

- reliability;

- value for money;

- level of customer service;

- fitness for purpose;

- attractive appearance or style;

- durability;

- conformance to design specifications;

- uniformity, with small variability.

These characteristics refer to two aspects of product quality: designed quality, which sets the quality that a product is designed to have; and achieved quality, which shows how closely a product comes to meeting the designed quality standard.

Quality management defined

Quality management is concerned with all the activities required to ensure that products and services conform to the standards set by the organization and meet expectations of customers. These activities include the steps taken to ensure that high quality is achieved (quality assurance), and the actions taken to check that defined quality standards are being achieved and maintained (quality control).

Contribution of the quality gurus

The approach to quality management generally used today owes much to the contributions of the quality gurus, especially Deming, Juran and Crosby, who spelt out the conditions and behaviour that promote quality as summarized in the following sections.

W Edwards Deming

Deming (1986) emphasized the importance of customers, the significance of continuous improvement and the fact that quality is determined by the system. He believed that customer satisfaction is created by a combination of responsiveness to customers' views and needs and continuous improvement of products, services and operational systems. He summarized his views in 14 principles:

1. Create constancy of purpose towards product quality.

2. Refuse to accept customary levels of mistakes, delays, defects and errors.

3. Stop depending on mass inspection and build quality into the product in the first place.

4. Stop awarding business on the basis of price only – reduce the number of suppliers and insist on meaningful measures of quality.

5. Develop programmes for continuous improvement of costs, quality, productivity and service.

6. Institute training for all employees.

7. Focus supervision on helping employees to do a better job.

8. Drive out fear by encouraging two-way communication.

9. Break down barriers between departments and encourage problem-solving through teamwork.

10. Eliminate numerical goals, posters and slogans that demand improvement without saying how it should be achieved.

11. Eliminate arbitrary quotas that interfere with quality.

12. Remove barriers that stop people having pride in their work.

13. Institute vigorous programmes of lifelong education, training and self-improvement.

14. Put everyone to work on implementing these 14 points.

Deming suggested that managers are in control of the organization and are responsible for its performance. The quality process is in two parts: the system, over which managers have control and which contributes 80 per cent of the variation in quality, and the workers, who are under their own control and who contribute 20 per cent of the variation in quality. Major variations in quality therefore come from managers improving the system rather than workers improving their performance.

J M Juran

Juran's main contribution to the philosophy of total quality was his concept of managerial breakthrough (Juran, 1988). In the traditional control situation, the typical managerial attitude is that the present level of performance is good enough or cannot be improved. The aim is therefore to perpetuate performance at that level. Management attempts simply to identify and eliminate short-term deviations from the usual performance.

Juran stated that in the breakthrough situation management adapts a completely different attitude. The belief is held strongly that change is desirable and possible in all aspects of operation. It is up to managers to make the 'breakthrough'. They must recognize and act on the need for what is, in effect, continuous improvement.

Philip B Crosby

Crosby (1978) emphasized that 'in discussing quality we are dealing with a people situation'. He suggested five factors that govern the management of quality:

1. Quality means conformance, not elegance.

2. There is no such thing as a quality problem.

3. There is no such thing as the economics of quality. It is always cheaper to do the job right first time.

4. The only performance measurement is the cost of quality.

5. The only performance standard is zero defects.

Quality management approaches

Quality management systems and techniques aim to deliver excellence to customers and thus make a major contribution to organizational success. The quality management approaches as described in this section are the standardized techniques of quality assurance and quality control, and the holistic concepts of total quality management and Six Sigma.

Quality assurance

Quality assurance aims to build quality into the system. It is based on procedures designed to ensure that the activities carried out in the organization such as design, development, manufacturing and service delivery result in products, services or other outcomes that meet the requirements and needs of customers. The underpinning philosophy of quality assurance is that right methods will produce right results (quality products or services).

Quality is also achieved by ensuring that individuals have the skills required to do their jobs. Careful selection, skills training and appropriate allocation of people to jobs are therefore important aspects of quality assurance. Job design is another key aspect of quality assurance. The jobs people do and the level of responsibility they are given must enable them to manage the quality of their outputs themselves without relying on other people, eg inspectors, to do it for them. As Maslow (1954) said: 'If you want people to do a good job, give them a good job to do' and 'A job that isn't worth doing isn't worth doing well'.

Quality control

Quality control involves the application of data collection and analysis to monitor and measure the extent to which quality assurance requirements have been met in terms of product or service performance and reliability. It can involve detailed procedural documentation that spells out how quality should be achieved and measured. The traditional approach to controlling quality is inspection. Control can be exercised more scientifically by means of statistical techniques.

Statistical quality control

Statistical quality control uses sampling techniques and mathematical analysis to ensure that during design, manufacturing and servicing, work is carried out and material used within the specified limits required to produce the desired standards of quality, performance and reliability. The main techniques used in statistical quality control are:

- Acceptance sampling, which ensures that items do not pass to the next stage in the process if an unacceptably high proportion of the batch is outside the quality limit. Sampling consists of taking a representative number of examples from a population and drawing conclusions about the behaviour of the whole population from the behaviour of the sample. Sampling techniques are based on statistical theory, including probability theory.

- Control charts, on which the results of the inspection of samples are compared with the results expected from a stable situation. If they do not agree, then action may be necessary. These comparisons can be recorded graphically on control charts, on which warning and action levels are marked. Control charts set out the control limits that either warn that a problem exists or indicate that action needs to be taken (warning and action limits).

- Control by attributes – attributes have only two states, ie whether an article or service is acceptable or not. The information required for control purposes is the number of defects and/or the number of defects per unit, which are compared with the desired level of quality – the acceptable quality level (AQL).

- Control by variables – variables can have any value on a continuous scale. Control by variables therefore takes place when there is a distribution of the features being measured rather than a go or no-go position as in attribute control. Variables are therefore measured, in contrast to attributes, which are counted.

Total quality control

Total quality control takes a comprehensive view of all aspects of quality through techniques such as zero-defects programmes or Taguchi methodology.

Zero-defects programmes

Zero-defects programmes aim to improve product quality beyond the level that might economically be achieved through statistical procedures. The ultimate aim is to eliminate defects so far as that is conceivably possible.

The principal features of such programmes are:

- Agreement is reached with all concerned on the quality goals to be attained and the quality problems that prevent their achievement.

- The participation of all those involved in establishing and running the quality programme is organized.

- Clear targets are set against which improvements can be measured.

- Procedures are established for providing prompt feedback to employees on their quality achievements.

- Provision is made for rewards to be given for achieving high-quality standards.

- Employees are encouraged to make suggestions on causes of errors and remedies, and arrangements are made for ideas to be implemented jointly.

- Work is organized and jobs designed to facilitate all of the above.

Taguchi methodology

This methodology was developed by the Japanese engineer Taguchi. Its main features are to:

- Push quality back to the design stage because quality control can never compensate for bad design.

- Emphasize design rather than inspection for control of production.

- Produce robust products with intrinsic quality and reliability characteristics.

- Prototype product designs and production processes.

- Concentrate on the practical engineering, not the statistical niceties of quality control theory.

Total quality management

Total quality management (TQM) is a systematic method of ensuring that all activities within an organization happen in the way they have been planned in order to meet the defined needs of customers. Its approach is holistic – quality management is not a separate function to be treated in isolation, but is an integral part of all operations. Everyone in the organization is concerned with quality. Its philosophy is that it is necessary to be 'right first time', ensuring that no defective systems are in use and that no defective units are made or inadequate services delivered.

TQM involves a change of focus from inspections at the end of a process to an emphasis at the planning stage on ensuring that the design allows high quality, and at the operations stage on ensuring that no defects are produced. During the process, operations departments take responsibility for their own quality. There is no separate inspections function. Each person is responsible for passing on units that are of perfect quality. This is quality at source, with job enlargement for operatives who are now responsible for both production and quality management and are rewarded accordingly.

The steps for introducing TQM are:

1. Get top management commitment. This is a key feature of TQM. Managers have control of the organization and they must realize that TQM is not another fad that will disappear in a few months, but is a way of thinking that improves long-term performance.

2. Find out what customers really want. Without knowing exactly what customers want it is impossible to design products or offer services that satisfy them. This goes beyond simply asking for opinions, and gets customers involved in the process, perhaps discussing designs in focus groups.

3. Design products with quality in mind. Organizations must design products that are robust and satisfy both internal and external demands.

4. Design the process with quality in mind. The quality of the product depends on the process used to make it, so this must work effectively and efficiently to produce perfect quality.

5. Build teams of empowered employees. Quality depends on everyone in the organization, so they should be recognized as the most valuable asset, with appropriate training and motivation.

6. Keep track of results. TQM looks for continuous improvement, with the adjustments to products having a cumulative effect over time.

7. Extend these ideas to suppliers and distributors. Organizations do work in isolation but are part of a supply chain, with the quality of the final product depending on every link in the chain.

Six Sigma

The main cause of quality problems is variation. To improve quality, variation must be measured, reduced and eventually prevented. Six Sigma, a name coined by Motorola Inc, is a statistical approach to the measurement of variations that has been expanded holistically to cover all aspects of quality in an organization. The Greek letter sigma (σ) is used as a symbol to denote the standard deviation or the measure of variation in a process. Statistically, six sigmas represent the range of values of a population with a normal distribution. Operations can be calibrated in terms of sigma level and the greater the number of sigmas, the fewer the defects.

The aim is to achieve a quality level of six sigmas. Businesses that want to impress their customers label themselves as 'Six Sigma organizations'.

General Electric Co. has carried out an ambitious five-year programme to promote the quest for six sigmas in all its business activities. The customer satisfaction objective is highly interdisciplinary, encompassing all activities in a modern enterprise. General Electric refers to Six Sigma as a product of learning. In a recent annual report the company stated that: 'We have invested more than a billion dollars in effort and the financial returns have now entered the exponential phase'.

Six Sigma uses a range of quality management and statistical tools to construct a framework for process improvement. The aim is to achieve the sigma level of 'critical to quality' performance measures that meet the needs of customers. This is done by following the sequence define-measure-analyse-improve-control (DMAIC).

Commentary

Quality management must start with quality assurance, and statistical quality control techniques can be used to check on the standards achieved and indicate where action is required. But quality assurance and quality control methodologies are best carried out within a holistic framework – TQM or Six Sigma. The problem with both these approaches is that they depend on strong top management, committed line managers and a continuing programme of communication, encouragement and training to achieve general commitment to the philosophies upon which these are based. This can be difficult to achieve, and if it is not, the impetus for total quality may not be sustainable.

Quality standards

Quality standards provide the basis for developing and measuring the effectiveness of a quality system. Their aim is to encourage organizations to think about their management processes and react to the changing demands placed upon them. The international standard ISO 9000 is the one most generally used. In addition an important quality standard has been produced by the European Foundation for Quality Management – the EFQM model.

ISO 9000

The requirements of ISO 9000 are structured under four headings:

- management responsibility – this includes particular responsibilities for ensuring continuous improvement, benchmarking and management review;

- resource management – this focuses on the effective use of resources, especially matching the skills of individuals to the demands of their jobs (the skill-based rather than procedural documentation approach);

- process management – this includes a requirement for risk analysis, recognition of the interactions between departments (the internal customer chain), capacity to respond to changing customer expectations, formal and documented reviews of capabilities and a focus on the delivery and post-delivery activity (organizations are expected to 'deliver it right' as well as 'make it right');

- measurement, analysis and improvement – this requires an appropriate measurement system to be in place that captures the adherence, or otherwise, of the product to the standards specified.

The EFQM model of quality

The European Foundation for Quality Management (EFQM) indicates that customer satisfaction, people (employee) satisfaction and impact on society are achieved through leadership, as shown in Figure 20.1. This drives the policy and strategy, people management, resources and processes required to produce excellence in business results.

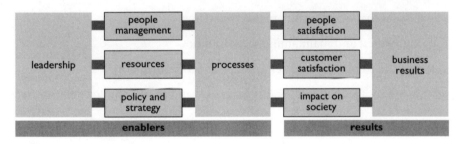

Figure 20.1   The EFQM model

The nine elements in the model are defined as follows:

1. Leadership – how the behaviour and actions of the executive team and all other leaders inspire, support and promote a culture of total quality management.

2. Policy and strategy – how the organization formulates, deploys and reviews its policy and strategy and turns it into plans and actions.

3. People management – how the organization realizes the full potential of its people.

4. Resources – how the organization manages resources effectively and efficiently.

5. Processes – how the organization identifies, manages, reviews and improves its processes.

6. Customer satisfaction – what the organization is achieving in relation to the satisfaction of its external customers.

7. People satisfaction – what the organization is achieving in relation to the satisfaction of its people.

8. Impact on society – what the organization is achieving in satisfying the needs and the expectations of the local, national and international community at large.

9. Business results – what the organization is achieving in relation to its planned business objectives and in satisfying the needs and expectations of everyone with a financial interest or stake in the organization.

Organizations that adopt the EFQM model accept the importance of performance measurement and work all the time to improve the usefulness of their measures, but they also recognize that simply measuring a problem does not improve it. Managers can often devolve their best energies to the analysis, leaving little left for the remedy. It is important to focus on both the enablers and the processes.

Quality management issues

The principal issues that affect quality management are:

- sustaining interest and maintaining momentum;
- developing the conditions and behaviour that promote quality;
- resolving the conflict between quality assurance and production or delivery targets;
- ensuring process compliance.

Sustaining interest and maintaining momentum

Total quality management or Six Sigma initiatives usually start on a wave of enthusiasm. This may originate from top management but it frequently happens as a result of the messianic zeal of a middle manager who convinces everyone from the top downwards that priority should be given to quality management.

A comprehensive programme then emerges involving communication, training and any other devices that will ensure commitment and engagement. Systems are designed, procedures are created and an infrastructure of full-time quality specialists, steering committees and improvement groups is set up.

The problem is sustaining interest and engagement after the first waves of enthusiasm have died down. Some people can become indifferent to quality, seeing it as an abstract concept and nothing to do with them. Others pay lip service to it but don't try very hard. Yet others resent the perceived bureaucracy of quality assurance and quality systems because they see them as taking up unnecessary time and interfering with their work.

If interest is not maintained, momentum will cease. So what can be done about it? The first step is to involve everyone from the start and keep them involved. Contributions to improving quality should be recognized and rewarded. Roles should be designed that emphasize responsibilities for quality and encourage people to be quality conscious. Competency frameworks should include quality and continuous improvement as a major heading, and performance management processes should ensure that the delivery of quality is specifically reviewed and assessed. Induction courses should emphasize the importance of quality and continuous learning programmes should equip people with the skills needed to produce quality performance. Bureaucracy should be kept to a minimum. If there are designated quality assurance or quality control specialists they should act on the principle that their job is to help people to deliver quality, not to police their performance.

Developing the conditions and behaviour that promote quality

The activities set out in this chapter will all contribute to the development of the conditions and behaviour that promote quality. This is essentially a matter of creating and maintaining a quality-orientated culture. Such a culture will be defined in terms of values and norms. The core values of the organization should give prominence to quality. The behavioural norms that characterize quality performance should be recognized, encouraged and rewarded. It is not enough just to espouse values. They must become values in use – accepted by everyone as governing behavioural norms in the realm of quality.

Resolving conflict between quality assurance and production/delivery targets

Quality assurance requirements may appear to restrict the scope for departments and individuals to pursue what they believe to be the best routes to achieving their production or delivery targets. There are three ways of dealing with this problem. The first is to ensure when setting quality assurance standards that they are relevant and realistic. The second is to involve line managers in setting and regularly reviewing the standards so that they can have their say on what they should be and how they should be applied. And thirdly, quality assurance should monitor the application of their standards not only to achieve compliance, but also to check with line managers for any problems they create that interfere with production or delivery responsibilities.

Ensuring process compliance

The aim of quality assurance is to set guidelines and standards for the levels of quality required. These are integrated within the total quality management or Six Sigma framework. There is clearly no point in having guidelines or standards unless they are complied with. Compliance is achieved by monitoring performance using quality control techniques as appropriate. But ensuring compliance should not be a mechanical 'policing' process that relies on extensive procedural documentation. Quality management is the responsibility of line managers; it cannot be imposed by a quality management function. In other words, it should be a self-managed process. This does not mean that line managers should be left to their own devices. Monitoring is still necessary but it should be monitoring with a light touch in line with the total quality management philosophy that quality is everyone's business.

References

Crosby, P B (1978) *Quality is Free*, McGraw-Hill, New York
Deming, W E (1986) *Out of the Crisis*, MIT Center for Advanced Engineering Study, Boston, MA
Juran, J M (1988) *Quality Control Handbook*, McGraw-Hill, Maidenhead
Maslow, A (1954) *Motivation and Personality*, Harper & Row, New York

Appendix
Alignment of Text with Managing for Results: CIPD Professional Standards

Professional standard A

Armstrong's Handbook of Management and Leadership has been aligned with the Chartered Institute of Personnel and Development's Managing for Results Professional Standards. The page numbers below indicate where the subject is covered in the text.

1 The practice of management

2 Delivering change

3 Enhancing customer relations

4 *Enabling continuous improvement*

Further Reading

Adair, J (1973) *The Action-Centred Leader*, McGraw-Hill, London

Appelbaum, E *et al* (2000) *Manufacturing Advantage: Why high performance work systems pay off*, ILR Press, Ithaca, New York

Argyris, C (1957) *Personality and Organization*, Harper & Row, New York

Armitage, A and Keble-Allen, D (2007) Why people management basics form the foundation of high-performance working, *People Management*, 18 October, p 48

Armstrong, M (2006) *A Handbook of Management Techniques*, 3rd edn, Kogan Page, London

Armstrong, M (2008) *How to be an Even Better Manager*, 7th edn, Kogan Page, London

Armstrong, M (2008) *How to Manage People*, Kogan Page, London

Armstrong, M (2008) *Performance Management*, 4th edn, Kogan Page, London

Atkinson, J (1984) Manpower strategies for flexible organizations, *Personnel Management*, **16** (8), pp 28–31

Bandura, A (1977) *Social Learning Theory*, Prentice-Hall, Englewood Cliffs, NJ

Barnard, C (1938) *The Functions of an Executive*, Harvard University Press, Boston, MA

Bass, B M (1985) *Leadership and Performance Beyond Expectations*, Free Press, New York

Beckhard, R (1989) A model for the executive management of transformational change, in *Human Resource Strategies*, ed G Salaman, pp 83–96, Sage, London

Beer, M (1980) *Organization Change and Development: A systems view*, Goodyear, Santa Monica, CA

Beer, M, Eisenstat, R and Spector, B (1990) Why change programs don't produce change, *Harvard Business Review*, November–December, pp 158–66

Bennis, W (1989) *On Becoming a Leader*, Addison-Wesley, New York

Bennis, W and Nanus, B (1985) *Leaders: The strategies for taking charge*, Harper & Row, New York

Bennis, W G and Thomas, R J (2002) *Geeks and Geezers: How era, values and defining moments shape leaders*, Harvard University Press, Boston, MA

Bessant, J *et al* (1994) Rediscovering continuous improvement, *Technovation*, **14** (3), pp 17–29

Birch, P (1999) *Instant Leadership: Reach your potential now*, Kogan Page, London

Blake, R, Shepart, H and Mouton, J (1964) Breakthrough in organizational development, *Harvard Business Review*, November–December, pp 237–58

Boxall, P F and Purcell, J (2003) *Strategy and Human Resource Management*, Palgrave Macmillan, Basingstoke

Bradbury, A (2006) *Successful Presentation Skills*, Kogan Page, London

Burns, J M (1978) *Leadership*, Harper & Row, New York

Burns, T and Stalker, G (1961) *The Management of Innovation*, Tavistock, London

Carlsson, S (1951) *Executive Behaviour: A study of the workload and the working methods of managing directors*, Strombergs, Stockholm

Caunt, J (2006) *Organize Yourself*, Kogan Page, London

Child, J (1977) *Organization: A guide to problems and practice*, Harper & Row, London

Cook, S and Bates, C (2002) How to create a customer orientated culture, *Customer Management*, **10** (2), pp 30–32

Crosby, P B (1978) *Quality is Free*, McGraw-Hill, New York

Cummins, T G and Worley, C G (2005) *Organization Development and Change*, South Western, Mason, OH

Deal, T and Kennedy, A (1982) *Corporate Cultures*, Addison-Wesley, Reading, MA

Deming, W E (1986) *Out of the Crisis*, MIT Center for Advanced Engineering Study, Boston, MA

Digman, L A (1990) *Strategic Management: Concepts, decisions, cases*, Irwin, Georgetown, Ontario

Dixon, N F (1994) *On the Psychology of Military Incompetence*, Pimlico, London

Drucker, P (1955) *The Practice of Management*, Heinemann, London

Drucker, P (1963) *Managing for Results*, Heinemann, London

Drucker, P (1967) *The Effective Executive*, Heinemann, London

Drucker, P (1985) *Innovation and Entrepreneurship*, Heinemann, London

Emery, F E (1959) *Characteristics of Socio-Technical Systems*, Tavistock Publications, London

Faulkner, D and Johnson, G (1992) *The Challenge of Strategic Management*, Kogan Page, London

Fayol, H (1916) *Administration Industrielle et General*, translated by C Storrs (1949) as *General and Industrial Management*, Pitman, London

Fiedler, F E (1967) *A Theory of Leadership Effectiveness*, McGraw-Hill, New York

Finch, B (2006) *How to Write a Business Plan*, Kogan Page, London

Follett, M P (1924) *Creative Experience*, Longmans Green, New York

Fombrun, C J, Tichy, N M, and Devanna, M A (1984) *Strategic Human Resource Management*, New York, Wiley

French, J R and Raven, B (1959) The basis of social power, in *Studies in Social Power*, ed D Cartwright, pp 150–67, Institute for Social Research, Ann Arbor, MI

Furnham, A and Gunter, B (1993) *Corporate Assessment*, Routledge, London

Ghoshal, S and Bartlett, C A (1995) Changing the role of top management: beyond structure to process, *Harvard Business Review*, January–February, pp 86–96

Goleman, D (1995) *Emotional Intelligence*, Bantam, New York

Goleman, D (2000) Leadership that gets results, *Harvard Business Review*, March–April, pp 78–90

Gowers, Sir E (1987) *The Complete Plain Words*, Penguin, London

Graen, G (1976) Role-making processes within complex organizations, in *Handbook of Industrial and Organizational Psychology*, ed M D Dunnette, pp 1201–45, Rand McNally, Chicago, IL

Gratton, L A (2000) Real step change, *People Management*, 16 March, pp 27–30

Gratton, L A and Hailey, V H (1999) The rhetoric and reality of new careers, in *Strategic Human Resource Management*, eds L Gratton *et al*, pp 79–100, Oxford University Press, Oxford

Grint, K (2000) *The Arts of Leadership*, Oxford University Press, Oxford

Hackman, J R and Oldham, G R (1974) Motivation through the design of work: test of a theory, *Organizational Behaviour and Human Performance*, **16** (2), pp 250–79

Hales, C P (1986) What managers do: a critical review of the evidence, *Journal of Management Studies*, **23** (1), pp 88–115

Halpin, A W and Winer, B J (1957) *A Factorial Study of the Leader Behaviour Descriptions*, Ohio State University Press, OH

Handy, C (1985) *Understanding Organizations*, Penguin, Harmondsworth

Handy, C (1994) *The Empty Raincoat*, Hutchinson, London

Harrison, R (1972) Understanding your organization's character, *Harvard Business Review*, **5**, pp 119–28

Harvey-Jones, J (1984) *Making it Happen*, Collins, Glasgow

Heller, R (1972) *The Naked Manager*, Barrie & Jenkins, London

Hersey, P and Blanchard, K H (1969) Life cycle theory of leadership, *Training and Development Journal*, **23** (2), pp 26–34

Hersey, P and Blanchard, K H (1998) *Management of Organizational Behaviour*, Prentice Hall, Englewood Cliffs, NJ

Herzberg, F (1968) One more time: how do you motivate employees? *Harvard Business Review*, January–February, pp 109–20

Higgs, M (2006) Change and its Leadership, Rowland, Fisher, Lennox Consulting, [Online] www.rflc.co.uk

House, R J (1971) A path-goal theory of leader effectiveness. *Administrative Science Quarterly*, **16**, pp 321–38

House, R et al (2004) *Culture, Leadership and Organization: The GLOBE study of 62 societies*, Sage, Thousand Oaks, CA

Huczynski, A A and Buchanan, D A (2007) *Organizational Behaviour*, 6th edn, FT Prentice Hall, Harlow

Hutchinson, S and Purcell, J (2003) *Bringing Policies to Life: The vital role of front line managers in people management*, CIPD, London

Industrial Relations Services (1997) Variety through continuous improvement, *IRS Employment Trends*, **624**, pp 8–16

Industrial Society (1997) *Leadership – Steering a new course*, Industrial Society, London

Ivancevich, J M, Konopaske, R and Matteson, M T (2008) *Organizational Behavior and Management*, 8th edn, McGraw-Hill/Irwin, New York

Johns, E (2008) *Out to Lunch: Back in six hours*, Institute of Customer Service, London

Johns, E, Wirtz, J and Johnston, R (2003) Singapore Airlines and the service template, *Customer Management*, May/June, pp 38–41, and September/October, pp 38–41

Juran, J M (ed) (1988) *Quality Control Handbook*, McGraw-Hill, Maidenhead

Juran, J M (1989) *Juran on Leadership for Quality*, The Free Press, New York

Kakabadse, A (1983) *The Politics of Management*, Gower, Aldershot

Kanter, R M (1984) *The Change Masters*, Allen & Unwin, London

Kelley, R E (1991) In praise of followers, in *Managing People and Organizations*, ed J J Gabarro, pp 143–53, Harvard Business School Publications, Boston, MA

King, J (1995) High performance work systems and firm performance, *Monthly Labour Review*, May, pp 29–36

Kinnie, N et al (1996) *The People Management Implications of Leaner Methods of Working*, IPD, London

Kotter, J (1977) Power, dependence and effective management, *Harvard Business Review*, July–August, pp 125–36

Kotter, J P (1991) Power, dependence and effective management, in *Managing People and Organizations*, ed J Gabarro, pp 33–49, Harvard Business School Publications, Boston, MA

Kotter, J J (1995) *A 20% Solution: Using rapid re-design to build tomorrow's organization today*, Wiley, New York

Lawler, E E (1969) Job design and employee motivation, *Personnel Psychology*, **22**, pp 426–35

Lawrence, P R and Lorsch, J W (1969) *Developing Organizations*, Addison-Wesley, Reading, MA

Levitt, T (1983) *The Marketing Imagination*, The Free Press, New York

Lewin, K (1951) *Field Theory in Social Science*, Harper & Row, New York

Likert, R (1961) *New Patterns of Management*, Harper & Row, New York

Lupton, T (1975) Best fit in the design of organizations, *Personnel Review*, **4** (1), pp 15–22

Luthans, F and Kreitner, R (1975) *Organizational Behaviour Modification*, Scott-Foresman, Glenview, IL

Management Standards Centre (2004) *Management Standards*, [Online] www. management-standards.org

Marks, B, Marks, R and Spillane, R (2006) *The Management Contradictionary*, Michelle Anderson Publishing, South Yarra, Vic

Mayo, E (1933) *Human Problems of an Industrial Civilisation*, Macmillan, London

McClelland, D C (1961) *The Achieving Society*, Van Norstrand, New York

McGregor, D (1960) *The Human Side of Enterprise*, McGraw-Hill, New York

Meindl, J R, Ehrlich, S B and Dukerich, J M (1985) The romance of leadership, *Administrative Science Quarterly*, **30**, pp 78–102

Miller, E and Rice, A (1967) *Systems of Organization*, Tavistock, London

Mintzberg, H (1973) *The Nature of Managerial Work*, Harper & Row, New York

Mintzberg, H (1983) *Structure in Fives*, Prentice-Hall, Englewood Cliffs, NJ

Mintzberg, H (1987) Crafting strategy, *Harvard Business Review*, July–August, pp 66–74

Mintzberg, H (1994) The rise and fall of strategic planning, *Harvard Business Review*, January–February, pp 107–14

Minzberg, H (2004) Enough leadership, *Harvard Business Review*, November, p 22

Nadler, D A (1993) Concepts for the management of organizational change, in *Managing Change*, 2nd edn, ed C Mabey and W Mayon-White, pp 85–98, Chapman/Open University, London

Northouse, P G (2006) *Leadership: Theory and practice*, 4th edn, Sage, Thousand Oaks, CA

Oakland, J S (1998) *Total Quality Management: The route to improving performance*, Butterworth-Heinemann, Oxford

O'Connor, Z (2003) The human touch, Topics, *ER Consultants*, pp 8–10

Pascale, R (1990) *Managing on the Edge*, Viking, London

Pedler, M, Burgoyne, J and Boydell, T (1986) *A Manager's Guide to Self Development*, McGraw-Hill, Maidenhead

Pettigrew, A and Whipp, R (1991) *Managing Change for Competitive Success*, Blackwell, Oxford

Porter, M (1980) *Competitive Strategy*, The Free Press, New York

Pugh, D (1993) Understanding and managing organizational change, in *Managing Change*, 2nd edn, ed C Mabey and W Mayon-White, pp 208–14, Chapman/Open University, London

Purcell, J *et al* (2003) *Understanding the People and Performance Link: Unlocking the black box*, CIPD, London

Quinn, J B (1980) Managing strategic change, *Sloane Management Review*, **11** (4/5), pp 3–30

Reddin, W J (1970) *Managerial Effectiveness*, McGraw-Hill, London

Revans, R W (1989) *Action Learning*, Blond and Briggs, London

Salovey, P and Mayer, J D (1990) Emotional intelligence, *Imagination, Cognition and Personality*, **9**, pp 185–211

Sayles, L (1964) *Managerial Behavior*, McGraw-Hill, New York

Schein, E H (1969) *Process Consultation: Its role in organization development*, Addison-Wesley, Reading, MA

Silverman, D and Jones, J (1976) *Organizational Work*, Macmillan, London

Sloan, A P (1986) *My Years with General Motors*, Pan Books, London

Stevens, J (2005) *High Performance Wales: Real experiences, real success*, Wales Management Council, Cardiff

Stewart, R (1967) *Managers and Their Jobs*, Macmillan, London

Stewart, R *et al* (1980) *The District Administrator in the National Health Service*, Pitman, London

Stogdill, R (1974) *Handbook of Leadership: A survey of theory and research*, Free Press, New York

Stone, M (1997) Evaluating the profitability of customer service, in *The Gower Handbook of Customer Service*, ed P Marley, pp 3–16, Gower, Aldershot

Sung, J and Ashton, D (2005) *High Performance Work Practices: Linking strategy and skills to performance outcomes*, DTI in association with CIPD, [Online] http://www.cipd.co.uk/subjects/corpstrtgy/

Tamkin, P, Hirsh, W and Tyers, C (2003) *Chore to Champion: The making of better people managers, Report 389*, Institute of Employment Studies, Brighton

Taylor, F W (1911) *Principles of Scientific Management*, Harper, New York

Tennant, C, Warwood, S J and Chiang, M P P (2002) A continuous improvement process at Severn Water, *The TQM magazine*, **14** (5), pp 284–92

Thompson, M and Heron, P (2005) Management capability and high performance work organization, *International Journal of Human Resource Management*, **16** (6), pp 1029–48

Thurley, K (1979) *Supervision: A reappraisal*, Heinemann, London

Tushman, M, Newman, W and Nadler, D (1988) Executive leadership and organizational evolution: managing incremental and discontinuous change, in *Corporate Transformation: Revitalizing organizations for a competitive world*, ed R Kilmann and T Covin, pp 102–30, Jossey-Bass, San Francisco, CA

Tyson, S (1985) Is this the very model of a modern personnel manager? *Personnel Management*, **26**, pp 35–39

Ulrich, D (1998) A new mandate for human resources, *Harvard Business Review*, January–February, pp 124–34

Urwick, L F (1947) *Dynamic Administration*, Pitman, London

Varma, A *et al* (1999) High performance work systems: exciting discovery or passing fad? *Human Resource Planning*, **22** (1), pp 26–37

Watson, G and Gallagher, K (2005) *Managing for Results*, CIPD, London

Weber, M (1947) *The Theory of Social and Economic Organizations*, translated by A M Henderson and T Parsons, ed T Parsons, Free Press, New York

Womack, J and Jones, D (1970) *The Machine that Changed the World*, Rawson, New York

Woodward, J (1965) *Industrial Organization*, Oxford University Press, Oxford

Woodward, J (1968) Resistance to change, *Management International Review*, **8**, pp 78–93

Worley, C G, Hitchin, D and Ross, W (1996) *Integrated Strategic Change: How organization development builds competitive advantage*, Addison-Wesley, Reading, MA

Zaleznik, A (2004) Manager and leaders: are they different? *Harvard Business Review*, January, pp 74–81

Index